What other people are saying

The Unsinkable Spirit…

"Not only is this book a heart-stopping read, it will enlighten, encourage and inspire you. It's a classic case of the true power of a dream. You will not only be inspired to dream big, but it will warm your heart, open your mind and send your spirits soaring."

… **Mark Victor Hansen**
#1 New York Times and USA Today
Bestselling Co-Author, Chicken Soup for the Soul Series

*"This book evoked every emotion I have. I laughed. I cried. I was mesmerized. It reads like a combination of **Angela's Ashes** and **The Perfect Storm**."*

… **Susan Jeske**
Ms. America 2000

"A powerful story. In this dynamic book, Boris and Shirley King certainly prove it pays to live your dream."

… **Dennis Connor**
Four-Time America's Cup Champion

"There is a man alive today who lives the spirit of Captain Cook, Marco Polo and Magellan! Boris King and his delightful wife, Shirley, bought a ship and sailed off to the South Pacific to discover the most exciting adventures. One of the best page-turners I have ever read. You won't be able to put it down. Better buy a carton – the best gifts you will ever give!"

… **Dottie Walters,**
Author, Speak & Grow Rich;
Publisher, SHARING IDEAS Newsmagazine

"An amazing book – three books in one. Wonderful storytelling ability. I first was attracted to the sailing stories but quickly became consumed by the amazing adventure tales of Boris and Shirley King. I can hardly wait for their next volumes!"

… **Peter Speck,**
Award Winning Publisher
Hollinger Group Newspapers

The Unsinkable Spirit

Episode I

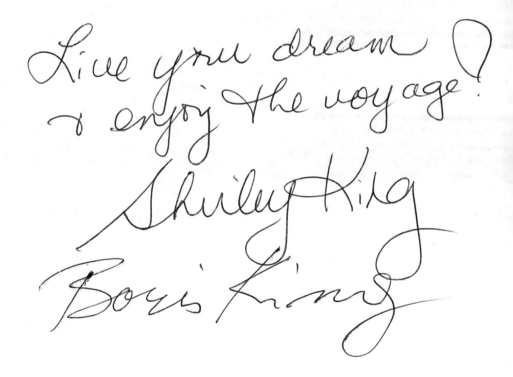

Live your dream & enjoy the voyage!

Shirley King

Boris King

The Unsinkable Spirit

Episode I

In Search of
Love, Adventure & Riches

by Boris King &

Shirley King

Boris and Shirley King
Toll free: 1-888-414-5464
Email: borisking@attglobal.net
Web page: www.theunsinkablespirit.com
or www.borisking.com
Mail: 111 East 1ˢᵗ Street, #20
       North Vancouver, BC
       Canada, V7L 1B2

ISBN 1-929925-06-9

Library of Congress Cataloging in Publication Number
00-106029

BORIS KING & SHIRLEY KING
The Unsinkable Spirit

Front and back cover designed by
GRAHAM COULTHARD

Inside page design by
JASON BUTCHER

Printed in Canada by Printcrafters Inc.

Canadian distribution by HUSION HOUSE
United States distribution by INGRAM

With love we dedicate this book to

Our parents,
Jakob and Mary Smrcek
&
John and Vera Duffield

May the gray hairs we caused bring you comfort,
knowing you allowed us to live
our dream!

&

Our sons,
Trevor & Ryan

May you dream big dreams,
set high standards for yourselves
and enjoy the voyage!

From the Author

... Captain Boris King

The reason Shirley and I wrote this book is multi-fold. Originally, after years of procrastination, I finally decided I wanted to write a workbook to support the theories I teach in my professional speaking presentations. Secondly, I craved to challenge myself to another level of thinking, another level of being and another level of doing – to become an author who could write something of benefit to the reader. And thirdly, Shirley and I wanted to leave a legacy for our two sons, Trevor and Ryan, who were there with us every step of the way, every minute of their lives.

Once I immersed myself into writing a workbook, however, an interesting phenomenon transpired. Once my mind relaxed, instead of highly technical and philosophical ideas flowing, it was flooded with memories of our adventures. I started to relive every moment of my life.

Even though this book is filled with short stories about our expeditions and adventures it has been written for you, the reader. Use this book as your navigational tool, your chart, compass and sails to guide you from where you are to where you want to be. My hope is that you will realize how important it is for you to have dreams, cherish them and live them out. As you read this book you may say, *"I can't do that,"* or *"I don't want to do that."* You don't have to. Sailing is not everyone's dream. I'm sure you have your own. And if you don't – dare to dream.

Decide what *you* want. What *are* your dreams and desires? Hang on to them tightly as they are the true treasures of life. Write them down so that the pirates of life, complacency and fear, can never take them away from you. Now they become your goals. To help you reach those goals, visualize yourself being in possession of them. It is much easier to reach your port if you can clearly see your destination. But don't go on the voyage through life alone. Form a mastermind alliance with one or more like-minded people to help you reach your goals. And as Mark Victor Hansen says, *"Put your team together, to get your dream together."* I chose my wife to be my number one mastermind partner; who is yours?

This is an adventure book. After all, what should any life be but an adventure? Helen Keller said, *"Life is either a daring adventure or nothing at all."* Don't let anyone or anything silence your dreams. Live your life out loud and on purpose. If you do what you love, if you are truly passionate about your dream, the necessary finances will follow and so will your enthusiasm, and the energy needed to make it a reality.

I want you to realize that *you* are the captain and CEO of your life's adventure. Consciously navigate your own way instead of being tossed about by the waves, winds and currents of someone else's dreams.

I hope to encourage you to make a plan for your own life, otherwise you'll become part of someone else's plan. If you don't know how, follow your feelings. Take a risk, wing it but just do it – take action. You will find that by plotting a chart for your own course you will be empowered and rewarded both spiritually and financially. Believe me I know how hard it is to cast off those mooring lines that keep us securely tied in safe harbors from sailing forth to take action. But with the support of your family and faith you will have the power to make it.

Trust that there is a true spirit of goodness in people and have faith that there is kindness, spirituality and love everywhere in the world. Continue to build and nourish your family but be aware not to limit it to only blood relatives. Extend your family to the people who love, trust and support you. Have the courage to give up the ones that don't.

Choose in favor of yourself to become a participant rather than a spectator in life. Strive each day to improve, to learn something new, to enrich the lives of others. Explore, discover, experience, and embrace change. Trust me. It will fire your neurons. Your energy will blow through the roof, and your consciousness will expand. You will accomplish things you never thought possible and the universe will sing you praises.

It's your life; take the helm and take charge. Set high standards for yourself, stretch your limits, and then rejoice when you accomplish what you once thought was impossible. Wake up and become alive. There is so much *out there* to learn, experience, and accomplish – things that will make your heart sing, dance, whistle and hum.

Now let the voyage begin!

From the Author

. . . Shirley King

When I grew up in the prairies in Alberta, never did I expect for a minute that most of my life would be played out on the high seas.

According to my parents, one thing was obvious. From a very young age, I had *ants in my pants* – so to speak. I couldn't sit still for a minute. I was curious and I wanted to explore. Yes, explore to the point that my mother had to put me in a harness whenever I played outside. It allowed me to run up and down the clothesline in our fenceless back yard. Without the harness, I was gone on my mission to explore.

In every other way, I think I was pretty average, growing up in a conservative catholic family of four children with very stable hard working parents struggling through the usual stuff in life. I wasn't the most popular kid in school. In fact I was kind of self-conscious. I was on the heavy side and sported coke-bottle thick glasses for my bad eyes (before the days of laser correction) and braces to straighten my buckteeth. My expectations for an exceptional life weren't high. Like my friends, I more or less drifted through my younger years, oblivious that I had the power to make any major kind of influence on the outcome of my life.

The powers of the universe have their ways of putting two people together, and I thank them for that. My life changed in a monumental way when I fell in love with Boris and we became a team working as *one* toward our aspirations and goals.

When Boris first told me about his dream to go sailing I had some major concerns to address before making a conscious decision that I wanted to share his dream. I was tempted, as I'd always harbored an adventurous travel bug within my soul and I felt *up* for the challenge. Of course my biggest dilemma was my responsibility as a mother to our eight-month-old baby, Trevor. However, after a visit to his pediatrician, a woman far beyond her years in wisdom, she not only gave me her blessing, but she encouraged me that Trevor's health would probably be even better than if we lived on land.

The other quandary I had was the fact that I had a tendency to feel very claustrophobic even under normal circumstances. To live in such confined quarters as on a boat didn't appeal to me at all. I thought it over, made my decision and discussed it with Boris. We agreed, I would give it a try. If I couldn't handle it, we'd go back to land-lubbing. Nothing could be lost from trying.

I was also concerned with our lack of sailing knowledge and our financial situation, but that would all sort itself out, as things always do in life. Once the procrastination was out of the way and the decision was made, everything else seemed to fall into place after we put our plan into action.

People always say, *"How could you be so brave?"*

I always feel a little undeserving of this comment. From my point of view it's all about perception. There we were *out there* – free from the bonds of routine life. We were alive – living our dream and thriving in the thrill of it. I almost felt a little guilty – as if we had discovered this big secret that nobody else knew about. The alternative, of course, was not to be living our dream. In my eyes I wasn't being courageous at all. I was just enjoying living life in full color.

I also get asked, *"How could you get pregnant?"*

In fact our doctor friend in the Hawaiian marina asked me if I was sure I wanted to have *that* baby. There was no question in my mind. I just went with the attitude that obviously women had been having babies since the beginning of mankind. After having a healthy pregnancy with Trevor, I felt confident to be pregnant while travelling the high seas. And not a day goes by without me feeling blessed for having both our precious sons.

Our voyage taught us a lot about life, but it also taught us about people. It was a comprehensive education. As crew mates we had to learn how to live harmoniously, in close quarters through such extremes as the doldrums and storms. And the lessons we learned would help us throughout complacent and difficult times in our life – and believe me we've had a few of those.

Now that I'm older and look back at what we managed to accomplish at such a young age, I am truly amazed. When Boris and I decided on each one of our goals, it first looked like a giant hurdle. But a funny thing happened. After we took action, the closer we inched toward our goal, the smaller the hurdle appeared. And of course once we reached it, we felt such a sense of accomplishment.

This book is another goal of ours, as we felt compelled to expand our horizons and share in writing our adventures. While working on this book it occurred to me that the process took on a similar configuration to the formula for our secret to a long-lasting marriage. We worked diligently together on a project in which we both shared the same goal. First Boris would input his stories, then I would revamp them. Then he would revamp them again. Then we'd sit down, talk it out, compromise and come up with our combined result. It's all about doing things together, sharing the same vision, working jointly toward it and last, but not least, compromise. How could we possibly not become soul mates?

Ours was a great voyage – yet one made by ordinary people. Our story highlights the fact that it doesn't take an extra-ordinary person to accomplish extra-ordinary goals or to live an extra-ordinary life.

It is my wish that this book will motivate you, the reader, to live your life to its greatest potential. I hope this book will be your motivator to challenge your soul – *to dare yourself to do the extra-ordinary.* Then hang on for an exciting ride and enjoy the voyage!

One and Only You

Every single blade of grass,
And every flake of snow –
Is just a wee bit different …
There's no two alike, you know.

From something small, like grains of sand,
To each gigantic star
All were made with THIS in mind:
To be just what they are!

How foolish then, to imitate –
How useless to pretend!
Since each of us comes from a MIND
Whose ideas never end.

There'll only be just ONE of ME
To show what I can do –
And you should likewise feel very proud,
There's only ONE of YOU.

That is where it all starts
With you – a wonderful unlimited human being!

James T. Moore

Table of Contents

Chapter 1

The Hurricane from Hell

"You know, we can't get out of life alive! We can either die in the bleachers or die on the field. We might as well come down on the field and go for it."

... Les Brown

It was a day we never looked forward to.

Shirley drove me to the Vancouver airport and once again parting was difficult. I knew I would miss her. I could tell her heart was aching – that she wanted to go – to be with me.

But that was impossible. We had committed to give our two teenage boys, Trevor and Ryan, the opportunity to have conventional schooling for a couple years before they were old enough to set out on their own. For many years Shirley had home schooled them on board our ship while we sailed the world. Now we felt it was important that their education be finished more formally.

We knew I had to earn a living, skippering our 110-foot traditional sailing ship, Latina, in the Virgin Islands. Unfortunately this

1

understanding did nothing to kill the pain of our separation. Ever since the day Shirley and I met, we had been inseparable soul mates, always yearning to be in each other's energy or love orbit, so being apart was a painful experience. She dropped me off outside the airport and as she drove off I could see her eyes cloud over with tears.

After a tedious 24-hour trip I was on my ship in the Virgin Islands, hastily preparing for Latina's upcoming charter. No matter how many times I had done it before, there was always last minute panic. Provisions had to be ordered, propane tanks filled, crew organized, cabins cleaned, decks washed down, and fuel and water tanks topped off. And then there was the machinery to maintain. Besides regular oil and filter changes something always needed fixing. If it wasn't the generator breaking down, it was the refrigeration.

Adding to the problem was the blasted humidity, a result of having had rain for the past few days. I wondered – *how in the world are we ever going to be ready for this charter? How will we manage to dry the bedding?* We had a washing machine aboard Latina but without a dryer we had to rely on nature's sunshine to dry our clothes on a line.

However the day the charter was to begin the skies were clear, the sun was hot, and the wind gently blew from the east. Within an hour of hanging up the laundry, everything was dry and the crew quickly made the beds.

Everything else clicked as well, mainly because most of the crew were seasoned sailors. Doris, who normally captained our 100-foot sailing ship Maverick, and her first mate, Gary, joined me aboard Latina because they didn't have their own charter that week. Having two experienced crewmembers on board, together with Robert, a keen novice, certainly had the makings for a great trip.

Normally the provisioning truck was on *island time* but today, it was punctual. I got out of the way while the crew efficiently stowed the fresh produce, meats, fish and dry goods. It never ceased to amaze me how they could find a spot for it all. With the coolers filled with sodas and beer, topped to the brim with ice, we were ready for the show to begin.

What a glorious day, I thought. W*hy had I been so worried about this charter?* Perhaps that's when I should have suspected something. There was something different in the air. The weather was just too perfect. I should have known better. As the old saying goes, *it isn't over until it's over.*

At noon our eager guests arrived. They were a group from North Carolina who would enjoy a week with us aboard Latina, sailing throughout the U.S. and British Virgin Islands. It didn't take long to discover that one of the women was picking up the tab for the entire group. She had recently inherited a substantial sum of money and decided to treat her friends to this unique vacation. Although it was their first experience aboard a sailing ship they immediately were impressed with the ship's generous cabin and deck space. It truly promised to be terrific charter, as everyone seemed so genuine and friendly.

After our guests settled into their cabins, we pulled up Latina's anchor and slowly headed out of the scenic harbor. The guests *ooed and awed* at the beautiful tropical setting. Colorful pink rooftops speckled the lush green mountains circling the bay. As we sailed past a row of giant cruise ships resting against the dock, many of their passengers were lined up against the ship's railing. They waved and cheered to us. It was a heartwarming send off. Amazingly, even after eight years of operating sailing charters out of St. Thomas, I still felt such an incredible thrill *going to work.*

Everything was turning out perfectly. I started to relax – to enjoy the sail. As we headed out to open sea, Latina's bow pounded into the oncoming waves sending an energizing shudder through the ship. Her stark white sails fluttered in the soft Caribbean breeze, contrasting against the cobalt blue sky. Tropical emerald islands, dotted here and there, took on the appearance of an oasis rising out of the sea. It was a sight I could never drink enough of. My guests' faces mirrored my excitement, totally unaware that our ecstasy was to be so short lived!

After barely setting anchor in Frances Bay on the island of St. John in the U.S. Virgin Islands, I picked up the first weather warning.

"...HURRICANE LUIS..." the VHF radio blared. At first that was all I heard but it was enough to catch my attention. I listened intently. Sure enough, a hurricane named Luis had formed in the southeast Atlantic, heading in a westerly direction.

"Oh cripes! That's all I need," I mumbled under my breath.

The report continued, *"It's extremely large in size and very organized."*

Great I thought. *Well at least it's far enough away and not likely to target us. But those poor buggers in its path...*

Feeling that there was no need to alert the guests I just carried on like usual. For the next couple days I closely but inconspicuously monitored the weather reports to track the hurricane's strength and direction.

Three days into our charter we were still having incredibly beautiful weather with cloudless blue skies. There was one variation – the trade winds. They had become light, forcing us to use engine power to propel us to the British Isle of Jost Van Dyke.

On the beach, Foxy, my good friend and one of the Caribbean's most renowned entertainers, dazzled us with his songs and comedy. My guests enjoyed the reggae music, dancing barefoot in the sand under the moonlight, contorting their bodies backward as they did the limbo well into the night. It was inconceivable to imagine that close by, out in the open Atlantic, a powerful hurricane raged. But it was true. Within 24 hours our lives would be altered forever.

The next morning I decided I had no other option but to alert the guests about the looming hurricane. The time had come to change our focus from enjoying their vacation to preparing for a serious storm. By now it was becoming obvious that we would be hit – how severely, no one really knew.

After breakfast we sailed from Jost Van Dyke to the little village of West End, on the British Virgin Island of Tortola to seek shelter. I gathered everyone on the aft deck to explain our predicament and to share my strategy for handling what now looked like an extremely dangerous situation. Surprisingly, they were very receptive to the news. In fact they didn't seem too concerned at all.

Obviously they have had no experience with hurricanes I thought. I had been in four – enough to respectfully fear them. I knew these people couldn't conceive that our beautiful windless weather was just the calm before the storm. I knew they couldn't comprehend the seriousness of the peril just on our doorstep. They didn't realize that a serious hurricane has enough power to provide the U.S. with enough electric energy for three years. That giant waves turn into death traps, and that the combination of the ocean spray and driving rain can easily drown a man. They couldn't fathom that a severe hurricane has so much force it could virtually sandblast a man to death. They just had no idea. Maybe it was just as well.

West End had an excellent reputation as a good hurricane hole with exceptional protection provided by high mountains on each side of the deep cove. It was said that pirates, buccaneers and other seafarers over the centuries had weathered great storms there. So I felt we were in good company.

Eager to help, the charter guests got into the spirit of things. They cleared the decks, stowing away anything that could possibly become airborne – windsurfers, cushions and chairs, and even a full-sized barbecue. Taking every precaution, we took off the sails and hauled one of the dinghies up on board. I was amazed how supportive the guests were. Not once did they complain about their vacation being interrupted by this huge inconvenience. They assisted in any way possible, and had a great time doing it – all in a spirit of cooperation. I truly had an exceptional group of people on board.

In our preparations to secure Latina we set three anchors off her bow, facing west and tied her stern to solid moorings on the beach facing east. Ashore, I searched for extra rope to triple our mooring lines. I happened to bump into another charter yacht captain. Surprised that my crew and I were planning to stay on board to ensure the safety of our ship he sneered, *"What's the matter Boris? Can't you afford a bottle of rum and a hotel room for the night? Don't worry about your ship. Come and join us – we're having a hurricane party!"*

I just stared at him, and then walked away. I had work to do. There was no way I was going to abandon my ship. I couldn't comprehend that kind of thinking. I loved Latina and I would never leave her. To me that would be like deserting a wounded friend on the battlefield while the troops were in retreat. I felt we were taking a calculated risk and my crew agreed with me. They all had the option to leave any time they wished.

As the hurricane crept closer, tension began to build on board. The charter guests decided after all to take my advice and seek shelter ashore. Predicting that would be the case, I had previously arranged land accommodations for them in a concrete building. They briskly gathered up their immediate personal belongings and left the ship. Only one guest was too stubborn to leave – Fritz was determined to ride out Hurricane Luis with me. His ancestors had been seafarers and even though he was a landlubber himself, he was compelled to stay on board. He felt he owed it to his deceased grandfather.

Maverick's Captain, Doris Bailey, with her steadfast determined character shining brightly through, also chose to stay on board. She was a strong, salty, hard working woman, the kind Boston breeds. Robert, our green deckhand, opted to leave the ship after I explained the danger in staying – not wanting to desert us in our time of need, but knowing it was the best thing to do. Tears rolled down his cheeks as I rowed him ashore. Gary being a long time loyal mate, agreed to take the last ferry back to St. Thomas harbor where he would fight the storm aboard Maverick. After the shuffle, only three of us were left on Latina – Doris, Fritz and myself.

Dusk set in and with it, a magic moment of peace before the storm. Magnificently the sun slipped over the horizon. Glorious pink and purple hues feathered across the sky and silhouettes reflected in the flat mirror-like water. Crickets sang to their hearts' content. The scene was one of tranquil bliss, an enchanted moment in time. And yet, in a few short hours, life as I knew it, so comfortable and secure, would be drastically altered.

Originally it was expected that Luis' eye would pass south of us. I hadn't been too concerned, but as the winds built up and new weather reports came in, it was obvious that the hurricane had changed its course. It didn't take long to realize that the worst case scenario was unfolding – *we were directly in the eye's path!*

Oh God! Not now! Not ever! I thought. I got that sick feeling in the pit of my stomach, as if someone had punched me. Shirley and I had worked so hard restoring Latina. When we bought her she was in much need of repair. She wasn't young, after all, being built in Italy during the Second World War. Yet when I first set eyes on her I knew I was sold. I could see her potential to be an excellent charter boat. She was big and spacious and gracious. And she had history. We were told that she had been the private yacht of Enzo Ferrari.

People had warned us, *"You're crazy to buy an old 110-foot WOODEN ship. That's going to be the end of your marriage – the end of your finances. That ship is going to drain you dry."* Well it just about did! We had worked hard. A lot of blood, sweat and tears went into upgrading and rebuilding her and with very limited finances. It had been an uphill battle – nevertheless a labor of love. And now the thought of losing her was too much. It made me nauseous. Now all we could do was wait and see what fate destiny was to deal us.

As a blanket of darkness covered us we experienced the first winds of the storm blowing from a NE direction. And within no time howling winds exceeding 75 miles-per-hour dominated the anchorage. Strong gusts laid smaller boats flat on their sides. It didn't take long for the storm to knock the power out and the stage was set. Total darkness created an eerie ominous feeling. My body was tense with anticipation, but at the same time, I felt charged – excited like a kid about to experience his first roller coaster ride.

"OK Luis – don't think you're going to get the best of me!" I taunted. But Luis just ignored me. His fury didn't subside.

In fact as the night progressed the wind increased in velocity and shifted to the NW. It was difficult to get about the ship. The violent wind now blew about a hundred miles-per-hour with gusts packing much more. So far we were holding our ground. I was pleased with the way Latina headed up to the wind, even though the gusts were rapidly shifting direction. We'd barely recover from one gust before getting blasted by another.

Giant waves constantly swamped the decks. I wondered how much abuse this grand old ship could handle before she'd start leaking between her planks. I wondered if the bilge pumps would be able to keep up. *Don't even go there* I thought. It was important to stay focused.

Rain pelted down, piercing my face when I went forward to check the anchors. It felt like bees were stinging me. *A couple of days after the hurricane I thought I was going through puberty again – my skin was breaking out. At first I thought it was a case of acne. Then I realized that sand and bits of debris, driven by 150 mile-per-hour winds, had actually embedded my exposed skin.*

Latina rode the storm like a bucking bronco. Everything seemed to be under control. Then suddenly in the darkness I could spot a white hazy swirling in the air and hear a horrific howling noise. It sounded like a jet revving its engine just before take off. It was deafening and frightening and I thought it would drive me mad if it didn't stop. It pinned Latina broadside and forced us sideways. We were no longer secure. It was obvious that our three anchors to the west had started to drag.

Hastily I started the engine. It was absolutely necessary to help us regain control. I ran back to the helm on the poop deck, shifted Latina into forward and steered directly into the wind. The gusts were so violent and constantly shifting direction that it became virtually impossible to hold Latina's bow into the wind anymore. *I knew we had to keep her away from the beach.* Adrenaline flowed through my veins. The fight was on to save her!

Somehow we managed and for hours the three of us – Doris, Fritz and I, took turns running the engine and spinning the massive wooden wheel from port to starboard trying desperately to keep Latina's bow into the wind. Working the wheel, located high up on the poop deck, we were totally exposed to the elements and were becoming exhausted in our battle against nature.

The wind was so strong it tried to blast us off the deck, and the driving rain so dense we had to wear snorkel masks in order to protect our eyes and faces. We had to turn sideways just to be able to breathe. At this point, I don't think we could even see our bow.

All along I feared the danger of other boats breaking loose and dragging into us. In the glare of lightening strikes, off in the distance I could see boats, *some belonging to my friends*, being helplessly dragged towards shore.

Suddenly in the spume of the ocean spray and rain, I spotted a boat, loose and out of control, being dragged at the wind's mercy. My stomach did a flip when I realized – *it was heading directly for us.*

"Full port! Steer full port!" I screeched into the deafening wind.

Charged with adrenaline, Captain Doris vigorously spun the wheel to port. I tried to jump from the poop deck down onto the main deck in an attempt to make my way forward. An intense gust stopped me, held me up, suspending me in mid air, then tried to fling me back onto the poop deck. Eventually, I managed to land on the main deck. Dropping on all fours I quickly crawled up to the bow with hopes of fending off the threatening oncoming boat. Fritz was close behind.

A small sloop rushed toward us out of the darkness, dragging just past our starboard side. It was an eerie ghostly sight, captured in short bright flashes of lightening strikes. The boat's mast was broken and dangling. A huge chunk was missing from its bow. It came so close that I could just about touch it, but before I could react, it darted by us and disappeared within seconds from sight. I stood shocked in disbelief. Fear overtook me.

This is serious stuff I thought. *What's our destiny to be? When is this hurricane ever going to end?* Hurricanes usually pass quickly. It's their only blessing. But this one seemed to be playing out in slow motion. And we had no choice but to endure it.

Remembering previous hurricanes I had survived I knew the water would become loaded with debris, either flooded into the sea from land or off battered or destroyed ships. It's one of the dangers associated with such violent storms. And Luis was no different.

Around 2 a.m. I knew we were in very grave danger. It was apparent that debris made up of other boat's snapped anchor lines and the like had wrapped around Latina's propeller, stalling her main engine. Without the assistance of the engine we'd lose Latina for sure. *What could I do?* My mind was racing. My heart was pounding. There had to be something I could do. I just *had* to free that propeller.

With not a minute to spare I dashed into the engine room to restart it, but each time I re-engaged the transmission, the engine would stall. The crew watched in horror and disbelief as I grabbed my dive tank and a hacksaw and leaped off the ship's deck into the darkness. I don't know how, but I felt my way through the black water to the stern of the pitching ship. I couldn't see a thing. How I found the propeller is beyond me. It was totally jammed with rope. Frantically, I tried to cut through it, but the hacksaw just wouldn't do the job.

The ship was pitching so hard that I had trouble hanging on to the giant rudder and cutting at the same time. One minute I was flying high above the water caught up in the vicious waves only to be plunged deep under the next. Each time Latina's monstrous stern fell down, I felt barnacles cutting into my head, back, shoulders and arms.

Forget the hacksaw; it wasn't getting me anywhere – it was a tool better suited for steel. It was just barely ruffling the rope. I cursed myself for bringing it. What I really needed was a sharp knife. Fritz and Doris helped drag me back up on board and I scurried off to the galley in search of a better tool. In seconds I leapt back into the water – this time clutching the largest knife I could find.

Blinded by the darkness I closed my eyes and let my sixth sense guide me. This time, lady luck was on my side. As I slashed the tightly wound ropes, I felt one layer after another giving way. It gave me such an adrenaline rush that I hacked away with the rage of a wild animal.

Suddenly a sharp pain shot up my right arm as one of my muscles tore. But I didn't stop. I was too close. Then another blow of Latina's 132-ton hull slammed down on top of me, knocking the air supply regulator out of my mouth.

I couldn't hear the rage of the storm anymore. Confused and barely conscious I continued to cut away at the rope, but my mind started to wander off.

My first thought was of Shirley. If she knew what I was doing right now she would be furious. If I were to die, she would kill me.

Then I started to ask myself. *Why was I doing this? Where did I get my drive – my passion for life? Where was it all coming from? Why didn't I, or why couldn't I care less?*

Perhaps the guy on shore was right. I should let go and not be so committed. *Why can't I? Where does my survival instinct come from? How did I acquire such an adventurous spirit?*

Perplexed, I shook my head and wondered what in the world a prairie kid from Croatia was doing in the middle of the Caribbean under a 132-ton ship in a raging hurricane? How did I get myself into this predicament?

Then my whole life flashed before my eyes...

Chapter 2

Jakob's Plight

"It is not what you have lost, but what
you have left that counts."

                             … Harold Russell

Innocent screams and laughter penetrated the Croatian schoolyard. The children were excited because they had completed their fourth year of public school, the conclusion of their formal education.

Now most of them at the age of 11 would stay at home and work on their family land. Others, fortunate enough, would be *given away* to wealthy tradesmen who would take them to apprentice as furniture makers, blacksmiths, carpenters, or wooden wagon makers. In today's terms, it would be the equivalent of child labor, as they worked fourteen to sixteen hour days. However, even though they weren't paid, they were the more fortunate ones as they were assured to be well-fed. Certainly other children wouldn't live that well at home.

Jakob's spirits were running high. He was to be one of the fortunate ones as he had been promised to a carpenter family. His parents were also delighted because they would have one less mouth to feed. Times were tough in those days of the *dirty thirties*. Their land didn't even yield enough to cover the taxes that were supposed to be paid to the local Count.

A group of children were playing a game of tag in the schoolyard. Jakob thought he could escape a boy who was chasing him by climbing way up high into the limbs of an old chestnut tree. However, the boy proved to be as agile as Jakob, and determined to catch him, followed closely behind. Jakob crawled out further and further onto a branch trying to evade his pursuer.

Suddenly there was a loud crack, like a rifle shot, as the branch broke. As if in slow motion Jakob started to fall, bouncing off branches, then falling again, further and further down. In his last moments of consciousness he realized he was hurling toward the earth, head first. Instinctively he extended his arms above his head as if he were diving into water.

He heard the crunching sound of breaking bones. His fingers were the first to snap, then the bones just above his wrists. The last thing he saw was a red flash when his forehead met the ground. For a few seconds longer he could hear the frantic screams of frightened children calling for help. Then the sounds became muffled as Jakob drifted into total darkness.

When the teachers arrived they found his little motionless body lying in a pool of blood. There was a big gaping hole in his forehead. His small mangled fingers stuck out in haphazard directions and the bones above his wrists punctured his skin. As they wrapped Jakob's still body gently into a blanket they dispatched a child to alarm his family.

When his father arrived on the scene with his wagon and team of horses, he was crushed to see his little son so mangled and vulnerable. The teachers thought the situation was hopeless. *"It's just matter of time before he dies,"* they broke the news.

On one hand Marko wanted to take Jakob home where he could die among his family. On the other hand, as any loving father would do, he hoped that maybe there was still a chance, a miracle that Jakob could still survive. Even if Marko did take him to the hospital he would never be able to afford a doctor. However Jakob's father was so committed to his little son that he set out on the six-hour journey.

Marko fought back tears the entire way as Jakob's unconscious body bounced around in the back of the wooden wagon. Not once on route to the hospital did Marko stop to see if his little boy was still alive. It just would've been too hard to bear had he not been. Instead he drove the horses as hard as possible.

Immediately when they arrived Jakob's limp body was rushed inside to be examined. And in no time the doctors decided that given the extent of his injury it was pointless to perform any kind of surgery. The nurses were ordered to hastily bandage Jakob's open wounds and wheel him into a dark room to let nature take its course.

"Mr. Marko," the doctor confided, *"I'm sorry but there is no hope. Jakob's scull is fractured from above his eye to the back of his head. He has a gaping hole right above his eye, two broken arms, broken ribs, and worst of all, he's bleeding internally. He has lost too much blood. There is no hope. Even if he lives, he'll never be right. Please go home. It's pointless to stay. When he dies we will bury him here at the hospital cemetery and send you his death certificate."*

Heart broken and defeated, Marko set out on his long and agonizing trip back home. He couldn't imagine how he was going to explain to his wife that all hope for their son was lost.

Days passed. Jakob lay totally motionless in that dark room. Once a day a nurse stopped by to check on his status, to see if his heart had stopped beating yet, and then she'd leave. On one of her routine visits she noticed something unusual. Jakob's right eye was swollen shut and the cavity over his eyelid was filled with dried blood. Then she examined more closely his left eye. Even though it was shut and bloody there were signs of some motion, as if there was rapid eye movement under his eyelid. Excited about her discovery she rushed to advise the doctor. Unfortunately he disregarded the news as an involuntary nerve twitch.

What transpired next was the noble work of a dedicated nurse, an unsung hero, one that took notice and did what she was trained to do – to truly care for the sick. On her next lunch break she ate sitting right beside little Jakob and nursed a few spoons of her own soup into his mouth. Using a wet cloth she gently started to wipe the dried blood off his face. She repeated this every day for the next few days and to her amazement, one day she found Jakob with his left eye open.

Even though he showed definite signs of life, his emaciated body still lay motionless. The doctors again ordered that he be left alone to die. However, now instead of obeying the order, even the other nurses secretly joined in on the mission to feed and nurture him. Quickly and inconspicuously Jakob became the nurses' secret obsession.

Jakob slowly improved and did so well that when he spoke his first words the nurses panicked. Now they would have to reveal their secret to the doctor. They feared punishment for not obeying his orders. Yet it was imperative to do so immediately because the bones on Jakob's arms still protruded out of his skin.

To the nurse's amazement, the doctor did not punish anyone, but instead proceeded to carelessly jab Jakob's bones back under his skin and roughly stitch the gaps in his body shut. He was totally in denial that the little boy would live.

Months passed by and Jakob continued to be the hospital pet in secret care of the nurses. Eventually he regained full control of his speech. Other than the fact that there was an obvious indentation on his forehead directly above his right eye, his head wounds had completely healed.

His crippled fingers, however, were inflexible and could never be straightened, locked forevermore in a semi-circular formation, as if in a permanent grip. Deep scars were left on his arms just above his wrists where bones had once protruded. Other than that, he seemed to be fine, suffering no permanent brain damage. Finally at Jakob's insistence, the doctor had no other choice except to release him from the hospital.

With the expectation that Jakob was to die, nobody had even bothered to notify his parents that he was still alive. Jakob had to figure a way to return to his family. Once again the nurses came through. Holding a private collection, they raised enough money for his train ticket home.

Thrilled to be alive and anxious to see his family again, he lost no time in saying goodbye to the angels that had saved his life and left, skipping from one leg to the next, leaving a dusty trail on his way to the train station.

With a final chug, the steam train screeched to a halt. Stepping off the train, Jakob waved good bye to the conductor who cheerfully responded with a wave. He was finally back in his village, exhilarated to be home. Yet as he walked along the dirt road toward his family farm he couldn't understand why everyone stared at him. They were speechless. Puzzled, he made his way toward home.

"Hi Mary," he cheerfully greeted a schoolmate that lived just up the street from him as he passed by her. Mary was perched up on the rail of a wooden fence. She froze in disbelief. Her mouth dropped open. Speechless with shock, she watched Jakob happily prance toward his home. What Jakob didn't realize was that to the villagers he had been dead for months now, and everyone thought they were seeing a ghost. He didn't care to stop and ask for an explanation. All he wanted to do was get home to see his parents.

Jakob's mom was the first to spot him. From inside the barn where she was working she saw him enter the front yard gate. Their eyes instantly locked into a stare. But instead of her running toward him to greet him, she suddenly spun around and ran the opposite direction to a field behind the barn. *"Marko, Marko,"* she screamed hysterically, *"Jakob is home!"*

Marko instantly dropped his work, leaving the horses and plow in the field. Both of them raced back toward Jakob, tears streaming from their eyes as they sobbed and cried their thanks to God.

Jakob never did have the opportunity to apprentice as a carpenter or anything else. Instead he worked on his family's land as much as he was able. He continued to grow, nevertheless very slowly, probably due to his injuries. Handling tools and other farm equipment proved to be a challenge with his permanently bent and rigid fingers. However, Jakob still remained a very amiable young man, even though he grew up in the shadows of his healthy older brother, Ivo, and his two attractive sisters.

Jakob's favorite sanctuary was up in the attic above the horse's stable. There he would lie for hours, tucked in among the fresh hay, reading anything he could put his hands on – which wasn't much in those days – perhaps bits and pieces of old newspaper, propaganda leaflets, or a few loose pages of a precious book. After reading the same things repeatedly, over and over again, he would carefully fold and hide his prized possessions in the hay.

It was customary that Jakob's family pray before their meal. One day the prayer took on a different tone when Marko bowed his head and solemnly announced, *"May God save us all. Today Hitler attacked our country and we are at war."*

However as time went on and the Germans advanced, Jakob was actually entranced with watching the columns march through his village where they met virtually no resistance. Being an impressionable young man, he was spellbound by their slick uniforms and shiny nazi helmets. Tanks roared by. Heavy trucks pulled cannons. Shivers of excitement soared up Jakob's spine.

Rumor had it that the Germans were going to recruit young men for their elite SS troops. The fantasy of himself in one of those uniforms danced in his mind and kept him awake at night. The first draft came and went, but Jakob was not called. Then a second and third. On the other hand, his brother Ivo had a choice, he could either enlist with the SS troops or the Croatian National Guard. He chose the Croatian National Guard who fought side by side with the Germans.

Jakob's spirit was crushed. Even at the height of the German losses sustained on the eastern front he wasn't recruited. Finally, close to the end of the war, Jakob got to wear the uniform of the Croatian National Guard Reserve Unit. In retrospect he was lucky. All fit and able-bodied men had been sent to the Russian eastern front, most of them never to return.

The war took a toll on Jakob's feeble body. Food was scarce. Whatever was available was sent to the front to feed the warriors. When rations of potato soup were dished out, Jakob swore it didn't contain a single piece of potato, nor could he taste any. His frail 5'1" body frame had shrunk since joining the reserves. With so many people contracting and perishing from tuberculosis it was a miracle he escaped its fury.

One day Jakob heard the news that Tito's partisans had captured his brother, just barely a year after he'd enlisted. Nobody had learned of Ivo's fate until now. The story went that he had been forced to join the partisan ranks. That came as a relief to Jakob as it was becoming clear that the Germans were losing the war on both the eastern and western fronts. Allied planes now regularly dropped propaganda leaflets announcing their victory in Italy and France.

Jakob never did see a battle even though he craved to. Like most young men, he was eager and caught up in the excitement of war. It didn't seem to matter to him who he was to fight, as long it was an *enemy*.

Virtually every night the partisans fired a lonely shot somewhere from the surrounding hills shattering the silence of the village night. In return, the Germans responded with a barrage of machine-gun fire from their bunkers. That was the extent of Jakob's experience with war action. Shortly afterwards the Germans, without warning, disarmed his whole regiment. Jakob was free to return home.

After three days of walking, wilted with exhaustion and ravenous with hunger, he arrived home. As he approached his house he expected to hear his mother's relieved voice, *"Marko, Marko, Jakob is back!"* But his mother was not to be found. To his surprise he discovered strangers living in their home. Devastated, his heart sunk. His eyes filled with tears. He assumed the worst.

Then he heard good news. His mind swirled in a fog as the strangers explained, *"Your parents moved to a place called Novo Selo 50 kilometers away. They got twice as much land there in exchange for this land. They left a message for you and Ivo to go join them if you survived the war."* Jakob in his exhaustion and confusion just stared at the strangers. *"Come inside now,"* they insisted. *"You must eat before you go."*

It was the best food Jakob had eaten in a long time – wheat-flour mush, similar to polenta, topped with a few drops of lard and fried onions. The strangers generously loaned him money for the train, and soon he was on his way to seek out his parents.

Weak from fatigue, Jakob struggled along the narrow muddy trail from the train station toward Novo Selo. Sticky clumps of clay clung to his worn-out army boots, like lead weights. He was exhausted. Just walking ahead of him was a woman having the same problem. She looked equally exhausted, as she carried a little baby and dragged along beside her two other small children.

Jakob desperately tried to catch up to the woman to ask if she knew where his parents lived. To his surprise when he opened his mouth to talk, he was lost for words. The woman before him looked so familiar. His tired mind just couldn't put it together. She also seemed to be dumbfounded. For what seemed an eternity their eyes were locked.

Finally the woman said, *"Jakob is that you? I'm Mary – you know – from your hometown. Do you remember me?"*

He smiled remembering the young girl that grew up down the street, *"Yes! Yes! I remember you Mary!"*

They beamed at each other with such a warmth in their hearts as neither of them had experienced before. A feeling of relief overcame them. Naturally they fell into each other's arms and hugged for long time. Jakob picked up one of the children and slowly they walked together toward Novo Selo.

Chapter 3

Mary's Curse

"Never bend your head. Always hold it high.
Look the world straight in the eye."

... Helen Keller

The little girl stood beside her mother's bed, knowing that something awfully wrong was happening. Her mom was silent – no longer answering her questions. She watched her mom's normally olive toned skin slowly turn ghostly pale.

Mary started to weep silently, tears streaming from her eyes. With all her might she tried to obey her mom's last request, to be strong and everything would be fine. She was trying, still how could she? She was not yet 10.

As the casket was being lowered into the grave Mary firmly gripped her father's arm. Somehow she felt that things would *not* be fine and for the first time in her very young life, she wished she were the one that was dead.

Her father really loved his daughter, but he was the playboy type – the kind that spends all his money on cards and booze. It was her mom who had worked hard, hand washing other people's laundry outside in the ice cold water in bitterly cold weather during the past winter, providing the family with some basic food and a few rags for clothes. *What was going to happen now? Who would take care of her and her brother?*

Mary mourned the death of her mom. She recalled watching her work in the cold, her body shivering without sufficient clothing to keep her warm. When she became sick her exhausted body was too weak to fight off illness. Now Mary sorrowfully yearned for her mom. What she did not know was her pain would seem so insignificant in comparison to the trials she was destined for in her own life.

Out of the blue one day Mary's father came home and announced, *"This is your new mother. Be nice to her."*

Perhaps it should have been the other way around. The stepmother was attractive except she couldn't stand these children. Not so much because they were bad or anything like that, but because she had an idea of her own. She wanted to start her own family and these kids were just in her way. She had a knack of knowing how to control her husband, who all of a sudden stuck close to home even though he didn't have to say too much without getting an earful. As a result he remained silent when his wife mistreated his children. Her efforts to get rid of them yielded some results when she managed to send Mary's older brother to live with a family to apprentice as a carpenter.

Now there was only one obstacle – Mary. With her out of the way the stepmother would control her own turf. Mary was a beautiful young child and even at the young age of 13 she was promising to grow into a gorgeous woman. However to Mary's poor fortune, a better-off wagon maker from a village some 50 kilometers away, noticed her fine qualities and potential. Every time he came to Mary's village he made it a point to visit her family and to share his feelings and intentions with her parents. Mary wasn't aware of her predicament. And it didn't occur to her be concerned because the man was more than 20 years her senior – an old man in her opinion.

In the meantime Mary's stepmother was losing her patience and became more determined to be rid of her. Yet what she didn't know was that the hatred she harbored for Mary and her brother would actually sabotage her sinister plot. She didn't realize her state of mind would create her state of results. Mary's stepmother got exactly what she constantly dwelled on – her mind was so filled with hate, it would prevent her from having any children of her own.

When Mary turned 14 the decision was made. She was to be given to Juca, the wagon maker, for just a small dowry. When she heard the news, once again she felt as if the world had slipped from under her feet. She felt betrayed and abandoned. She constantly cried but the pain just wouldn't go away.

Then one day Juca came to pick her up. Mary had no choice. She began the journey to her new home on a farm 50 kilometers away. As the horse-drawn wagon rolled through her village, she could see through her tears a boy with a deep scar on his forehead hanging over the fence waving goodbye to her. A thought flashed through her mind remembering his name – Jakob. She recalled seeing him that day, when he was younger, walking down the street after everyone thought for months that he was dead. Now all she wanted to do was to be dead herself.

The Second World War was in a full swing now. The only things interrupting the two-day journey to Mary's new home were regular German roadblocks. Juca tried to initiate small talk with Mary along the way yet she constantly cried.

Finally arriving at her new home there was another shock. *She was expected to sleep with Juca*. Nobody had forewarned or prepared her. At first she slept alone. Trembling in fear she would curl into a ball on the very edge of her bed. She was only a child. She didn't know what to do – and had no mother to tell her what to expect.

Fortunately Juca was a nice enough man to treat Mary with respect and eventually with indifference. He became distracted, busy with making a living. Juca's widowed mother was not mean to Mary, however she would not readily communicate with her, except to dish out orders to work. She also treated Mary with indifference.

The expectations of Juca and his mother overwhelmed Mary. They expected her to labor on their land, hoeing in the fields indefinitely from early in the morning until late into the evening. Also she was to maintain the livestock, garden and cook the meals. She would barely fall asleep before it was time to start all over again. Things would not improve for Mary anytime soon.

Within a year Mary, still a child herself, had her first baby – a boy. Again nobody prepared her for her home delivery or taught her how to care for her newborn. She didn't even have diapers or baby clothes. Only through sheer desperation she found her way through this quagmire. As the war dragged on Mary gave birth to another child just about every year until she had three children, two boys and a girl.

By now Mary had settled into a routine and respected the fact that Juca was innovative and creative enough to provide just enough food to feed his family when others did not fare as well, going to bed hungry. Then one day even that little bit of security vanished.

Word was out that the Germans were coming into town to collect the Jews. Those not having a certificate from the town Commissioner that certified they weren't Jewish were to be taken to a concentration camp. Mary didn't know why, but for some reason the town Commissioner didn't want to give her nor Juca and their children the certificate. However, she felt confident she'd be able to get them out of this jam as most of her family was of German origin. In contrast Juca did not want to take the risk. He felt the town Commissioner might have ulterior motives, perhaps even eyeing their property, and was not prepared to risk what he treasured most – his children.

That night Mary readied their children while Juca harnessed the horses to their wagon. They silently slipped out of town with only a few precious belongings. As Juca drove his team of horses throughout the night he wondered if he would ever see his mother again. Driving the horses hard, he wanted to be as far as possible from his town by daybreak where no one would recognize them.

Juca had a good friend, Peter, who lived a day and a half away.

He was a wealthy merchant, a landowner and wine producer. Juca hoped that Peter would give them shelter and hide them for a while until things settled down. As it turned out their timing was perfect. Peter had been ill for some time and welcomed Juca and his family with open arms. He was delighted to have help running his business. Most of all he felt fortunate to utilize Juca's skill in fixing his poorly maintained fleet of wagons.

Mary and the family had a home again. It consisted of one large room on the second floor of Peter's house for the five of them. Things were going well. Peter was so impressed with the way Juca had secured a family that he started to think about it himself. He was an only child brought up in a wealthy family and like Juca, he was in his early forties. He had never been married and now he was all alone since his parents had died. His health was very poor and he constantly coughed. Perhaps it was time to find himself a wife like Juca had.

One day one of Peter's business clients offered to give him his daughter's hand but Peter would have to pick her up. As she lived in Croatia's interior the journey took him days. To Peter's delight his new bride turned out to be a beautiful girl and the dowry was beyond what he ever expected.

Stefie was 18 and also from a better-off family. She did not like her father's choice of husband but was assured that she was marrying into wealth and security. In preparation for her journey to her new home she packed two large wooden trunks of clothing and bedding. Little did she know what significance those trunks would have in the future.

When Mary first met Peter's new bride she admired her fine features and was taken by her beauty. Stefie fast became her good friend. It was a long time since Mary had such a friend. As an additional bonus Stefie adored the children and would baby-sit them while Mary worked in the fields.

Everything was going exceptionally well. The two families got along wonderfully, though as the months passed Peter's health deteriorated to the point that he became bedridden most of the time.

Everyone expected him to recover as he was still a young man and could afford the services of the town doctor. To everyone's surprise, only six months into her marriage, Stefie became a young widow. All Peter's wealth was now hers. But she was lonely. She felt no reason to stay any more and decided to return to her parent's home.

In preparation for her departure, Stefie decided to only take one of her wooden trunks with her on the train. She discussed, both with her baker friend across the street and also with Mary and Juca, storing her other trunk in safekeeping until after the war. Then she would have it sent to her.

Stefie finally decided to leave the locked trunk with Mary and Juca. Carefully they placed it in one corner of their room and actually used it as a base for the bed of one of their small children. Mary never suspected that innocent looking trunk would alter her life so drastically.

Days passed, then months. One day a sharp rap at the door startled Mary disturbing her from her daily routine. Who could it be? Juca was not expected to return from the vineyard until dark. It was such a commanding knock that Mary imagined only the worst. *Did the Germans finally find them?*

Then there was a second round of vigorous thumping. Mary reluctantly opened the door. To her surprise and delight it was only her neighbor, the baker. *"Mary I came to pick up the trunk,"* he said. *"Stefie asked me to keep it for her."*

"I know Stefie talked to you about it too, but just before she left she said she wanted Juca and me to keep it for her. I feel obliged to safeguard it," Mary explained.

"I'm taking that trunk now!" the baker growled.

"I can't let you. I promised Stefie," Mary held her ground. An argument flared up.

The baker tried to push Mary out of his way yet she held her position. Even though he towered a foot higher over Mary's small 5'1" frame she wouldn't give in. Finally the baker left cussing into his beard.

When Juca returned Mary told him about the incident. Immediately he went to speak with the baker. Again he demanded to have the trunk. Juca refused. The baker warned Juca he would create problems for them unless they gave in to his demand. Juca didn't budge.

The next day the village Mayor came by their room and demanded that the trunk be turned over to the baker. Juca and Mary were now more than ever determined to keep their promise to Stefie. They couldn't imagine why someone would want a chest of clothing and bedding so badly. And why create such animosity? After that they were harassed constantly and the baker refused to sell them anymore bread.

One day, out of nowhere, rifle and machine gun fire could be heard throughout the town. Grenades thundered. Mary quickly scooped up her kids, went inside and locked their door. *What was going on?* Never before had she experienced fighting like this. She knew Tito's partisans were in the hills but normally they would fire one or two shots on the bunkers located close to the railway station. The Germans then would respond with a barrage of firepower back toward the hills.

However, this time the fighting was very serious and Juca was not at home. She cursed the poor timing. The fighting went on a few hours. Mary, with her children huddled in a corner, suddenly heard the heavy pounding of a gun-stock against their door. Fear shivered through their bodies.

"Open the door," a loud voice commanded.

Mary kept silent. Her children followed her example.

"We will blow this door open. Open it now!"

Mary had no choice. Slowly she drew the door open. Three men towered over her. Their pointed caps displayed a red star indicating they were partisans. Gun barrels raised, they aimed directly at Mary's head.

"Please don't kill me, I have young children," she pleaded.

The partisans barged their way in and went directly over to the chest as if they knew what to look for. With just one sharp whack of their gun-stock, the lock broke open. After a quick inspection of the chest's contents, two partisans quickly lugged it away, leaving the other partisan to guard Mary and her kids at gunpoint. Mary silently prayed for their lives. She had never seen partisans before, although she knew about their reputation for being brutal fearless fighters.

Just then Juca returned home. He discovered his house besieged and his family under house arrest. Without explanation the partisan locked them inside their room and stood guard at their front door. They wondered what was to become of them.

The next day the scam unfolded. The partisan Commander, pronouncing them traitors, ordered them to leave their home immediately. Juca's request for his horse-team and wagon was denied, so the family had no choice but to escape on foot with only the clothing on their backs.

With no idea of where to turn for shelter, they thought of their little daughter's godparents who lived in the next village. It was a long walk, however to their good fortune Irene, the woman of the house, welcomed them. She was a kind soul who loved the children, especially her little godchild, Nada. However, it became clear to Mary and Juca that they would have to move on soon as Irene and her husband barely had enough to eat themselves, never mind feeding five more hungry souls. As it turned out they would not have to make that call.

On the third day after their arrival, early in the morning the same partisan Commander that had ordered them to leave their home burst into the yard with a half dozen soldiers. They were looking for Juca. *"We've been told that you are a good horse team driver. We need you to drive our wounded soldiers. The Germans are mounting a counter offensive so we're heading into the hills."*

Juca immediately declined. He feared their reputation. There were many stories about partisans forcing people to join their ranks – never to be seen again.

"I'm ordering you," the Commander said, *"but I promise that once we are safe in the mountains you can return back home to your family."*

Once again Juca declined, claiming he could not leave his children. *"This is an order. If you don't come you will be shot right now – on the spot."* Juca still didn't budge.

The Commander sternly nodded to his men. Two soldiers grabbed Juca and lined him up against the wall while the others readied their rifles. Screaming hysterically, Mary ran in front of Juca and begged the soldiers not to shoot.

The Commander gave Juca one last chance. Fearful for his life and also for his family, Juca agreed to go. Hastily the partisans escorted him down the street. Mary, holding onto her three young children cried, and watched hopelessly as her husband disappeared into the distance. She was never to set eyes on him again.

Juca had no idea what his future was to bring. He was forced to harness a team of horses and load the wounded soldiers onto a wooden wagon. One of the wounded caught his attention. Juca felt the young man couldn't have been more than twelve or thirteen. He placed the boy lying in his stretcher on the wagon with his head close to Juca's seat. Perhaps they could talk on the ride toward the hills.

"Let's go. Let's go. We can't hold these Germans much longer," the Commander ordered his column.

They started on their journey. Juca was in the third wagon, and as they made their way out of town, gun and mortar fire slowly faded in the distance. Everyone was relieved when they reached the hills and started to enter the thick forest – the partisans' traditional safe haven.

Suddenly, without any warning, a barrage of firepower burst out of the forest on the high side of the road.

"Ambush! It's an ambush!" everyone screamed.

Juca leaped off his wagon and into a ditch on the opposite side of the road, away from the firepower. Although he was protected in the ditch, he decided to return to the wagon to help the wounded over to the safety of the ditch as well. Amazingly he managed to get them all except the young boy. Alone, Juca didn't have the strength to carry the boy's stretcher.

Huddled against the embankment of the ditch, Juca and the wounded were totally defenseless, with no guns to protect themselves. The fighting raged on for hours. The partisans at the front of the column struggled. They needed support from their men behind trying to make their way forward. Only then did they manage to push the Germans back into the forest.

As the fighting receded the partisan Commander gave the order to move. One of the other wagon drivers yelled out, *"OK Juca let's go! Let's go!"*

Juca was still in the ditch. He didn't move. The driver gave him a shake. Juca just rolled over and continued to roll – lifeless, down to the bottom of the ditch. He was dead.

The partisans lost some of their men and others were wounded, but everyone in the ditch survived without a scratch – everyone except Juca. One lonely bullet went astray and managed to hit him right behind his left ear. Nobody was even aware when it happened.

Many days later one of the wagon drivers returned to Juca's home and broke the sad news to Mary. *"Oh God – NOOOooooo!"* she wailed as she ran back into her room.

She cried for hours. Her three little children looked on, not comprehending what was happening. Being one, two, and three, they were just too young to understand. Their mother was a widow and she was barely 17.

Now they were alone. One thought permeated Mary's being. She wished *she* were dead. In her prayers she repeatedly asked God why couldn't He let *her* die.

Still ostracized by her family, Mary's only option was to return with her children to Juca's family home – if there was anything left of it. She did return, finding Juca's mom in good shape, and she actually received Mary and the children quite well.

To her surprise, now with Juca dead, Mary found herself in the leading family position, one she was uncertain of how to handle. Perhaps it was the first time in her life that she actually felt important, someone who was needed, and who could make a difference.

Raising her three tiny children was a challenge itself. There wasn't a day that went by without some kind of crisis. Mary worked hard. The weaker she grew physically from laboring, the stronger she became mentally and spiritually.

Then one day she noticed something that just didn't seem right. German soldiers were scurrying about, not paying much attention to the local populace. Later in the day columns of wagons filled with wounded German soldiers started passing through the village, though they did not stop. The commotion continued throughout the night.

Speculation had it that the Russians were on the offensive and might be pushing the Germans back toward Germany. Yet word spread like wildfire that the Russians were out of control, raping local women and killing any men even slightly suspected of collaborating with the Germans.

The next morning an explosion from an artillery shell bolted Mary out of bed. It had completely destroyed their barn. That was just the beginning as the whole village and surrounding area burst into fire from the constant shelling.

Mary and her family hid in the only safe place in the area – their wine cellar. Other neighbors dashed over begging for shelter also. Soon it was full of people. The battle for control of the village lasted the entire day. In the cellar, they could hear voices out in the street shouting orders in Russian, as the fight raged on, to take over each house one by one. Mary, her family and neighbors sat in the darkness paralyzed with fear.

A loud bang on the cellar door made everyone shriek with terror. Speaking in Russian, and obviously irritated, a man yelled as he pounded his fist rapidly against the door. Everyone froze – men and women alike. But Mary thought she recognized one word the Russian was yelling – *"Rakia!"*

She said, *"I think he wants some plum brandy. Let's give him some brandy. I have some here in the barrel."* No one stirred.

Meanwhile the Russian just kept yelling and banging on the door with his gun-stock. Mary didn't waste any time. She immediately grabbed an empty bottle and siphoned some brandy into it.

"Don't open the door. Don't do it Mary!" Everyone was mortified but no one else offered to go themselves. She slowly creaked open the door to find a man pointing a rifle directly at her chest. He reached and yanked the bottle out of her hand and tasted its contents. Obviously delighted with it, the soldier ran up the steps and back onto the street.

Phew! Everyone felt the relief. That time they were spared, nevertheless what if it happened again? *Would they be found?* Those were their thoughts as they huddled silently. The fighting lasted all night – in contrast the morning greeted them with an eerie silence. As quickly as the Russians had come, they had left.

Mary was the first to climb out of the cellar. She immediately saw a dead body slumped against the wall of her house. It was the Russian soldier she'd encountered the night before. He had barely taken a few steps before a bullet found him. His fingers still clenched the brandy bottle as if it were a precious possession.

Finally the war was over. It was time for Mary to pick up the pieces and carry on with her life. The first thing she wanted to do was to find her husband's grave, yet to her regret and sorrow she never did. The wagon driver who had buried Juca could not find the exact location. He knew Juca and the dead partisans were buried somewhere beside the road, but brush had since overgrown their resting place.

Back at Irene's house Mary discovered the mystery about Stefie's trunk – the trunk that had caused so much hardship and turmoil in her life. It turned out that both the baker and the town Mayor were secret partisan collaborators. Apparently the reason they wanted the trunk was to smuggle it to the partisans since they were so desperate for clothing. And more importantly, they needed material of any kind to be used as bandages for their wounded soldiers. In those times the contents of that abandoned trunk were a valuable treasure and the partisans were prepared to go to any length to get it. For Mary it was all about integrity and the promise she had pledged to her friend.

The war might've been over however for Mary the pain was not. She couldn't decide whether she was happy or sad when she heard the news that her dad and stepmother had sold their land in the village where she was born and moved to a town called Novo Selo, 12 kilometers away. She missed her father but could not forget the psychological abuse and pain her stepmother had caused her. However, it wasn't really a matter of choice. She could barely feed her three children and winter was coming. Maybe – just maybe her dad could help.

Mary started out on her 12-kilometer journey to Novo Selo, walking on the road with her three young children. She tried not to be anxious and fearful about seeing her stepmother again. There were just too many painful memories. It had to be the longest 12 kilometers she ever walked. The mud on her shoes felt like lead weights dragging her down. Slowly she trudged on, carrying Nada on her hip and towing her two little boys behind.

She didn't notice when a young soldier slowly caught up to her. Her burdened mind almost didn't respond when the soldier asked, *"Excuse me madam – do you know where Novo Selo is?"*

She looked at his tired frail face and thought she recognized him. Then she noticed the deep scar on his forehead and without hesitation she said, *"Jakob is that you? I'm Mary – from your hometown. Do you remember me?"*

Jakob smiled. Yes, he remembered the young girl who grew up down the street, *"Yes! Yes! I remember you Mary!"*

They beamed at each other with such a warmth in their hearts as neither of them had experienced before. A feeling of relief overcame them. Naturally they fell into each other's arms and hugged for a long time.

Jakob picked up one of the children and slowly they walked together toward Novo Selo.

Chapter 4

Mary and Jakob

"What does not destroy me, makes me strong."
… Friedrich Nietzsche

When Mary told her parents of her desire to marry Jakob, she was surprised by their response. Her stepmother was delighted yet concerned. Delighted because she liked Jakob but concerned because she wondered how on earth the five of them, two teenagers and three small children would be able to feed themselves. World War II was over however food was so scarce it was a matter of bare bones survival.

To Mary's surprise her stepmother offered to help by looking after 18 month old Nada, her youngest daughter, until they were settled. Neither Mary nor Jakob suspected an ulterior motive.

With the help of their family and neighbors, Mary and Jakob built a basic one-room mud and straw house, and just in time. One month after they moved in, Jakob's dream would come true – the birth of his first son! Unfortunately his joy would not last.

Mary and Jakob were only 19 years old raising four young children. It was the coldest winter in years and their house wasn't warm enough for the harsh environment. It was like a classic winter scene from Dr. Zhivago. Wind howled between the sparsely layered clay roof tiles under the rafters, blowing freezing cold snow into their house. Any water left in the bucket froze solid. The small wood stove just couldn't keep up.

Nada was the lucky one as she lived with Mary's stepmother and father full time now. Meanwhile her two older brothers huddled in bed, covered with a feather comforter in order to survive the bitter cold.

The newborn baby did not fair so well. One sad morning Mary found him dead. As much as she had tried to keep him warm it just wasn't enough. He simply froze to death. There just wasn't enough clothing and blankets to protect against such extreme conditions.

Jakob was shattered. Dealing with the constant hunger, poverty and cold, and now the loss of his baby son. It was just too heavy a burden to carry. Every night Mary and Jakob cried themselves to sleep. However Jakob would soon have a second chance.

The following year, 1947, Mary gave birth to twins, Luka and Vera. Improvements were made to their mud house, however not enough to adequately withstand another harsh winter. The twins developed whooping cough and Luka's condition steadily worsened. Mary's tears and prayers could not stave off fate. Luka died and Jakob's life was once again devastated.

He cried and mourned the loss of a yet his second son. He cursed the poverty he was born into. He cursed his job that everyday exhausted his frail body. However, one thing he cherished and was thankful for was his baby girl, Vera.

One day Jakob returned from work to find Mary sobbing uncontrollably.

"Mary what in the world happened?" Jakob asked.

"I went to pick up Nada to bring her home but my stepmother accused us of not being capable to take care of our other kids. She wouldn't let me take Nada! She said she's going to adopt her and raise her as her own." Mary shoulders heaved as she cried.

It was a fact that Nada had lived the last two years at the home of Mary's stepmother and father. She was well looked after and loved, though Mary dearly missed her. Even in her poverty and misery, she could not envision giving up one of her children forever.

On the other hand, the stepmother now considered Nada as her own daughter – the one she was never able to give birth to. Perhaps she even felt she was helping the matter by taking a load off Mary and Jakob. Or was it just a rationalization to cover up the real truth that she had wanted to keep Nada all along?

Jakob invited his in-laws over to discuss the situation, hopefully to negotiate a peaceful solution. There was no compromise with either Mary or her stepmother. Mary would not consider giving up her child and her stepmother refused to give up custody.

Little Nada must've wondered what was happening when the two women played tug-o-war, with her in the middle. The stepmother won. She scooped up Nada into her arms and took off running down the village street with Mary running in hot pursuit behind.

"Give me back my child. I want her back," Mary wailed as she caught up with her stepmother at the gate of Ivo's house. A fight ensued and the roles were reversed with Mary running back to her home, Nada in her clutches, with her stepmother racing behind. Eventually Mary was able to lock herself in her house and refused to open the door for anyone.

Finally her stepmother and father left, however not before her stepmother threatened to pay Mary back. Mary had no idea what that meant at the time. Jakob, however sensed that his father-in-law's wife was out for cruel revenge, and he was right.

The little support that they used to receive from Mary's stepmother and father, mainly in the form of milk and cheese, never happened again. They had Nada, but the reality was that Jakob and Mary had one more mouth to feed and Mary was now totally rejected by her family.

Jakob didn't fare that well either. His parents were very poor and old, unable to help in any way. His brother, Ivo, and his wife had never agreed that Jakob should marry a woman with three children in the first place because he would never be able to support them. Of course that was just their excuse not to help. Never would they share a crust of bread, a log for the fire, or offer support in any way – yet were quick to dish out criticism and ridicule.

Jakob's older sister's husband who lived across the street wasn't any more sympathetic. He insisted that Mary, Jakob and all their rotten and raggedy kids would never amount to anything.

Jakob was a diligent hard worker at the local sawmill, unloading and stocking huge logs. He hoped to work his way into the plant to get an easier job. But because of his permanently bent and inflexible fingers, he couldn't perform some of the more tedious jobs and was therefore stuck with hard labor in the log yard.

Through all the adversity Jakob had become a man of determination. He promised Mary that one day he would build her a new house, one that would keep them all warm to survive the winters. In order to back his promise he worked nights molding and firing bricks for a brick-manufacturing co-op. In return for his labor he received the equivalent value in bricks. Every day Jakob patiently stocked his share of little red bricks. With each one he earned he became closer to his goal.

Six years passed and in 1953 Mary became pregnant again. Jakob decided the time had finally come to build the house. It was the beginning of summer and the children temporarily moved in with their godparents while Mary and Jakob diligently worked. Every night they nestled in the hayloft above their barn and shared their dreams of what their new three-room *palace* would look like. Then their exhausted bodies would fall deep into sleep.

It didn't take much to tear the old mud house down although it took a lot of back breaking labor to build a new one. By October 1953 the walls were up and two overlapped layers of red clay roof tiles graced the structure. The rafters and eaves were all finished, with the gaps filled in for protection from the cold winter winds and drifting snow. Even though the interior was incomplete and there were no ceilings, the family's comfort was immeasurable. The children now had a room of their own where all four slept in one bed, cross wise. And for the first time in their lives, Mary and Jakob had a room all to themselves.

That didn't last long. On December 12, 1953, another baby boy was born. Once again Jakob was ecstatic that he had a son, and vowed that he would do everything possible to keep this one alive.

He was true to his word. The whole family closely watched over me, loved and protected me. Each of my older brothers and sisters were assigned to baby-sit around the clock to assure my health and safety. The first years of my life I was always riding on my brother's shoulders or propped up on my sister's hips while Dad labored in the log yard and Mom in our farm fields.

My parents still had their challenges. Each day they worked themselves to the point of exhaustion just to provide enough food for us children to survive. Things must've looked hopeless and they must've felt helpless – each day wondering if they were ever going to pull out of their chronic poverty.

Chapter 5

Remembering the Hunger

"I cried because I had no shoes until I met a man who had no feet."

… Persian saying

By the time I was five, things were supposed to get better for us, however they didn't. Feeding and clothing a seven-soul family proved to be too much for Mom and Dad. We were experiencing more hunger than full tummies. Our clothes had more patches than original material.

It was an embarrassment that shamed us all but it was especially heartbreaking for Mom and Dad. They constantly prayed that our life would improve, yet as history would show, instead of getting better, things got worse. We were about to experience a true trial in life.

It was a late summer. Mom and Dad went to visit some neighbors for the evening while we kids stayed home. While they were gone my older brothers and sisters, now teenagers, became very hungry. The watered-down soup we'd eaten for dinner wasn't enough for the young teenagers' hunger.

They searched the house in vain for something edible, only to discover some stale bread and a 16-ounce jar of sour cream. Mom had been slowly saving it, a spoonful each day, for an upcoming special occasion. We did own a cow, however we weren't allowed to drink its milk or eat any dairy products. They were considered precious commodities to be sold which would allow us to purchase other staples we couldn't grow – things like sugar, salt, oil and such.

Everyone knew that eating the cream would be an enormous no-no, so we all agreed that each of us would sample only one small dip of bread into the precious treat. We had good intentions yet our agreement didn't hold. Once we savored the tasty morsel we couldn't stop ourselves, even though we all knew there would be hell to pay. When it was all said and done, to our horror all the bread was gone and so was the cream!

Dead silence greeted Mom and Dad when they returned home. They immediately sensed a problem. We couldn't believe our eyes when Mom marched straight into the pantry before she even asked what was wrong.

"Jakob, the kids ate the sour cream!" she screamed from inside the pantry. She came running out furious, crying hysterically, wielding my father's old army belt and slapping everything in her path. I was the only one to escape her rage.

When she was finally finished she curled up in the corner behind the door. Defeated, she broke into uncontrollable sobs. My father never physically disciplined any of us. He was a philosopher type. I would guess that they had an agreement that he wasn't to interfere when she used her style of discipline.

Dad looked at the sorry sight – us kids whimpering in one corner of the kitchen while my mother cried her heart out in the other. *"That's it. I am going back to school Mary, and this time no one will talk me out of it!"* Dad proclaimed.

We didn't know what on earth that had to do with the cream, but Mom burst into even louder sobs. What Dad meant and did was, he signed up to return to school to get a degree, which would enable him to get a better job. Finally he came to the realization that he couldn't feed his hungry family on a laborer's salary. He made the bold move to leave us at home, move onto the school campus and totally immerse himself in his studies. What a challenge he gave himself – with only having a pre-wartime grade four education.

Dad struggled with his challenge. He studied day and night. On Sundays he would take the train home to spend time with us. He would eat the meager food Mom prepared for him and then instantly fall asleep, relieved and exhausted from the hunger he endured during the week. The nourishment of his Sunday meal would have to carry him through the rest of the week. Other students on his campus had food packs given to them by their families. It was common knowledge that the little bit of food provided at school was not enough to sustain the students. However, my father had to return to school empty-handed.

We barely had anything to eat ourselves. The little amount of money Mom made, combined with some from Dad's student loan, was not enough to even pay our monthly bread bill.

Somehow every Sunday morning Dad managed to bring home a small treat for each child. At his school students received a slice of bread for breakfast, a glass of milk and an individual portion of jam, packaged somewhat like a cube of butter found in today's restaurants. Dad would save his little jams and bring all six of them home, one for each of us kids and one for Mom too.

On those Sundays I, as a six-year-old tike, would religiously walk two miles to the train station to greet my father and receive my precious treat. I would savor it, licking the sweet jam slow enough to last me most of the day. That way I could show off to my friends how Dad brought me a very special delicacy. Of course the other kids didn't think it was such a big deal, but I did. I never had anything so pleasant tasting in my life. And I loved my dad for it. We would hold hands as he walked and I skipped along beside him all the way home from the train station.

Dad's school days were hard on him. At the beginning of his re-education, one of the most humiliating things he experienced was the fact that he was over 30 years old and they made him study children's poems, paint watercolors, sing in music class and such – all basic grade stuff. He felt it was degrading and a waste of time but unfortunately he wasn't able to write his exams and progress through the grades until he finished those assignments.

He admitted years later that one of the most difficult things about his schooling was that it was so hard to concentrate on studying while constantly feeling hungry. Tediously he studied anyway from early in the morning until his classes started. Then again after school until the wee hours well after midnight. After a few hours sleep he'd be back up and at 'em again to study before school. Dad's friend said sometimes in class Dad would collapse to his desk or to the floor, exhausted.

Meanwhile, on the home front it looked as if the struggle would never end. All those years my mother worked extremely hard. She held it all together, keeping up our land and caring for the livestock. A couple years into Dad's schooling she even worked at a flower farm; it was only temporary work, in summer when flowers were in bloom. Nevertheless she tried her very best to feed her kids.

It was too much – too hard on everyone. Mom wanted Dad to stop his schooling but he refused to quit. In those days of poverty and hunger I didn't know how we could have survived if it weren't for the help of our neighbors. They organized a food collection drive for us, going from house to house with a tin can asking to donate of a spoonful of pork fat so we could have something to cook with. Likewise with flour.

I remember my mother needing to wash my clothes – a weekly occurrence. Of course she didn't have a change of clothes for me to wear so I had to strip stark naked and go to bed. I hated those days. They seemed to last for an eternity. It was difficult for me, a restless child, to wait for Mom to hand-wash my clothes and hang them outside to dry, all that time having to sit still, waiting and keeping warm in my bed.

On one of those wash days it was a beautiful sunny crisp winter day, just after a great snowfall. I could hear the laughter of my friends playing as they tobogganed down a hill near our house. I peeked through my window and witnessed their fun. It was just too much. I couldn't resist the temptation any more.

Even though my clothes were still wet on the clothesline, I quickly put them on and without permission, I slipped on my mom's wooden clogs, and ran outside to join my friends. Finally I was in heaven. I took a run and slid down the hill gliding on Mom's wooden clogs like a skater on ice. I was in ecstasy, just having a blast, as I propelled much further than anyone else in their regular winter boots.

My clothes were frozen stiff and so were my little toes. When I bent over, my pants crackled under my knee joints and likewise with my shirt and little jacket. But I was having fun! I played until finally the cold became unbearable.

To my misfortune I returned home just at the time Mom came in from the barn. When she saw that I was wearing her wooden clogs, she went ballistic. They were her dress shoes, only to be worn for special occasions. And there I was – guilty of using them to *play* in the snow. She wasn't impressed. After a good spanking, I ran off to bed crying. My young mind just could not figure out why all my friends seemed to have it so much better than us. Why were we so different?

One day I came home from school crying. I was traumatized. Mom held and hugged me, trying to sooth my pain. She wondered what had gone wrong. I told her that at school, one of my patches on my pants was torn. The teacher had given me a really hard time ridiculing me in front of the class, asking *what kind of a mother did I have – one who didn't even care enough about her child to sew a good patch on my pants?* The whole classroom laughed. I was humiliated. I wished so much we could afford nice clothes.

Mom just hugged and reassured me with her warm deep voice that one day, when Daddy finished school, we wouldn't have to worry about old worn-out clothes any more. In fact she said we wouldn't have to worry about money, or even going hungry. She promised to buy me a bicycle and some toys. I just couldn't believe her. I didn't own one store-bought toy.

I certainly didn't feel like going back to school again even after Mom sewed another patch on my pants. By now even *I* was getting to hate the curse of poverty. I thought it would never end.

My father's studying and hard work eventually did pay off. After four years of agony it was finally time to celebrate. He received his degree in economics.

Immediately after Dad finished college our lives changed dramatically. He was offered a job as Director of a farm co-operative and earned a lot of money by comparison with what we were accustomed to. I vividly remember the proud day he received his first pay envelope. He sat me on his knee and let me count the cash. I clenched the small fortune in my hands – so proud of my father.

Then he hugged Mom and promised that from that time on the dark cloud of poverty would never visit us again.

Chapter 6

Breaking Family Ties

*"Twenty years from now you will be more
disappointed by the things you didn't do than
by the ones you did. So throw off the bowlines.
Sail away from the safe harbor. Catch the trade
winds in your sails. Explore. Dream. Discover."*
… Mark Twain

Tears leaked from Dad's eyes but he didn't snivel. His bent fingers dug deeply into my back as he hugged me hard. Mom couldn't bear to watch and turned away, sobbing loudly, just about hysterically. When it was her turn to give me a hug, she just squeezed me and wouldn't let go. Her body jerked uncontrollably as she cried. I hugged and kissed her in return and reassured them both that everything was going to be just fine.

I was so keyed up about my first airplane ride that I didn't really understand what the fuss was all about. In my youthful innocence, at the age of 17, I just had no perception of the pain I was causing my parents. I had no point of reference, no experience or feeling for the magnitude of love that parents harbor for their child. According to tradition, as the youngest male in the family, I was their only hope to stay with them, to inherit their house and farm and to look after them in their old age.

What I really didn't realize at the time was I was my father's pride and joy – his only surviving son, someone he wanted to nurture, guide and help educate. I couldn't relate to the kind of pain and suffering he endured when my two older brothers had frozen to death. Finally he got to keep me, love and protect me, but now – now I was slipping out of his hands.

It was true he was a philosopher type. Often we would engage in discussions about why I should or should not leave my homeland. Even though I drove him absolutely crazy over this issue he never lost his cool. He had a vision of what I should become in life, believing that my future was in mechanical engineering. However, engineering was the last thing on my mind.

I'm sure he speculated that if I went for a higher education, by the time I would finish I'd be mature and forget about leaving home. However, already at my age I realized I wouldn't subordinate myself to certain goals unless they made my heart sing, dance, whistle and hum. No other person's wishes, not even my father's, would interfere with that.

Being the youngest of five children, I was the last one to leave home. My other brothers and sisters were forced to find their own way through life early in their lives because of the poverty they were forced to live in at that time. I guess that attitude rubbed off on me too.

The truth is I didn't really have to leave. Now the circumstances at home were much different. After receiving his Degree in Economics, Dad became a well sought after business leader, yet more importantly, a respected community leader of high integrity. He inspired people to take action to build roads, bridges, youth centers and such in their community.

Even though prosperity finally smiled on Dad in business and public life he never lost track of his roots. He knew that education was the magic ingredient for success and it was what he wished for me. He was selling, but I wasn't buying.

It didn't help the situation from his point of view that when I was 13 my sister, Vera, left Croatia to marry a fellow in Canada. They sent home letters on a regular basis confirming prosperity and opportunity. The kind of money they took home each month with Mario working in a butcher shop and Vera as a laborer in a factory, would take my dad years to earn.

Scenes of *the good life* in North America danced on a screen inside my mind every day. There wasn't a moment that I wasn't campaigning with my wishes to emigrate somewhere, either to Germany, Australia, the U.S. or Canada. It drove my parents crazy. Of course they felt I was only 13 and much too young to go anywhere.

On the other hand I thought *what's the big deal? I'm capable of working hard and looking after myself.* After all I was used to hard work on the farm. We had worked like slaves. From the minute we were old enough to pick up a hoe, there was no time to go play. Vera swore that she had worked much harder back in Croatia than she did in Canada. If she could do it I felt I certainly could, regardless of the fact that I was only 13.

My father was a determined and focused kind of person. If I pushed my luck too far he would put his foot down and say, *"No go – until you are 21."* I was crushed. For a young person eight years was a long time to wait.

Still I never quit dreaming. I spent my nights fantasizing what it would be like to be in North America. I visualized myself already there having a well paying job, driving my own car, riding a white stallion through the prairies and being chased by Indians. Of course no arrows would hit me. OK, OK, I had a good imagination!

I totally focused on my goal. I kept the topic of immigrating to North America alive and frequent in our family conversations. Finally at the age of 16 when I enrolled in my first prep year of college education my father said, *"Now-a-days you have to be educated before you can make it in this world. Once you have a degree or diploma then you can go to North America."*

Bingo! For the first time my father expressed a definite outline of his terms for my freedom to leave. Now it was up to me to deliver, to take action in that specific direction.

I immediately had a meeting with my teachers and shared my ambitions and desire to immigrate to North America. Not only did they agree to accept the first year of mechanical engineering I had completed toward a three-year trade school diploma as a mechanic, they allowed me to combine the next two years into one.

Now I was on my way to becoming a mechanic. I went to school in the morning, apprenticed in the afternoons and weekends, and studied during the evenings.

I made an offer to every teacher in my school. Whoever had a car, I'd repair and maintain it for them, free of charge, as a part of my practicum. I remember the look in their eyes. They seemed entranced with my ambitious nature and enthusiasm about completing my schooling so quickly. I am sure it had been a while since they saw a teenager with so much conviction but they understood where I was coming from. They knew about my goal.

The opportunity to leave home and emigrate had been denied me for so long that now, with my father on board, wasn't the time to drag my feet and run the risk of losing it. I wasn't prepared to wait one second longer than absolutely necessary.

Finally the big day arrived. I was 17 – three months short of 18, and ready to go! My sister, Vera, had mailed me $550, a loan for a one way air ticket, and Dad gave me $30 for pocket money – all he could afford. I thought I was rich.

Now that we were actually at the airport, I was excited yet frightened at the same time. On one hand my dream was becoming a reality. However, on the other hand I was frightened because I didn't know where I was going or how I would be able to manage in a foreign country when I couldn't speak the language. The only words of English I knew were *OK* and *thank you*. I didn't even know how to say *you're welcome*. The future was one big question mark! Yes I was scared, but fear didn't matter. Nothing really mattered. I was going to America and that was all that counted.

By way of some miracle, my dream was becoming a reality. Deep down I always knew it would happen. My conviction was so strong that it had to. Yet I was living with a fearful feeling every day – that somehow I shouldn't expect it, as if I wasn't worthy of a better life – that having a great life was an option only for others, not for me. Even though I wanted to believe I would make it somehow, I was afraid it would simply slip out of my hands. I had lived with that fear constantly every day, and everywhere I looked there were obstacles. Although at night I could dream.

Now as I walked across the tarmac toward the plane I realized my feeling of fear had vanished. Only feelings of excitement and expectation enveloped me. I looked over my shoulder, back up toward the airport observation deck to see my pretty sister, Nada, with her husband cheerfully jumping up and down and waving goodbye.

Beside them Dad firmly hugged Mom. She slipped a black scarf over her head. With her right hand she hugged Dad back. All the fingers of her left hand were in her mouth. Their bodies trembled as tears ran from their eyes. Suddenly looking so vulnerable. I felt their pain spilling over the rail, encircling me, drawing me back like a magnet.

My eyes filled with tears yet I just couldn't stay, I *had* to go.

Chapter 7

Working at the Slaughterhouse

"Do the thing you fear and the death of fear is certain."

... Ralph Waldo Emerson

Each day after I left Croatia, it seemed like I was taking an apprenticeship in life. Perhaps I was trying to do things in such a way to please my parents, to prove to them that I was capable of running a great life for myself, even at the age of 17. Or maybe I consciously wanted to make myself a better person today than I was yesterday – and better yet tomorrow. Because of that, my life has been full of change and uncertainty.

Consciously or subconsciously (I don't really know which) I embraced my new life with a different kind of zeal – with an adventurous spirit. Perhaps because of that, my life took many turns I never dreamed were possible. Like anyone else, I've had my crosses to carry, but overall it has been a very rewarding way to live.

I arrived in Winnipeg, in the heart of Canada, on a beautiful September day in 1971. It was Friday evening. The following Monday, my sister Vera took me to the local employment office to register. By the next day I was at work assembling farm machinery for export to Cuba and getting paid $1.75 per hour. Wow! This was great. I felt so fortunate, so privileged and honored to have my very own job at 17. And I managed to get it without speaking more than two words of English!

It didn't take me long to learn more English and discover that the slaughterhouse across town paid $2.40 per hour. The thought of switching jobs was difficult because in Croatia it was considered imprudent not to hang onto your job for life once you got one.

After being so lucky as to land a job at 17 you sure don't blow that kind of privilege, I kept telling myself. Except the thought of a better job opportunity just killed me. I wanted to take it, yet I was too scared to give up my present job – too frightened of the consequences.

One day, at the urging of a friend, I gave in to the temptation. It had to be one of the toughest things I'd ever done – to quit my first real job. The very thing I came to North America for, I was betraying, throwing away. But like a hermit crab wanting to trade its smaller shell in for a larger one, I quit my old job and made a dash for the new one.

Soon I was working at the slaughterhouse and was downright grateful for it. It was a big leap in earnings for me. My spirit soared. It was true. North America *is* the land of opportunity. The quantum leap I made in earnings in such a short time period was incomprehensible to me.

My work wasn't as glamorous as my pay, however it was worth it. After the animals were killed, they were hung upside down and transported on an overhead conveyor track from the killing area to the processing plant, a hundred or so feet away. Blood gushed out of the animals' sliced throats, spilling down onto the floor and walls, curdling into a pile. My job was to shovel the curdled blood into a large garburetor in the floor. The stench rising from the steamy heaps of blood made me gag.

At the end of the day my job was to hose the area down. I didn't care for the bloodstains that streaked down the white walls so after my regular working hours I found some Ajax and scrubbed away until the stain disappeared. I figured if I was going to work there it might as well be as clean and pleasant as possible.

I accepted the gory reality of my job because I knew that I would enjoy the money I was making. I had no way of knowing how quickly things were to change.

The very next morning the foreman came and was curious who had *painted* the room. I explained that I had just scrubbed it clean with Ajax.

"Boy," he said with his fists propped up on his hips, *"you like things pretty clean. I could use a man like you on the production line."*

Wow, the next day I was learning how to sharpen an enormous butcher knife and separate a cow's liver, kidneys and lungs from its intestines. Along with the new job came another increase in pay.

But like the way things usually go in life – there is a hitch to every success. Bud was my hitch. He worked beside me on the processing line. He was an exceptionally attractive guy – too good looking to be doing this kind of a job. He was a bulk of a man in his late twenties. His muscular body, resembling Arnold Schwarzenegger, towered over me in an intimidating manner.

It didn't take a genius to figure out Bud didn't like me. In fact he hated me. Why? I didn't know. Perhaps he was one of those guys who hated the world.

Splat! A piece of slimy innards that Bud had flung hit me on the left side of my face. As our eyes met he said, *"You F...n DP"*. The whole processing line of butchers burst out laughing.

"F... YOU!" I replied in my ever so rapidly expanding English vocabulary.

Boom! An unexpected blow from his fist on my shoulder sent me flying smack into a huge butcher on the other side of me. Not impressed, the butcher huffed as he heaved me back. I clenched my fist and creamed Bud's shoulder. Infuriated, with choice words flying aplenty, he leaped at me and a wrestling brawl broke out.

I didn't really fight back, I just tried to keep my balance as he attempted to slam me to the ground. Deep inside I was hoping this was just a ritual of being accepted into the Fraternity of Intestine Separators, the *brotherhood of butchers*.

A crowd gathered and cheered. Bud's attempt to wrestle me to the ground was abruptly stopped when our crusty old foreman walked over to see what was happening.

Unimpressed he shouted, *"Break it up! Break it up!"*

I didn't understand what Bud said to him although I could sense he was trying to convince our foreman that I started the fight. Our foreman probably knew better. He gently patted my sore shoulder and said, *"Ok, let's get back to work."*

Bud wasn't impressed with the fact that I was able to resist him. He continued to threaten me, flinging innards at me accompanied with remarks like *"F...n DP"*. At the time I wasn't aware of the meaning of *DP* but it didn't take long to get the general drift.

Each time our foreman passed by he assured me with a warm smile, as if he approved of my resistance to Bud.

I guess that crusty old foreman really took a liking to me. On one lunch break he came over, slapped my back and said, *"Young man would you like to make some real money?"*

"Yes sir!" I eagerly quipped.

"Everyday from 4 to 8 a.m. you can load frozen pork halves and beef quarters into the reefer. It pays double time. Don't forget I'll also need you on your regular shift at 8 a.m." I felt honored to be given the opportunity.

I was bursting out of my skin with happiness. I had goose bumps that had goose bumps! You know what I mean. The image of all the money I would be making was dancing on a screen in my mind.

However, my ecstasy quickly faded away at 4 a.m. the next morning when I realized that Bud had also been chosen to load the reefer. Only the strongest were given that job opportunity. Bud couldn't stand the fact that I was there. Maybe he didn't think I qualified. Or maybe he felt I was a threat or competed with him. I don't really know.

Days passed and I continued to take the harassment – tripping, bumping, punching and verbal abuse – with my jaws clenched. I hoped that time would change Bud's attitude toward me. My fear of him amplified on the loading shift. I hated that early morning session because my only savior, our foreman, didn't arrive at the plant until 8 a.m. I tried to avoid Bud and he knew it. If I happened to be in the lunchroom when he came in he would demand I go elsewhere.

One morning I didn't succeed in evading Bud as he walked up behind me. I was carrying a heavy beef hindquarter when I felt my right foot being tripped behind my left. Losing my balance, I slammed to the ground flat on my face, the beef quarter landing on my back. The pain briefly knocked me out but when I came to, I could hear roars of laughter.

When I realized what had happened rage overwhelmed me. I leaped up at Bud knocking him and the frozen carcass he was carrying to the ground. We wrestled and fought each other fiercely. My punches tamed Bud to where he was just trying to block them. His nose bled. I don't know where this fight would've ended if onlookers didn't drag me off Bud to stop the fight. To my surprise the other loaders congratulated me on my victory and for the rest of the shift they teased Bud.

It was a magical transformation where others now paid me respect while Bud avoided me. In a way the feeling of victory was great. However the experience of working in the slaughterhouse and dealing with the abuse has lodged in my memory as being one of the most unpleasant times of my life.

From then on things improved a great deal. The foreman promoted me to the Meat Cutting and De-boning Department, which again earned me more pay. At times Bud and I would pass each other. His head would slump down as he tried to avoid eye contact.

Two months later I left the plant for another opportunity to work with a stone mason who introduced me to the bonus system based on piece work performance and pay-on-completion. This time it wasn't so hard to quit. I just couldn't believe how many jobs were out there if one just wanted to work.

The stone mason job was much nicer than working at the slaughterhouse, though much harder. However it was worth it as I my earnings were even higher and I never had to face Bud again.

For years Bud worked at the same job, separating beef innards, until the slaughterhouse shut down for good. Word has it he got a better job at another meat processing plant where he still works today, 25 years later, in the Smoked Meat Department. The story goes that after our fight he totally withdrew and never bullied anyone again.

I sometimes think about my reaction which led to our fight and wonder if the incident degraded Bud's self-esteem to the point where he never attempted to do anything to upgrade his life. I hated that fight so much and wish it never had happened. Even today I get teary-eyed just thinking about it and wonder how many other Buds are out there.

That was one of the more painful experiences of my life, yet it forced me to face adversity and discover other opportunities. In the process I began to understand that one can improve their circumstances to unprecedented levels as long as they are willing to improve themselves.

Chapter 8

Let the Love Adventure Begin

*"Love does not consist in gazing at each
other but in looking together in the same
direction."*

… Antoine de Saint-Exupery

It was one of those lazy gray fall days on which you just don't
feel like doing a thing.

The cool mist in the air and the solemn darkness of the early
evening weren't conducive enough to motivate me to go out on the
town and paint it red. So when my cousin Steve called and asked me
if I wanted to go to a university dance, I flatly declined.

"Funny you don't feel like going out. I don't either," Steve quipped,
*"but I thought since it was Saturday night, I better do something.
Your friend, Mel Degan, in the rock band Privilege will be playing so
I thought we'd go and have couple beer and listen to the music."*

Beside the fact that I didn't feel like going out, I was also on a
strict budget. I had just teamed up with a real estate company that
was going to train me to be a realtor. The prospect of making money

in the short term looked pretty grim, so anything that involved spending wasn't synchronous with my present condition. I continued to refuse Steve's offer. Eventually, I gave in when he pointed out that since my friend's band was playing we probably wouldn't have to pay the cover charge. I agreed to go just for one beer.

Sure enough we were successful in gaining our entrance for free. The band was Edmonton's best but I still couldn't get into the mood. Obviously Steve was in better humor. Immediately he got up and danced while I sat there listening to the music and slowly nursed my beer.

"Boris you've got to come and help me," Steve pleaded. *"There are seven single girls at this table and there's one I like. I know she'll never separate from the others unless she has at least another girlfriend with her."*

Not so keen on my cousin's request, I nonchalantly asked an attractive blonde to dance just to help him and to keep peace in the family. She responded with a friendly smile and in no time I was dancing, my joints twisting and contorting in every extreme direction. She was curious to know where I was from.

When I responded with, *"Croatia",* she enthusiastically told me a girlfriend she was sitting with had just returned from a six month European trip that included Croatia.

"You should come and meet her. Her name is Shirley," my dancing partner suggested.

After the dance I nonchalantly strolled over to the table full of girls and pulled up a chair next to a cute, longhaired brunette. Before saying a word I reached over, helped myself to a cigarette, lit it up, and exhaled a massive cloud of smoke *(I can't believe I did that)*.

In my broken English I bellowed out with my not so shy voice, *"I hear you just came back from six months in Europe and you visited my country?"*

I didn't expect what was about to happen.

The minute she spoke to me it was as if I could see her heart.

Instantly I felt we were in tune with each other – so in sync. Drawn together like magnets we continued to talk. Our interests, our ambitions and our desire to travel were so mutually harmonious that I forgot all about the blonde. Shirley's warmth encircled and enlightened my heart. I knew from that moment on my focus in life had changed. I would never be able to settle for anything less than being with her.

Shirley's shy yet confident personality captivated me immediately. I couldn't quite match her travel accomplishments with her personality. The remote places she and her girlfriend, Nancy, had traveled to in an old Volkswagen they purchased in Germany clearly indicated a very adventurous and determined person. We quickly bonded as we compared stories of our past travels and shared plans for future ones.

Shirley explained how she had disciplined herself not to blow her money on entertainment and unnecessary things and instead saved it for her European trip. I told her how I just about hadn't come to the dance because I was saving my money to become a real estate salesman. That's when we discovered we both shared the same goal. It was our heart's desire to save enough money to travel Australia.

It was magic when we danced. Our moves exactly matched the rhythm. I couldn't take my eyes off her as her body flowed in sync to the music. However it was when we closely danced a slow dance that I felt our energies blend, flowing through us, enveloping us, holding us together. My rough laborer's hands wanted to crush her tight against my body but in her shy way she wouldn't let me. Yet the gentler we touched, the more our feelings surged. Wherever she laid her hand on me it was like ET's finger, glowing, spreading the healing power of love. By the end of the night I knew it was our destiny to be together.

Before I left Croatia my father had shared some of his wisdom about selecting a wife. He said, *"Son when you fall in love with a woman and you wonder what she'll be like in the future – how she'll treat and love you, whether she'll stand by you when life gets tough – just take a good look at her parents. Examine her family. Discover what their life values are all about. If you like what you see, that's the woman you should marry."*

That advice stood out in my mind when I met Shirley's parents, John and Vera. I'm sure they still wonder what happened that day they met me. I was hungry to know them, feeling the void of not having my own parents on the same continent with me. The more questions I asked, the more information I gathered, and the more I fell in love with the family.

Amazingly, I had more in common with John and Vera than with their four children. The way I grew up on our farm very much resembled their childhood, before they moved to the big city – with horse drawn wagons and plows and old steel-wheeled tractors and threshing machines. I didn't think anybody here had worked as hard as we did back home, yet Shirley's parents had also fed livestock and hand-milked cows and scythed grass and grain.

Scything had been one of my favorite farm chores except I disliked waking up so early. However it was necessary because it was best to scythe grass early in the morning before the dew evaporated – like shaving a moist beard. Dad would wake me up at 4 a.m., an ungodly hour for a young boy. Together we would ride our bikes in the darkness to our field and by the time our scythes were sharpened the first rays of the day would give us just enough light to start.

No words in the world can describe the feeling you get when a sharp scythe, in one swoosh shaves a thick swathe of grass and neatly deposits it in a straight row. Of course since I was a competitive 13-year-old my swathe had to be at least a bit wider than Dad's.

I remember it as being a peaceful time. In silence we would work as the aroma of the freshly cut grass infused the early morning air. The swooshing sound awoke the first birds, alerting them to our presence. They would take on the appearance of comical kamikazes diving behind us to pick up the newly exposed worms. Picturesque pink hues in the sky over the green fields would recharge my spirit to push forward faster.

After two or maybe three hours of scything my father would leave to start his day at work and I would go to school. The next morning we'd repeat it all over again.

Shirley's parents could relate to all of it. They were hard working and honest middle class people with a strong sense of humor. The love and dedication they had for each other and their children was unmistakable. The more I got to know the family, the more I loved them all, and the deeper I fell in love with Shirley.

Adversity was not a stranger to this family. John had been an electrician who damaged his back in a work-related accident, causing him to be unemployed for a few years. Having young children to feed and with no funds coming in, things were pretty tough on the family. Of course this was before times of government assistance from such programs as unemployment insurance or workmen's compensation. Welfare was out of the question.

Vera had no choice but to get a job. During the day she would care for her children and husband, then catch a bus downtown to work the night shift as a full-time telephone operator at the MacDonald Hotel. It was clear where Shirley's determined spirit came from.

John, never physically able to work in the field again, upgraded his education and became a white-collar worker, an electrical estimator. His faith became stronger as he thanked God's blessings for allowing him to recover enough to once again earn a living, and be an active father, spending many years coaching boy's hockey. He impressed me as being one of the most kind and diligent persons I had ever met.

Each time I visited the family I gave them a warm European handshake and hug. What John and Vera didn't realize was I was ecstatic because I was building a relationship with their daughter based on the strength of theirs.

At first I received a conservative welcome. I sensed they were skeptical about our relationship, perhaps because of my limited English, or perhaps because they felt I was a bit of a dreamer with my high expectations in life. Or maybe it was our cultural and religious differences they were concerned about. Whatever it was it didn't worry me. I knew things would change once they got to know me better.

On the other hand Shirley's older brother, Jim, and the younger kids, Wayne and Joan, warmly accepted me. From my vantage-point, each time I came to visit, I was at total ease and on purpose. I felt like I was coming home – that I belonged there. This family had the all the qualities Dad told me to look for, and I was delighted.

After only a few short days I told Shirley she was the woman I was looking for – that I had serious intentions of marrying her. She looked at me skeptically, wondering if I was feeding her a line. I know I was coming on pretty strong. She didn't realize that even though I had just turned 19 I already knew what I wanted. Eventually she trusted me and liked the idea.

At this point in time it was impossible to imagine what turn our lives would take. Shirley and I had many dreams although our financial situation was bleak. Like any young couple just starting out in life we were broke – just two prairie kids from opposite sides of the world with a common goal to travel to Australia.

What was to become of us would be left to destiny – *or would it?*

Chapter 9

Perfect Wonderland

"I am free to be what I want to be and to do what I want to do."

... Jonathan Livingston Seagull

When we tell our story to other people, the response we receive is always the same. *"How could you guys do that? How was that possible? How could you afford it? How did you know how to even go about it at such a young age?"*

Those questions also arouse my curiosity. When I look back over the last 25 years of our marriage I am just as astounded as others are. How *did* we manage to pull that off? After all there was nothing special about us. We were just ordinary people trying to make a living like anybody else.

As a young man there had been times when I had doubts about my future and the choices I had made. I wondered if my father was actually right that I should have finished my education before leaving home. Most of my new Canadian friends had some kind of university education going for them, whereas I didn't.

I felt confused. Two feelings collided – one that I needed a formal education and the other that there were so many opportunities out there to enjoy, to just go for, to just do and I'd learn what I needed along the way. Well the second one appealed to me much more because I just couldn't decide what I wanted to do! Everything in this new country was appealing. There were so many choices, so much opportunity everywhere that I just didn't know which way to turn or what to do next.

Once I got over my initial fear of changing jobs, and once I conditioned myself to take action and do the thing I wanted most, I was on my way. All that was left to figure out was *how*? Once I figured that out, I worked hard until I got it. It was a natural progression.

That whole process started the first day I arrived in Canada. I guess coming from a country where opportunities were so limited, I was able to recognize such an abundance of them when I saw them.

Shortly after my plane had touched down in Canada, I started to sum things up. I thought to myself, *"My God this is THE place, this is where dreams come true. This is where I belong. This is wonderland!"* I was just about swept off my feet by everything I saw and by all the opportunities around me.

From that time on, it was as if my sole purpose in life was to live out all my dreams, because in North America it appeared possible. The more I observed, the more I realized opportunities were bountiful, and the more I knew I was in the right place! If there was something I wanted to have or experience, all I had to do was make a conscious decision to work hard toward attaining it.

Hard work was not a problem – it was something I was accustomed to – and so were having dreams and desires. In the poverty of my youth I lived to dream, to escape from everyday reality. So to figure out how to achieve those dreams, that was my challenge. Back home I was familiar with the rigid communist system, all their rules and *inner-circle-only* mentality. Here in North America things were different.

Here you were free to be free if you wanted to be. The invisible danger was becoming a prisoner of your own mind. (*I can't do that, I'm not good enough, and it's not for me... that kind of thinking.*) Here I realized that if you wanted something, you just had to ask. I observed that success was attainable to anyone, not restricted to only one particular class of people. I realized I could do all the business I wanted, with whomever I wanted, as much as I wanted, and wherever I wanted.

Opportunities were limitless. After all, that was why I had wanted to come to North America – for opportunity – nothing else. All I needed was opportunity and I was prepared to do the rest.

In Croatia I had been taught to hold onto a job, if I was lucky enough to get one, for dear life. Here, rather than fear changing from job to job, I transferred into the mode of seeking many different types of work, which challenged my ability and intellectuality. My insecurity of being a foreigner (or DP as some ignorant people preferred to call me) quickly subsided as most employers treated me with respect and rewarded me based on my contribution to their organization and not on my lineage or heritage.

Positive attitude, enthusiasm and willingness to try new things I'd never done before erased the negative doubts roaming in my head, like – *I can't do that, I'm not good enough, not smart enough, not educated enough.* I'm sure it helped me win the job I pursued.

I was at the energetic age of 19 when I heard that real estate was the business to be in. After two years of working my way through the labor ranks I truly felt I had mastered English adequately to evolve to sales. However, what I thought and what reality was, were two totally different things. Simply put, in my blissful ignorance, I didn't know that I didn't know how to speak English very well.

When I first arrived in North America I made a major mistake. The government offered a free program for new immigrants to learn English, which I didn't take advantage of, thinking I could learn it well enough just hanging out with English-speaking people. Wrong! Now 25 years later, I finally admit that I still haven't mastered the language.

When I inquired about a career in real estate, it was obvious those people spoke another language. In those circles, unlike the labor force, there was an obvious absence of four letter F words. Nobody seemed to know where I could find an *F...n job* as a salesman...!

Another obstacle became obvious – my age. That was easily adjustable. Being 19 didn't work so I tried the magic age of 24, which seemed to have much better appeal, yet still no luck. I continued to apply but to no avail.

Determined, I persisted. After awhile the real estate offices started to all look the same so I really wasn't sure if I had called on them previously or not. Thankfully I didn't comprehend the true meaning of the word *NO*. If I had to face that much rejection today, surely I'd break down, give up and cry.

Finally my persistence did pay off, and in the meantime I learned a valuable lesson. *If you desire to upgrade your life, have a mentor in the form of a mastermind partner.* Don't expect a hand-out from that person. But be assured the superstar in your life will be willing to give you a hand-up if you're prepared to work hard to help yourself.

At last I found my mentor and mastermind partner, Larry McCutcheon. He was an owner of a small real estate company in Edmonton. Before I passed the realtor exam, Larry took his time to teach me the tools and techniques of the trade. Most importantly, he spent countless hours explaining unfamiliar terminology – words like purchaser, vendor, caveat, mortgage, interest rate, bungalow, triplex... and on and on it went. To this day I'm bewildered why he helped me so much.

What I do know is that he opened the door to a whole new world. He taught me how to make the kind of money I never thought possible. More importantly he sold me on the art of selling. It was the most significant purchase I ever made in my life – the day I bought into the new profession of becoming a salesman. Every day hence I have used the same sales principles Larry taught me for selling products, services, ideas and even myself.

It wasn't the easiest thing to break into a real-estate career, but sometimes blessings come in beautiful disguise. Shirley supported my desire to upgrade my life. She insisted we rehearse contract terminology on our dates. If she sensed I wanted to give up, she would encourage me to try harder. For some reason, she saw more in me than I could in myself. She intuitively understood the persistence principle and knew that if I tried hard enough I would make it, and I did. And our love for each other flourished as we nourished and grew together.

Real estate proved to be a great profession, yet over time, like a kid in a candy store, I was tempted to move on and test my selling skills in a number of different markets. Possessing a new tool, sales savvy, I decided that if I wanted to drive a new car, I would just get a job as a new car salesman. If I wanted to drive a new Ford, I sold new Fords. If I wanted to travel, I became a traveling industrial equipment salesman.

Increasingly, I wanted to spend all my time with my sweetheart. Shirley and I became so close and shared the same dreams. Foremost on our list was travel. We constantly dreamed and schemed about it. Our ultimate ambition was to visit Australia. And soon our sole focus was to save enough money and elope to Sydney to get married.

We worked diligently at our jobs, Shirley as an executive assistant to the Chief of Police, and I, as a new Toyota automobile salesman. But we were dissatisfied at the rate our money was being saved, even though we refused to spend a penny on frills.

One day I sold my boss on having Shirley and me work in the evenings after the car lot closed. I proposed we wash the wax off the newly shipped cars and prep them so they would be ready for me to sell during the day. At $10 a car, if we worked with our noses to the grindstone, we could make an extra $40 a night.

Even with that we weren't satisfied with the pace of our progress. Then I convinced the dealership owner of the idea of allowing Shirley and me to do their janitorial work. So in our spare time (what spare time?) we cleaned toilets and washed floors. Now with three jobs each, we finally were getting somewhere.

I admit my surprise that Shirley was willing to wash toilets alongside me – not everyone would've. But she had a good upbringing and was obviously not afraid to work for what she wanted. I was proud of her flexible attitude and work ethic and knew she'd be a good mother to our children one day. And in the meantime Shirley and I became soul mates working toward our goal together.

To further accelerate our net worth and to personally cash in on my real estate knowledge, we started to buy old houses, repair and sell them, in addition to holding down our other jobs. Again Shirley was beside me, learning how to scrape and paint. Both of us were so strongly infatuated with our desire to travel that our hard work was worth the effort if it was the vehicle to our goal.

As things turned out we never did elope to Australia. Instead we had a big family wedding that included my parents coming from Croatia. Then two and a half years later Shirley and I had saved enough money to set out on a year long expedition around the world. It was a mind-blowing accomplishment – to work toward our goal and then to actually attain it. It felt like a dream or fairy tale. It was wonderland. We were young, proud and ready to reap our benefits – to travel.

However, a peculiar thing happened. After attaining what we had strived so intensely for, a cloud of guilt ate away at me. In my upbringing I was forever told to work hard, be persistent, hold on to that job, don't ever quit, don't be wasteful, save for old age, be content with what I have, don't be greedy, and on and on my conditioning went. Even though I wasn't familiar with the term inferiority complex or low self-esteem, I was suffering from it.

Deep within I believed since I was born into poverty, I wasn't worthy of anything better. Now through what must've been sheer luck or a fluke, we had attained something better than poverty, and the benefits shouldn't be wasted on travel. While striving for our goal, the struggle and hard work were synchronous with my upbringing. However, now that we were at the point of enjoying the fruits of our efforts, I felt it pushed the limits of what I thought was possible to achieve in our lives.

Guilty thoughts that I didn't deserve to have such a good life started to wreak havoc in my mind. It was something I would constantly struggle with. Every time Shirley and I reached one of our many goals in life, overcoming the obstacles along the way, I had conflicting feelings – one of accomplishment but also one that we weren't deserving of the rewards. Not that every goal we strived for was easy to accomplish; in fact we had more than our share of tough times of failed ventures. Though looking at the big picture, those failures were merely stepping-stones to even greater achievements that I feared we were not deserving of.

My guilt was such that after quitting work for our year of travel, visiting over 30 countries around the world, Shirley and I were almost embarrassed to share our adventures and excitement with our friends. We downplayed the whole thing or sometimes skipped the topic all together. It just didn't seem right to rub it in.

Finally returning to Canada, Shirley and I decided it was time to quit acting like *juvenile delinquents* and settle down to one job for the rest of our lives and start a family. Making that decision was almost a relief. We were ready to exist the way we'd been conditioned for after all. We wouldn't be required to try new things, learn new ways, search new possibilities and I wouldn't feel guilty about our accomplishments. Ahhhhh, that felt sooo gooood, so sooothing. For our perfect wonderland would be no more, but a place to exist.

Fortunately the universe has its own laws to uphold, over which we have no control. The feeling of our accomplishments, coupled with our travels, certainly had an effect on our souls. It was like an aphrodisiac. Yet we weren't the only ones that were affected.

A strange thing developed. Even though we'd spent most of our meager savings on traveling around the world, people now seemed to treat us differently. They based their opinion on who we were and what we had accomplished rather than on what we owned, and respected us for our courage to trade security for living out our dream.

The exact company Shirley quit to go travel hired her back, in fact promoting her over others who had stayed put and were just as qualified. She was adored and respected by her peers. Our bank manager, knowing what we had done, was more liberal in lending us money even though our net worth was much less. It accelerated our real-estate investments even more.

Instead of the passive existence we expected, our lives in fact took a major turn upward to another phase in our lives – entrepreneurship. We became preoccupied with our new trade and with plans to start a family. We were free to be free.

Chapter 10

The Impossible Dream

*"All our dreams can come true – if we have
the courage to pursue them."*

… Walt Disney

The birth of our son, Trevor, marked the beginning of a new era and the end of our lives as *juvenile delinquents*. I was happy and content with that! *Or was I?* Having a family was certainly something I truly desired. It was synchronous with my ideology of a truly satisfying life and I wouldn't want it any other way. After all, Shirley and I had sewn all our wild oats before settling down to have our baby.

Merely nine months earlier we had returned from a year-long trip that took us through the USA, Mexico, Belize, Guatemala, El Salvador, Honduras, Costa Rica, Panama and then over to Europe and North Africa – visiting a total of over 30 countries. Basically we were satisfied with travelling and our focus was now to settle down and raise a family – to live a normal conventional lifestyle. So I thought!

To my surprise, the harder I wanted to be the *norm* in society as a new parent, the more I felt my chest tighten and even a feeling of panic set in. What was my panic all about you may ask? I didn't quite understand myself why I felt the way I did.

I did have something nagging at me. But it made no more rhyme or reason than someone wanting to fly to the moon. You see, since I was a young boy I had a dream. Except it was so unconventional. So bizarrely different that I didn't even reveal it to Shirley for a long time because it was just too weird.

I dreamed of going on a sailing expedition – not just any expedition but one throughout the South Pacific, following in the footsteps of Captain Cook, visiting enchanted islands and meeting civilizations visited only by the lucky few. It was the darnest thing. I didn't quite know where it was all coming from or why I had such a strong desire to do it. It certainly didn't make much sense.

It was so far fetched. Neither Shirley nor I grew up near the ocean. We were both prairie kids, for heaven's sake. We didn't know the first thing about sailing! And truth be known, we didn't even have a clue how to go about buying a ship capable of navigating the Pacific – never mind the navigation skills needed to locate a tiny island in the far reaches of that huge body of water.

Back in the real world, Shirley and I were living close to the Rocky Mountains in Calgary, and had just purchased our second house as a revenue investment. We both worked during the day downtown. I sold new Fords and Shirley was an executive assistant at Shell Oil. Always, the first person home after work would pick up Trevor from the babysitter and start cooking dinner. After our meal Shirley would care for Trev while I went to our revenue property to build a basement suite for a mortgage-helper. I would dream about the expedition while I worked.

I felt so privileged that life had treated us well – that the infinite powers of the universe had allowed us to accomplish so much at such a young age – that I regarded my dream as a childish, foolish fantasy. We had a great start in life for a couple in their early twenties. We were even envied by many of our friends. So why would I want to disturb this setup? And honestly I didn't really think I wanted to do it. If only my nagging thoughts would leave me alone.

Daily I struggled with my dream, yet I confided in no one. My desire to be a good father and a good husband kept my thoughts and feelings in check. *This whole idea of going on an expedition is ridiculous anyway* I kept telling myself. *I have a family now.* And when I played with my son I wondered if it was even possible to go with a child only a few months old. *Of course not! It's ridiculous. Preposterous!* I would tell myself. Then my mind would shoot back, *And why not? Throughout history children sailed with their families across the oceans and seas and many were even born at sea! Remember the story of the Mayflower?*

I just give up! I resigned. I couldn't get through to myself that we didn't belong out there in that big foreign ocean. For that very reason, for the longest time I never shared my dream with Shirley. In fact I tried to hide it. There was no point to alarm her.

I wasn't pleased with myself over this whole sailing thing. It was ridiculous – based only on fantasy, movies I'd seen, books I'd read and memories of old history classes. It had nothing to do with the reality of today. I kept telling myself – *Come on now Boris be reasonable. You live in the prairies, 1,200 kilometers from the Pacific, and you have a family, a job, and two mortgages. You don't know how to sail, navigate or even how to go about buying a boat. And your son – you have to look after your son.*

Every time those thoughts permeated my mind, my chest tightened, feeling the burden of a heavy weight sitting on my shoulders. It drove me nuts. It was the first time in my life that I remember feeling the true power of self-rejection. It's the worst kind of rejection when *you* reject you. When you don't trust yourself, when you don't believe in yourself, when you don't like yourself, and in my case, when you don't follow your dream.

Finally one day at dinner I unloaded my burden. I couldn't stand it any longer. I revealed to Shirley all about the internal struggle I'd been having with my sailing dream. I explained that ever since Trevor's birth I felt claustrophobic – like my dream would never materialize. Immediately I saw relief on her face.

She said, *"I did notice that something wasn't quite right, but I thought you just hadn't adapted too well to the responsibility of raising a child yet."* She laughed with comfort in her voice and reaffirmed, *"Honey there's nothing wrong with having dreams or fantasies."*

Her response shocked and surprised me. For some reason I had expected ridicule.

"You really don't think it's wrong to have dreams like that?" I asked in disbelief.

"No, of course not," she reassured me.

"Does that mean you'd consider the idea of someday undertaking a three year expedition through the South Pacific if I could figure out a way of doing it?"

"Sure! Why not? You know I'm hooked on travel as much as you are. Some day we'll probably do it." And so she agreed.

That was my green light to openly explore the possibility of my dream. I reassured her that if I ever earned enough money to get our expedition off the ground, she and Trevor would be part of the crew package. I wouldn't consider going without them.

Many years later Shirley confided that she only agreed because she, NEVER – *in a million years* – thought it would ever materialize. At the time she was just content knowing that I wasn't having cold feet about our marriage and the responsibility of raising a child.

Right now, with Shirley's support, it was a great relief just knowing that my dream was not dead. The possibility of it happening wasn't great. Still it was something I could continue to fantasize about.

And so I did. In my mind I actually visualized scenes of a ship sailing, plowing through ocean waves. However the ship wasn't real. It looked more like a drawing made by a second grade child. The vision of Captain Cook was a little more vivid. In my mind I replayed some scenes I remembered from movies and pictures I'd seen of him being rowed into shore by his crew. I saw him stoically standing in the middle of the rowboat, his hands crossed over his chest, with natives curiously lined up on shore awaiting his arrival.

Again I thought the concept was ridiculous. I'd never even lived close to the sea or any great body of water. In fact, in order to learn how to swim in the little ankle deep creek that passed by our house in Croatia, my father and I had to dig the sand away to make it deep enough to tread water. Yet each time my mind had a chance to sojourn into its own tangent it would create yet another image of the voyage.

Since Shirley hadn't gone ballistic, I continued to share my visions with her more often. And later I started also to share it with my co-workers at Metro Ford. I started to buy sailing magazines and made inquiries with yacht brokers in Canada and the U.S.

Trevor had been born on October 16, 1978, though my dream didn't really begin to take shape until that following Christmas. Shirley's brother, Jim, and sister-in-law, Ann, visiting us from Edmonton, thought the idea was fabulous. Instantly they became mesmerized just like us. They wanted to be in on it.

We promised to keep in touch. Soon afterward we all decided to visit Vancouver during Easter to check out the availability of ocean going vessels – just to look! I reassured Shirley we were just looking – nothing more. Easter week arrived, and Jim and Ann, their two daughters Cara (three) and Marci (one and a half), together with Shirley, Trevor (five months) and I drove the 800 miles to Vancouver to inspect boats.

To our dismay it was obvious that anything we could ever hope to purchase was either too small or derelict, taking on water and sinking slowly at the dock. My hopes faded but I consoled myself because after all, deep down it was only a fantasy. It wasn't really meant to happen! *Maybe it was only the kind of dream you're supposed to fantasize about, to tinker with* I thought.

Like the others, I ended up with a bitter taste of disappointment. If only our lack of finances wasn't such a hurdle between our goal and us. Yet overall I was proud of how well I handled the letdown. *Maybe it was a way the supreme powers kept order by restricting certain things from those people that aren't meant to have them* I justified.

Anyway, I felt totally out of place aboard the ships we inspected – like a fish out of water. It wasn't something I was comfortable with. I lacked adequate boating knowledge and struggled with the terminology.

Finally our time to visit Vancouver was coming to a close. With an *oh well, we tried attitude* we decided to go for a nice meal at beautiful Coal Harbor where we could dine while enjoying the view of the ships in the marina against the backdrop of Stanley Park.

It was a beautiful sunny day. And I felt kind of mellow as we all strolled through the marina on our way to the restaurant. Suddenly a boat caught my eye. As I stood admiring the traditional design of the sail boat, the captain popped his head out of the companionway and asked, *"Can I help you?"*

"Not really. But I am in love with your boat," I gushed.

"My ship, you mean!" the proud owner beamed. *"Ships can carry boats. Boats can't carry ships. That's the difference young man."*

"I 'd sure love to see your ship," I gushed some more.

"Well come on board. Permission granted to board ship."

Eager as ever, I whistled my way onto the ship. The rest of the group closely followed. Like young children, wide-eyed and mesmerized, we intently absorbed everything the captain told us about his voyage to Tahiti. We fell instantly in love with the 57-foot wooden ketch. Nausikaa III had mighty fine lines with a sheer proud bow – perfect for our kind of expedition. And she'd already been proven capable of crossing the ocean. She wasn't currently on the market, however the owner and his wife had been toying with the idea. He promised they would discuss it and let us know later that evening if they were interested in selling her.

Immediately we postponed our plans to return to Calgary as a test sail on Nausikaa was planned for the following day.

And what a marvelous day that turned out to be. The sun sparkled like diamonds on the water and Nausikaa sailed like a charm. There was no doubt about it – she would make a perfect cruising ship. The entire time I couldn't control the perma-grin on my face. No matter what, I just couldn't quit smiling. Shirley was also totally into it – as were Jim and Ann and the kids. We were in our glory.

Needless to say, I think you know what happened next. We were sold! I left the captain a deposit toward the purchase of the ship, with one condition – that he promise to teach us how to sail once the balance of the deal was paid.

We were to take possession on the first of June. We merely had two months to sell our houses, car and furnishings in order to come up with the money. It was unclear how we were going to manage that, but for now it didn't matter. Right now nothing mattered except that we were on our way.

Never in my wildest imagination did I think that I would actually get this close to seeing *my dream* materialize. Except now it became *our dream* as Shirley was totally on board. And working as a team, our determination fueled us to see it through. How? That was yet to be resolved.

Chapter 11

You Guys Are Nuts!

"Live 20% outside the 'proper' zone; remember that the great wise men of the past held no respect for today's conventions, and neither will the great men of the future."

... Anonymous

It probably wasn't intentional, nevertheless I never felt so humiliated in all my life. Most people we shared our plans with ridiculed us. It didn't seem to matter how much or how hard we tried to explain the level of our commitment to the success of our dream, the response was almost always the same. Instead of encouragement and support we received discouragement, accompanied with comments like, *"You guys are nuts! It can't be done. And even if it could be, what makes you think you can do it?"*

Here we were trying to accomplish something that would surely give us peace of mind, with great belief in our expedition and in ourselves. But we were being told *it couldn't be done*. Who said that? I think you know – the doubting Thomases.

"It won't work and you're crazy for trying." I felt we were being psychologically persecuted for having different goals and desires in life by those people who had no great achievement to their credit and

had never experienced the true power of their own belief in themselves.

It wasn't easy to continue. In those trying times we came so close to giving up. At night I lay in bed, eyes wide-open, feeling defeated, dealing with my own fears that feasted away on my exhausted brain. I was having difficulty raising sufficient funds for our expedition. On top of that it was heartbreaking to sell everything we had worked so hard to acquire – those things that had provided our security. We certainly didn't need further discouragement in the form of pessimism and ridicule.

We also sensed apprehension from our closest friends and family, those that loved us and cautiously supported our decision but had their own concerns for us. It was understandable. My parents wrote us a heartrending letter from Croatia. It, alone, almost destroyed my self-confidence. In essence this is what they wrote …

"Dear Son, Shirley & our Dear Grandson Trevor:
Whatever we may say in this letter is not meant to
offend you but to show our concern for your safety.
We love you all and wish you all the best. Son, you
were a joy to have as a son while you were with us
though we wish you weren't going to sea. The sea is a
dangerous place, one you know nothing about. We are
so proud of all your accomplishments in life but we
regret that you are throwing away everything that you
and Shirley have worked so hard for. We also regret
that we will probably never see you again. We wish
there were a way to talk you out of this whole sailing
thing, as we don't want to lose you. If you must go,
please leave Shirley and our grandson with us. We
will miss you forever, we will think of you forever, we
will love you forever. Good bye dear son… Your loving
parents, Mom and Dad."

Inside the letter they had enclosed a check for $1,500. Later, we were to learn it was their whole life savings. They knew we didn't have enough money to complete the sale, yet they knew how desperately we wanted to go.

That letter just crushed me. It was like a final good bye, as if they would never see us again – finished, finito, fini. I was certain that if it had been possible they would've erected a tombstone for us to see before we died to show how much they cared for us. I understood their concern, their pain and uncertainty. Deep down I understood Dad's fear of losing his only surviving son. Although from my perspective, I thought they had nothing to worry about.

It wrenched my heart – their suggestion to leave Shirley and Trevor behind while I went on the expedition myself. That was out of the question. I loved them way too much to be apart for any length of time. After all, this expedition was meant to keep us together – to share our adventures and adversities together, to bond as a family. How could I even consider leaving them behind? I couldn't. At the very root was the foundation of my promise to Shirley – regardless of what was to happen we would stay together. I would not allow anything to stop us from raising our family, just as if we lived on land.

Shirley's parents especially didn't give me too many hugs and kisses. Shirley's brother, Jim, and his wife, Ann, and their two daughters were also coming with us on the first leg of our voyage from Vancouver to Hawaii. In essence my in-laws were dealing with the fact that *all* their grandchildren were being taken to sea by an inexperienced and very naïve crew. We understood their concern also, but thought it was unnecessary.

Now looking back, I see it quite differently. I realize it must've taken every effort for them to contain themselves from insisting that we stay put! They obviously understood how much we wanted to go. Very unselfishly, they held themselves back and didn't interfere. Oh the gray hairs we must've caused!

In a relatively short period of time Shirley and I had sold our two houses, car and furnishings. Regardless we were still miles way from possessing the necessary finances to complete the sale of the ship. Things didn't look good. We weren't going to make it. We could understand why people didn't want to lend us money, but couldn't understand the ridicule.

This wasn't the first time we had been laughed at. We had already accomplished many things outside the usual, not conforming with other people's expectations. I thought by now we'd be used to the mockery. However it seemed that the bigger our goals become, the greater the scorn.

At the ripe age of 24 we were fortunate enough to realize that people don't intentionally try to be discouraging. They just think on a different level. They think they are doing a favor by alerting you, to avoid disappointment and failure. Yet actually in the process they can destroy the very thing that makes you happy and successful. It was almost enough to break down our willpower, to change our minds.

I didn't want to be *pigeon-holed* (stay as you are and don't dare change) by society. For that reason we started to share our dream only with those that were likely to support our expedition, those that wanted to share our excitement with us. We needed that encouragement to support us to victory over our fear of the unknown.

Miraculously the grand boost we needed came when Jim and Ann sold their own house to complete the purchase of Nausikaa. The deadline was so close I'd almost lost hope. I was even prepared for the possibility of losing our down payment. But now Jim and Ann were into the adventure of the voyage as much as we were and our fears of how it was ever going to materialize faded.

Our expedition was finally becoming a reality.

Chapter 12

Caution
to the Wind

"Why wait? Life is not a dress rehearsal.
Quit practicing what you're going to do,
and just do it. In one bold stroke you can
transform today."

… Marilyn Grey

It was a London-misty kind of morning. Even though it was only days away from being the longest day of the year it seemed the shortest. Emotional good-byes were exchanged as our families bid us farewell at the Edmonton train station. Cautious enthusiasm mixed with somber thoughts, coupled with an overcast day and rainy night, made our 30-hour train journey through the Rocky Mountains a mystical one. There was a certain aura of magnificence in the air shrouding an even greater mystery, soon to be revealed to us. How were we ever going to learn to handle a massive 57-foot sailboat?

In my mind and probably in all our minds we wondered – *What did we get ourselves into? Were we nuts?* The reality of our predicament was setting in fast. Fear of what our future was to hold was at its peak as we found ourselves at the crossroads between two lifestyles – our familiar one, the one on land that we were leaving behind and the unfamiliar one at sea. One we didn't know anything about yet but had pledged to embrace at any cost.

It was a strange sensation. My heart wanted to jump out of my body as the emotion of fear collided with the emotion of extreme excitement, of burning desire. In either case I felt like crying, but as any captain would do I displayed an outward appearance of having things under control. And why not? First of all Shirley and I had solid support and encouragement from Jim and Ann. And secondly, the owner of Nausikaa III had promised to teach us how to sail after we closed our deal. We planned to circumnavigate Vancouver Island, a four to five hundred mile trip, to gain experience in coastal navigation and inland and open ocean sailing. Maybe we'd even experience a storm. Gale force winds were pretty common in that area.

Reed Point Marina, located just outside Vancouver, was shrouded in a thick morning fog. Nausikaa III's captain had brewed a fresh pot of coffee on the ship's diesel stove. Inside the ship it was toasty warm. It seemed to soothe my shivers, coming from where, I didn't really know. Maybe it was the chill of the early morning air. Or maybe it was my fear, or excited anticipation at closing our deal. I still feared it might not go through, that something would go amiss – like the owner changing his mind at the last minute or something. I also feared the whole thing was just too good to be true. But right now that didn't appear to be the case. We were being warmly greeted and well treated.

The good captain took us on a tour throughout the ship from stem to stern showing us that all the equipment, including the spare sails, was accounted for according to our agreement, which would enable us to start our expedition. He gave us a quick demonstration how to turn off and on the engine and explained how the transmission worked in forward and reverse. Tickled to death, we all signed the contract and traded our final payment, a certified check, for the ship's registration. The deal was done.

We celebrated with coffee blessed with sugar and more importantly, for an occasion such as this, a generous shot of Lemon Heart rum. We were now the proud owners of a 57-foot sailboat. Unbelievable! It had been barely six months since I originally had approached Shirley about my dream. It seemed impossible that it all came together so fast. *Surely I must be dreaming* I thought. But each time I pinched myself I knew it was real.

There was one concern looming over our celebration. Everyone handled our new home just fine except Trevor who was now 8 months old. While Marci and Cara comfortably played on the boat, Trevor constantly wanted to be held. Each time we put him down on the deck he screamed. *What's the matter with that kid?* I thought. The boat barely moved. We were tied to the dock for heaven sake! But every time we put him down and the boat rocked ever so gently, he started to cry again. His little arms stretched upward, tears pouring out of his eyes, begging us to pick him up. In his little way if he could, he would have jumped right back into the comfort of our arms.

My heart fibrillated and I started to wonder. *What did we get ourselves into?* I started to doubt the practicality of my dream. How we were going to handle this problem, I did not know. I just wished it would go away. After all we had just bought the boat and it was time to celebrate, not to think about giving up.

I walked the good captain to the end of the dock and bid him good bye. When I inquired about the next time we would see each other again, he warmly patted me on my back and replied, *"Don't worry Boris you'll do just fine."* I wondered what he meant by that. He turned and slowly walked down the dock and like a classic scene out of a mystery movie, he disappeared into the thick fog as it swallowed up his image, that first day of June.

It didn't take long to figure out what the captain meant. As early as the next day he was *too busy* to show us how to practice docking our ship.

However the good news was that Trevor was up contently playing with his toys in our aft stateroom. That delighted me no end because we were anxious to take Nausikaa III out on the bay for our first test run.

My teeth locked together tight as Jim and some people in the marina helped give Nausikaa a good shove away from the dock. I didn't know what I was more sensitive about – the snickers we received from the onlookers (waiting like vultures for us to do something wrong) or the anticipation of what was going to happen once I engaged the transmission. I quietly thanked the infinite powers for our safe passage out of the marina and then turned the helm over to Jim while I tried to control my involuntary shaking. After spending some time practicing various maneuvers, forward and reverse, circling port, then starboard, we were ready to return to the marina.

This time, however, the infinite powers were not with us. The more times I approached the dock unsuccessfully, the louder the laughter, and the larger our *welcome* group became. *"How far are you going to take this ship, sailor?"* they shouted.

Like a smart-ass, with a bitter smirk on my face and in total frustration, I shouted back, *"All the way to Australia!"* They laughed some more. I tried to dock once again.

It was a big lesson I learned that day. It doesn't pay to share your grand goals with others so early into the challenge. It virtually seemed as if they preferred to see us fail before we even got started. Maybe it wasn't intentional but that is how it came across, and right then I had enough challenges to deal with. I certainly didn't need to be mocked, too.

The next day we didn't bother to ask for assistance. We were able to sneak out of the marina early in the morning before the fog lifted and before most people were awake. That was a great success. But once we were out in the bay different challenges presented themselves.

It was time to rig up the sails. Jim and I were as proud as peacocks when we managed to hank the jib and figure out how to hoist it. We all cheered. Our young children, playing in the cockpit, wondered what all the fuss was about. But after observing the situation closer we decided we cheered too soon. When we compared our hoisted jib with a drawing in our *How to Sail* book I knew something was wrong. This time we laughed hysterically. The joke was on us. *The sail was upside down.*

When the fog lifted we were blessed with a gentle breeze, which allowed us to practice *coming about* (turning around under sail). The summer sun caressed our faces and the wind filled Nausikaa's sails. We loved it. We cherished the day away. Slowly I felt the seawater seep into my veins and into my soul. I was hooked.

Daily we made it a point to go out and practice. As the days passed, we realized we were our own teachers and would have to do the best with the knowledge we had. Our time to sail around Vancouver Island was limited and quickly diminishing. There just wouldn't be enough time to do it. It was imperative to follow our time schedule, to use the open weather window to make our passage across the North Pacific to Hawaii before the gale season set in for the fall. As it was, even in the middle of the summer it was quite unlikely to cross the North Pacific without experiencing at least one storm. Typically, the later into the season it gets, the more frequent and violent the storms become. For novice sailors like us the likelihood of any storm made us shake in our shoes.

Probably if we had thought things through more rationally, we wouldn't have ended up getting to this point. Think about it. When we were considering buying a boat, other boat owners described the most beautiful things about sailing and the lifestyle – the pristine anchorages, uninhabited islands, great fishing, great quality of life and how fortunate we would all be.

However, now that we had purchased our ship, we were hearing the other side of the story. We were filled with negative stories – things like storms were a constant reality. That it was hard to find a good anchorage that wasn't overcrowded. That the sea was studded with sharp reefs and rocks that could tear huge holes in a boat's hull and sink it in minutes. That the seas weren't as abundant with fish thanks to commercial fisheries. And as for the quality of life, forget it. We would be forever enslaved to our ship. What a contrast in concepts.

Being so naive and having such big plans, we were probably the laughing stock of the marina. We as green sailors didn't know what to make of it. Perhaps it was our inexperience that attracted so much negativity from others. Or maybe they truly meant well, trying to make us aware of the possible dangers. However in the process they were destroying our self-confidence. Our enthusiasm for our expedition just plummeted. We knew that we had to get away from all the negativity in that marina.

Our wives had one stipulation before we left – to ensure the ship was safe for our children. Jim and I worked rapidly on hand-tying a large net that encompassed Nausikaa. After tying thousands of knots the ship took on the appearance of a huge playpen. And we were all in it. It was perhaps one of our best improvements to the boat. Over the years it would not just keep our children safe but it would also catch flyaway cushions, sails, buckets and even keep adults from being washed overboard.

Finally with the netting complete we were ready to move from Vancouver to Victoria on Vancouver Island. There we would be a small step away from the open Pacific. Our spirits were recharged with renewed excitement and wonder, speculating on the unknown adventures that lay ahead of us.

Anxious about our crossing, we were relieved when Nausikaa's original owner agreed to help us make the one-day passage to Victoria. We arranged to pick him up at another dock on our way in West Vancouver. He warned that we'd be passing under a railroad bridge – the type that is raised and lowered to the appropriate height, as needed. As we were approaching the narrows we were to contact the bridge watchman via VHF radio, to ensure the bridge was raised high enough for our masts to clear. The only way to make it under the bridge was to pass during the outgoing tide. With a flooding tide the current would be too strong to allow us through.

It was six in the morning when we quietly slipped out of the marina. Even though it was an overcast misty day, the excited atmosphere on board charged us all. Even the children knew something special was happening.

Armed with a chart and tide tables I steered the ship toward the bridge with great pride and confidence. It was the correct time for the outgoing tide and seeing other boats also heading toward the narrows confirmed it. However, our attempts to reach the bridge watchman were unsuccessful. He wasn't answering our calls. The bridge was raised but we couldn't tell if it was high enough. Smaller recreational boats and commercial fishing boats zoomed under it with plenty of room but we would need more clearance than they did.

Just to be cautious I slowed right down to let a smaller sailboat pass us by. Slowly we followed. The leader's masts passed under the bridge with no problem, but I didn't feel confident there was enough clearance for us. I decided to wait for yet another sailboat with taller masts to lead the way. Just to be on the safe side, I engaged the transmission into reverse to stop us from moving forward. However we didn't slow down. What was happening?

Panic set in. *It must be something mechanical* I thought. Trying to troubleshoot, since we were still going forward in reverse I switched to forward. I was shocked to see us shoot toward the bridge with even greater speed.

"We're caught in the current!" Jim yelled. My heart sunk to my feet. In total alarm I jammed the gearshift into reverse and applied full throttle until it screamed. A cloud of black smoke spumed out of the exhaust port. I panicked even more! I never saw so much smoke come from the engine before, but that wasn't my concern. I just wanted to stop Nausikaa from moving forward. I couldn't.

In disbelief I watched the bridge deck draw closer and closer to our masts. I held my breath. My mind frantically raced trying to come up with a solution to our crisis yet my body was paralyzed in fear. I was in such a state of shock that I couldn't hear the screaming engine any more. My eyes fixed on the bridge. I stood helpless and watched what was to happen. As if in slow motion, ever so slowly, the radio antenna atop Nausikaa's main mast just managed to skim underneath the railway bridge.

I stared up at the top of the masts, still intact, then burst into joyous relief. With the bridge now behind us I collapsed onto the helm seat, my head slumped over the wheel, my white knuckled hands still tightly gripping it. I couldn't believe it. This could have been the end of our expedition before we even had a chance to get away. I was totally ecstatic, relieved, and thankful that our little adventure for the day ended favorably.

What I didn't know was that this adventure was just the beginning, a tiny drop in the bucket. An ocean full of adventures lay just ahead.

Chapter 13

The Maiden Voyage

"My own experience has taught me this: if you wait for the perfect moment when all is safe and assured it may never arrive. Oceans will not be sailed, mountains will not be climbed, races won or lasting happiness achieved."

... Maurice Chevalier

Victoria, with its large Pacific salmon-fishing fleet, was an excellent location to provision Nausikaa III for our maiden voyage to Hawaii. We were anxious to stockpile charts of areas that we'd only dreamed about so far. They would be our friendly guides to reality. A clerk at the local marine store seemed fascinated with the uncommon charts that interested us. He wasn't even aware he had some of them in stock until we requested them. That's how rarely they were sold.

We examined the charts with great interest. It was the ultimate treat. I felt like kid in a candy store. I just couldn't get enough of it. Some island chains appeared not to even exist anymore because their names had changed since the charts were published. The Gilbert Islands were now named Kiribati. Others like the Bikini Islands were marked as a prohibited area as they were once used for nuclear testing sites. Christmas Island near the equator was also a nuclear test site but now was accessible, allowing sailing ships to stop and re-provision. Only 22 years earlier the British had carried out surface nuclear explosions. *I really want to stop there* I thought. I was curious what it would look like now.

At first the clerk kind of snickered to himself as he watched us. We must've looked like four very naive dreamers wasting our money on a foolish unrealistic dream. Over the years in his business he must've seen many new sailors renege on their plans of cruising the South Pacific after experiencing just a taste of the open ocean. *"Some make it little way down the west coast, some even make it to Hawaii,"* he said, *"but you don't hear too often of people making it that far south."* As amused as he must've been he was still professional enough to assist us. However, the cost of the charts was a reality check, depleting our limited finances.

At the fishing tackle store the clerk was not so kind. When we requested his professional opinion for appropriate fishing gear for our voyage he blatantly burst out laughing. *"You are going where? And you want to catch what? Out there?"* He laughed so hard, it made his big salmon belly jiggle like Santa's. *"Why would you want to buy all that fishing gear when there are no fish out in the open ocean? Fish only go out about two hundred miles into the Pacific and that's it. If you're smart, let me save you some money. I talk with those fisherman all day long and they ought to know,"* he crusaded.

The harder we tried to buy fishing gear, the more aggravated he became. At that point I am sure his pride was on the line. If we bought the tackle, it would be obvious that we didn't believe a word he was saying. Under normal circumstances I would've just walked out on the idiot, but the reality was that he was a fishing fleet wholesaler and could save us a lot of money. He was so convincing and I would've probably believed him had I not known of Kon Tiki and other seafaring stories confirming that people had depended on the fish they caught for their very survival. Finally with great reluctance the annoyed clerk sold us a 1,000-foot spool of 200-pound test nylon fishing line, a

600-foot spool of quarter inch nylon rope and a bunch of fishing hooks, lures and weights.

The clerk's action was another example of how people reacted to our voyage. I couldn't believe it. Being on top of the world wasn't as much fun as I expected. We were on our own emotional high but other than a few salty sailors, most people continued to try to dissuade us from going. We became very frustrated with their discouraging attitude. That was the reason there was no fanfare the day we left Victoria. There was no media coverage, no publicity, no flowers or warm goodbye hugs. Nausikaa III, ever the beautiful traditional sailing ship, with her dark blue hull and indian-red sails, quietly slipped out of the harbor leaving Victoria behind sparkling in the early morning sun.

As I look back at the history of our first voyage I just don't know where we found the courage to embark. We were barely adults with the responsibility of three young children, ages three and under. We were so naïve.

Just because we departed Victoria it didn't mean that we were in the clear to set out on our voyage to Hawaii. No sooner did we enter the straight of Juan De Fuca that we heard on the VHF radio that a very strong gale was in the forecast. There was a warning for all small craft to stay in port for the next three days.

Without hesitation, we immediately pulled into Neah Bay, Washington, a quaint Indian village that hosted a large Pacific salmon fleet and also a large US Air Force and Army observation station. We ended up staying for three days and those were the first rewarding days in our young sailing career. Here everyone we met supported our dream and encouraged us to carry it through.

On the last day of our stay our Air Force friends invited us to a party at the officer's mess. Forty new-found friends treated us to a great dinner and good cheer and wished us a safe voyage. The next morning some even came to see us off, but others had celebrated too much the night before. There was so much excitement and so many last minute things to say and do that we finally left port around mid-day.

Later that afternoon we would learn a lesson never to be forgotten. It was our inexperience that caused us to leave the protection of the harbor so prematurely after the storm. No sooner did we round Neah Bay point, than we were faced with humungus swells left over from the storm. There was little wind but an abundance of confused seas. Nausikaa bounced around like a small cork. Our stomachs churned. *Boy – were we ever stupid to party the night before our departure* I thought. That was our first big mistake; leaving port hastily was our second. However nobody felt we were in danger in the rough seas, just uncomfortable.

We decided to push on using engine power with our sails to help propel us as fast as possible away from shore where the water was shallow and the seas confused. Really we didn't have to endure such discomfort. We should've swallowed our pride, not letting it get in the way of our instinct and common sense. We should've turned around and waited another day but after such a beautiful send off, decided not to.

It wasn't long before we experienced the worst feeling one can have at sea – seasickness. There's an old saying, *the only people that haven't been seasick are the ones who are going to be.* It hit us all just about the same time. We were complaining of feeling nauseous and within seconds Shirley, who hadn't been feeling great to begin with from celebrating the night before, leaned over the rail and started vomiting violently. Jim and Ann closely followed her. It was a sight I'd never seen before and don't enjoy remembering. They vomited until there was nothing left to vomit, then they suffered dry heaves.

I felt so miserably sick myself that I wanted to lean over the side and join them. The feeling of nausea pushed the food from my stomach up to the back of my throat. I was inches away from losing it, but I just wouldn't allow myself to let go. I kept swallowing it back down. It was a total mind game. I wouldn't allow myself to be sick for two reasons. First I didn't want to burden the others with having to helm the boat, and second because I felt responsible for their misery. After all I was the person that originally instigated the expedition, selling them on my dream.

Another reason I didn't want to be sick was because I felt my captainship or leadership role would be compromised which would make the situation appear even more hopeless. Horrible thoughts encircled my mind. I wondered if the seas were always so rough. *No wonder very few are able to adapt to life out here* I thought. I cursed the day I conceived the whole idea. If there were a way to roll the clock back I would've paid any price to do it. But for now the only thing I could manage was to keep our course heading west and hope for the best.

Jim became so sick that he didn't even notice when his eyeglasses slid off his face and into the ocean. It had to be one of the most sad, helpless times in my entire sailing career. There we were, the four of us with our children helplessly stuck on a little cork bobbing along in the vast ocean not having much confidence in where we were going or how we were going to get there.

Perhaps it was the fact that night fell that saved our expedition from failing. In my mind I was prepared to quit, to turn around, return to port and just walk away from the boat never to return. However, I had a problem. I didn't know how to find our way back to the safety of the harbor in the dark. We had no choice. We had to stay out until morning and then that would be it.

O God, I hated myself and I hated the thought that I had exposed us all to such danger – especially our children. Tears filled my eyes as a reality check confirmed that our expedition was only a foolish dream and not a realistic one. What God-given right did I have to ask life for such a privileged gift when I hadn't acquired enough experience and knowledge to make it a reality?

I kept swallowing hard to avoid being sick. That night I constantly changed my mind whether or not we should turn around and head back home. A few times I changed our course back toward the east but couldn't see any lights or other signs of land. Just to be on the safe side I headed west toward the open ocean. One thing I knew for sure was that a sailor's greatest danger was not the sea itself but running aground and being shipwrecked.

It was a peculiar thing but the children were not seasick. They must've known something was wrong, and instinctively stayed quietly out of the way. To my amazement they contently played on the floor down below in the main salon. I thanked God for that, because if they'd been sick and needed more attention, I don't know what we would've done.

I couldn't believe how Trevor handled the rough seas without uttering a whimper of complaint. It was quite a contrast to his reaction the very first day we moved on board. Then he had cried as the ship rocked just the slightest even though we were tied up in the marina. There is a theory children up to the age of four or five don't get seasick because the motion of the ocean resembles the motion in their mother's womb. It would prove to be our experience sailing with young children.

For dinner the children sported big smiles on their faces. Never before were they given free access to the cookie container. That night however, it was all we could do to get the container out of the cupboard and plop it before them, letting them go to it. At least, we justified, the cookies were hearty with raisins and oatmeal. It filled them up and kept us out of the galley – an area we felt deathly ill in.

On an ocean voyage the wheel has to be manned 24 hours a day. We took turns on four-hour watches to ensure someone was continuously at the helm throughout the day and night. That first night at sea we were exhausted from the motion and weary from seasickness. Everyone curled up in the most comfortable corner they could find and fell asleep waking up only to man their watches. By the time I fell asleep I was so trashed, both emotionally and physically, that I didn't even hear Jim shut the engine off in the middle of the night. Finally when I returned to the cockpit I realized someone had generously cut me some slack covering my watch, as it was well into a new day, and a nice one at that.

Nausikaa III was under full sail and still heading west. The seas had flattened nicely and a gentle yet steady wind propelled us through the water at five knots. A few lonely clouds lazily cruised across the sky. I walked the deck and surveyed the horizon 360 degrees. Land was not in sight. Yesterday's ghostly pale faces now looked normal with big grins and sparkling eyes revealing the feeling, *it was great to be alive!* Our children played nicely in the cockpit and Ann, on her watch, kept a good eye on them.

With new energy filling my soul I looked at everyone and said, *"I guess we aren't going back are we?"*

Chapter 14

Where Are We?

*"If you don't know where you're going, how
will you know when you get there?"*

... Unknown

It was sheer joy to watch our children play safely on deck as
Nausikaa's bow sliced through the waters of the North Pacific.
Everybody was finally over their motion sickness after three days at
sea. The winds and seas had calmed down and we were settling into
a steady routine. The adults kept busy with their watches and everyday
chores like cooking meals, washing diapers and tending to all three
children.

Jim and I were astounded how many cotton diapers Marci and
Trevor generated daily. Every day we washed them out by hand in
salt water, rinsed them in fresh, and then tacked them onto the lifelines
to dry. *"Thank God,"* we joked, *"we're out at sea where nobody can
see our gypsy boat."* We also carried a small supply of pampers on
board for emergencies in case we found ourselves in a storm or if we
ran out of dry diapers.

The days were perfect for sailing. The skies were clear, but the
North Pacific winds were bone-chilling cold, demanding full winter
clothing attire complete with toques. It was difficult to keep warm on

95

night watches even after we rigged up a canvas tent over the cockpit and wrapped ourselves in thick blankets. After watch we quickly retreated below to enjoy the comfort generated by our diesel stove. It kept the coffee hot and us warm.

We were pleased the way the both families adapted to life at sea. With each new day it looked more like the picture I had envisioned of my fantasy. We embraced our expedition with the same spirit as the old sailors. Just like they did before us, we were pleased to discover that we were covering about hundred and twenty miles per day by the sheer power of nature's wind. Determined not to waste fuel we were committed not to use engine power except in the case of an emergency or to idle the engine in order to recharge the house batteries that provided light at night.

So far we hadn't caught any fish and I wondered if by some chance the old fishing tackle salesman in Victoria was right, we were too deep for fish! Not giving up hope yet, we checked our hooks regularly and experimented with different lures and hoochies. We had two lines in the water, one off each side of Nausikaa. An alarm system was in place whereby we tacked a section of the fishing line with a clothespin to the ship's lifeline. If a fish hit, it would yank the fishing line out of the clothespin, making a snapping sound and alerting the helmsman. It was a primitive arrangement but we felt that if there were any fish in the ocean it should work.

A couple false alarms revealed some seaweed on the hook. Finally we were really excited when we awoke one morning to discover the starboard line had snapped sometime during the night. Such a fuss was made as the heavy line was being pulled in. Everyone gathered around for the big moment, but as the *fish* was pulled out of the water we were all shocked to see Ann's favorite jeans snagged on the end of it. Ann was thrilled. She'd hung her jeans out to dry on the rail the night before and the wind blew them overboard. We all had a good laugh about our big catch of the day!

It was a bizarre sensation not to see a soul out in the open ocean, just one vast horizon all around us. Every day a heavy uncertainty loomed over my head making me uncomfortable – navigation. Truth be known I didn't know where the heck we were. Oh how I wished and dreamed for a road sign along our route to confirm at least that we were on the right track. The uncertainty killed me but I had to project confidence that I knew where we were in order to keep morale up. Perhaps I was right about our location, but I didn't know for sure and it was eating me from inside out.

I kept our dead reckoning position and updated it twice a day based on our speed log and compass heading. That method of navigation didn't allow for drift, current or imperfection in steering the ship. What bothered me was that the dead reckoning position never corresponded with my celestial navigation calculations. Before leaving port we purchased an extra sextant so we would have two on board in case one was damaged or lost overboard. I constantly referred to the *Celestial Bodies Tables* and the book, *Celestial Navigation* by *Mary Blewit*.

The complicated process of calculating latitude and longitude to determine our position challenged me even though I felt I was a pretty good mathematician. But each time I went through the process of calculations and tables extractions I would come up with a different result. For the life of me I could not figure where I was making a mistake. So back to the books I went, over and over day after day.

One day Ann, who was watching the children play, spotted something far on the horizon. It was a large structure about forty degrees to our starboard. Without hesitation I changed our course heading directly for it. Everyone on board, especially me was so excited that there was actually someone else in the same waters as we were. *Perhaps they can confirm where we are,* I hoped.

"This is Canadian sailing vessel Nausikaa III calling any station. Do you copy?" I asked over the VHF radio.

Silence.

"This is Canadian sailing vessel Nausikaa III calling any station. Do you copy?" I repeated over and over but to no avail.

I was anxious. I didn't want the ship to escape over the horizon. Large ships moved much faster than we did. However this one just increased in size as we sailed closer toward it. As we approached we were able to make out the ship's features. She seemed to be stationary and looked deserted with no signs of life on board. The ship looked neglected, rusty and old, except for her unusually busy superstructure loaded with what I identified as a complex array of spinning radar dishes and a forest of communication radio antennas. The whole thing appeared odd and chilling.

By now our curiosity really had us. We were right next to the ship and yet nobody answered our repeated radio messages. No flags were flying, as would be the normal procedure to identify the nationality of the ship.

Persistently I tried again for the umpteenth time, *"This is Canadian sailing ship Nausikaa III calling the vessel on our starboard side – requesting a position check please."*

Finally to our surprise our VHF radio blasted to life in full volume, *"To the vessel calling, this is the Russian fish packing ship Vladivostok. We are anchored on top of Sea Mount Cobb and that is your position."*

The voice was gruff with a thick Russian accent. But he had a good command of English, much better than I had – that's for sure. At first I felt cold shivers run through my body at the thought that we were actually conversing with a Russian ship. After all we were at the height of the cold war.

Then it hit me like ton of bricks – this had to be a Russian spy vessel camouflaged as a fish packing ship! I was puzzled by the fact that the ship was able to anchor in waters so far away from the North American continent. On a large scale chart, it showed no shallow water anywhere, but then after talking with the ship, I examined a close-up chart that had Sea Mount Cobb marked. Our depth finder still wasn't registering shallow water so just for conversation sake and to break the ice I asked, *"How much water do you have under your keel Vladivostok?"*

"Sixty feet, " he replied.

Now that we were really up close we could clearly see their radar hardware in full spin. *Surely they'd seen us coming from a long way's off* I was convinced. *Why didn't they respond earlier?* But it was obvious. This was the perfect location for Russians to sit and spy on the U.S. west coast Navy and their shipping activities.

I desperately wanted to instigate small talk, if nothing else, just to break up our daily routine. But all I received in return were brief snippy replies. It wasn't until I divulged that my name was *Boris* and that I had immigrated to Canada from Croatia that the conversation opened up and became friendlier.

But initially the Russian radio operator hinted scorn at me betraying my country. He asked how I could ever leave a communist country to embrace a capitalist system. Then more directly – how could I leave my home, my family and friends, and my village? The whole concept was too incomprehensible for him. He went on comparing his life and tried to illustrate what I had done was wrong, and how he could never do such a thing.

But his tune changed, once I described the kind of freedom and opportunity I found in North America. I described to him what the feeling was like to have total personal freedom. To have the independence to live life the way I wanted. How stimulating and liberating it was to have a choice of where to live, work, play, shop and pray.

I explained the only down side was that there was even the freedom to choose not to work and still get paid for it as in the case of welfare abuse. And after living under the heavily regulated communist system the first 17 years of my life, I felt so energized to have all the freedom in the world to sculpt my life the way I wanted it to be, to the best of my ability, ingenuity and depth of desire.

Now the tone of our discussion changed. My Russian *tovarish* (friend) and I were deep into a friendly conversation exchanging philosophical ideas. After a while he divulged his fascination toward the concept of what we were striving to accomplish. He agreed it would be impossible to do such a thing if I still lived in Croatia. And he was astounded that we were just ordinary people, two families with our young children, able to afford a sailing ship, never mind the fact that we were able to roam the world at will.

Our great philosophical conversation continued. Shirley and I, listening intently to the radio, became teary-eyed, touched by his remarks. The Russian was also moved. His voice started to tremble as he agreed it was a shame politics got in the way of people from different countries getting along. We concluded that inherently most people are good, wanting only a peaceful life for themselves and their families. Our conversation became lengthy and revealed emotions I didn't expect. It seemed as if we would be missed once we were out of radio range. As it was we were drifting away from the ship.

Then the Russian wondered if we wanted anything. Well, we were out of fresh meat and fresh milk. With no refrigeration on board other than our small icebox we weren't able to keep such things for long. We did have plenty of canned meat and evaporated milk but the thought of fresh milk at least for the little ones seemed wonderful.

I queried if they had any meat or milk that we could buy. The officer was delighted they would be able to assist us and refused to discuss money. A plan was made. We were to come about to pick up the supplies. In the time it would take us to reach them our package would be ready. They readied the crane they planned to use to swing our package out over the ship's side and lower it down onto our deck.

As we approached the Russian ship we were actually able to see the ocean bottom through the shallow water. Suddenly our fishing alarms alerted us, as both clothespins snapped. Simultaneously Ann and Shirley screamed, *"Fish! We have fish on our lines!"* We had to bring Nausikaa into the wind to bring us to a complete stop, because it was impossible to haul the lines in.

Whatever we had caught was much stronger than we were. The timing couldn't have been more awkward as now the once vacant decks of the Vladivostok were alive, teaming with curious crew hanging over the rail waving to us and awaiting our arrival. They were as interested in us as we were in them.

As hard as we tried we just couldn't haul our fishing lines in. Momentarily we would gain a few feet of line but then lose it. All of a sudden it became obvious what our problem was. All we had to do was look out into the water to see what was happening. Shark fins infested the area. They were everywhere. The large beasts swam nonchalantly around us; like in the movies, the sharks circling their prey before a feeding frenzy. It was an eerie sight. Surely it was hopeless to retrieve our fishing gear so we just cut our lines. The two protective moms stood clinging onto their curious babies, holding them back from the ship's rail.

On our final approach to the starboard side of the Russian ship we realized we were in for danger. Even though the wind wasn't very strong and the waves and swells weren't very big, Nausikaa's mast tops swayed back and forth – enough to pose a threat of colliding with the large ship's hull. They would've snapped for sure and spelled a disaster we didn't need. But the promise of fresh meat and milk was enough of a lure to make a fool attempt it, so I did.

Rough water slapped up between the two ships, tossing Nausikaa around like a toy. I cringed every time the ocean swells rocked us too close, our masts coming within inches from crashing against the Russian hull.

Luckily for us, not a package but a pallet of goods landed on our decks on the first try. Jim immediately cut off the line that lowered the load down to our deck, and we sped out of harm's way.

It was an emotional time for us all as we continued on the radio repeating our thanks and good byes over and over. Finally two hours later we were out of radio reach.

We were delighted with our Russian friend's generosity, but were disappointed with the contents. We were surprised that our package included one solid 200-pound brick of frozen red snapper, which we didn't have much use for except for eating a few fish. They also gave us dozens of cans of heavily sweetened evaporated milk. I burst out laughing, amused with our expectation. *What did I think – they had a cow on board?* It was obvious the Ruskies didn't have fresh provisions either. They were in the same predicament we were in. In fact they probably hadn't provisioned for months.

However the true gift we did receive was friendship. And peace of mind. Because at least for now, we knew exactly where we were.

Chapter 15

The Deep
Blue Pacific

"I have stood on the shore of time picking
up a beautiful sea shell here and there.
While all before me lies the great sea of life,
undiscovered."

... Sir Issac Newton

The further we sailed offshore the less seaweed we observed drifting in the water, and the bluer the ocean became. In sheer delight we watched Trevor slowly learn to walk. Using the netting Jim and I had woven around the deck, Trevor would pull himself up, hang onto it for support and gingerly waddle sideways along the rail. It was a sight to see how incredibly well he was able to control his balance as the boat rolled back and forth and up and down.

At no time was he free of tottering and it appeared as if the motion of the ship actually assisted him. Each time Trevor was about to fall Nausikaa seemed to rock just the right way to compensate, keeping him upright and allowing him enough time to dash to the next piece of rigging to again hang on for support. Under the same conditions adults seemed to have more difficulty getting around yet Trevor, barely 10 months old, was just cruising the decks.

Shirley and I beamed with pride and delight that our biggest of all fears turned out to be one of our least concerns – that Trevor had adjusted so well to this life. The thought of taking Trevor offshore had been a major consideration for Shirley when she first realized I was serious about going. With her adventurous spirit, she was *up* for the challenge, but she was torn over her responsibility as a mother to her son. How could she take a helpless baby to sea? Only after Shirley visited Trevor's pediatrician, who surmised that he would not only be OK but be healthier than if he lived a normal life on land, did she feel relieved about it.

Shirley also had feared her tendency to feel anxious or claustrophobic in small areas such as in the tight quarters as we had aboard Nausikaa. For the first two weeks she would find herself in the middle of the night, suddenly outside on deck gasping for air (not knowing how she got there) in the midst of little panic attacks. The last thing she would remember was going to bed, but she would wake up outside on deck. Eventually her panic attacks became fewer and fewer until they petered out to nothing and she overcame her claustrophobia.

Oh how thankful I was that we hadn't given in to fear of the unknown, the invisible killer of dreams.

Another fear we had before leaving on our expedition was how were we going to handle constantly being around each other day in and day out. Since the first day we met, Shirley and I were very compatible and cherished our time together. Neither one of us wanted to disturb that. However, we had never spent 24 hours a day non-stop together and wondered how that would affect our relationship. But in actuality that fear was also unjustified. We thrived on it and treasured sharing special times, from waking up to sun rays gleaming through our porthole at the start of each new day to witnessing brilliant red sunsets as we sat wedged in the bowsprit pulpit dreaming about our next destination.

Nausikaa's bowsprit was also a magnificent place to observe schools of dolphins that loved to swim just inches away. They would crisscross in our bow wave for hours as if playing a game of chicken. Some days they entertained us for what seemed like hours. It was one of Trevor's favorite things to do and for us the most romantic. And it was on one of those enchanted days when we were on the bowsprit that Ann, who was at the helm, yelled out, *"We have a fish on the line!"*

Jim was the closest to the line and was well on his way hauling it in by the time we arrived on the scene. To everyone's delight Jim flipped a beautiful yellow and blue colored 25-pound fish into the cockpit. It was a sight of absolute delight – children screaming, adults laughing and excitement overflowing. Blood spattered on the deck as the fish flopped around. I quickly handed Jim the fish bat and he subdued the fish with a couple hard blows to its head.

Jim was a great fisherman with lots of experience fishing at Calling Lake in northern Alberta where his parents had a summer cabin. He immediately volunteered to gut the fish but before he could proceed, the clothesline peg on the port side of the ship snapped with a loud *ping*. This time it was my turn to haul it in. We couldn't believe our luck. Two fish on the same day! My fish was a bit smaller than Jim's and we contemplated throwing it back but decided instead to use it to make fish jerky. That way we'd be guaranteed not to run out of fish for the next few days.

"Yippee!" We were ecstatic. Yes, there were fish out here in the deep ocean. We joked and plotted how we should take a picture and mail it from Hawaii to the salmon-bellied fishing-gear salesman, just to set him straight.

Jim and I unhooked our fish and once again we slowly let out our lure. Jim's was barely past Nausikaa's stern when incredibly, another fish hit. *"We got another one,"* he yelled. The kids screamed and we laughed and jumped for joy. I was still letting out my line when suddenly it bolted out of my hands, catching me totally off guard and scaring the hell out of me. Yet another fish had hit the other line. This was surreal. We felt so lucky – so on top of the world. Just realizing that if we were ever in a position that we needed to rely on the ocean for a source for food in order to survive we could. It sent shivers of delight throughout my body.

However we didn't have much time to revel in our glory because no sooner did we release the second pair of fish that another batch hit. We were dumbfounded. With Jim on one side of the boat and me on the other, we just kept pulling them in one after another. Now we were into the game of *how many fish were there in the ocean?* After awhile we started to wonder if the same fish we were releasing were hitting our lure again. However that was impossible. The fish were different sizes, ranging from about ten pounds up to forty-five.

In the meantime, Shirley and Ann referred to our fish book and decided we had stumbled on a school of yellow fin tuna. Jim and I finally had enough. We were blissfully exhausted after catching and releasing about forty fish each. I don't think there's a gauge in the world that could've measured the level of our excitement and joy.

At first, with all the commotion, we hadn't noticed the seawater was much warmer today than yesterday. But when I was getting buckets of water for Jim to clean the fish he commented on how warm it felt. It was a revelation. Then everyone noticed that even though it was just about dark, with Jim relying on a flashlight to finish filleting the fish, the air was also much warmer. I had expected the transition between cold and warm temperatures to be a more gradual one, but instead it was as if we crossed over a magic line and presto, it was warm.

Even though it was night I washed my sticky hair for the first time at sea, using a bucket of salt water and rinsing with a single glass of precious fresh water (our lifeblood). I didn't realize at the time but this exercise was the mere beginning of a trend known as *Boris' famous sea bath* that would be taught to and enjoyed by many in the future worldwide.

Another first was experiencing our freshly caught tuna feast. By now it was getting late and since we had been sidetracked by our fishing marathon nobody had prepared dinner. In order to curb our hunger and hold us over I decided to prepare an appetizer. Quickly I sautéed a couple tuna fillets in butter and seasoned them with garlic and lime juice. I passed a steaming hot plate of tuna up to the cockpit. And all I heard from down below were moans and groans, and before I knew it they handed the plate back down ready for a refill. Basically they inhaled the two fillets. Even the children loved the tender soft butter-like tuna. I continued to cook. Everyone continued to eat. I don't know how much mouth-watering fish we packed away that day. We ate as if there was no tomorrow. Certainly there was no need anymore to prepare anything additional for dinner.

After feasting, two very content families cuddled up, each on their own side of the cockpit. With bulging tummies and a deep sense of satisfaction resonating from their being, they settled in to witness a symphony – the rebirth of another star studded evening.

Chapter 16

The Imperfect Storm

*"Life – you've got to ride that thing like
a bucking bronco."*

... Rick Potter

It was now so sunny and warm that as a rule we wore our bathing suits during the day and only in the evenings were we forced to dress more warmly. No longer was there any need to have a temporary cover to protect us in the cockpit or to wrap ourselves in blankets. At night a light jacket and a pair of shorts with a towel draped across our knees was plenty.

Sea-baths became an everyday delight, a healthy pastime. We developed a system where one person (known as the bucketeer) would scoop a bucket of water from the sea and generously pour it (trying to duplicate a gentle waterfall) over the head of the person having the bath (also known as the sweaty one). Regular shampoo generated a humungus quantity of suds, which the sweaty one would spread all over their body. (Warning – regular soap does *not* lather in salt water and leaves you feeling stickier than before you started.) Using two applications of shampoo guaranteed the shampoo company's profit margin and at the same time made the sweaty one squeaky-clean. Carefully applying no more than one cup of fresh water over the sweaty one's hair and body allowed for a mini-rinse removing some of the salt. Next, a final good rub down with a towel and presto, the sweaty one would feel like a million bucks and the captain was happy because water conservation was in full effect.

The children loved it also, wanting bucket after bucket poured over them for hours on end. In fact so much so that there were not enough bucketeers to satisfy them. We loved to see them enjoying the water so much. After all that was one of the reasons for our voyage, to enjoy the delightful highlights of life at sea. But after a few days we ran for cover the minute the bucket game was requested by one of the children. We solved the problem, realizing the kids were just as happy to play with their water toys in a bucket or with other containers of water. Little Trevor adopted a five-gallon bucket because he could get right inside it, sit down and splash around with his toys. For him it was a miniature pool.

For days we were mesmerized with life at sea, enjoying warm sunshine and good sailing – so much so that we let our guard down. We didn't notice the ocean swell gradually rising from the NW until it became clearly obvious. By the next afternoon the swell had built up so much that it was like sailing through rolling foothills. Actually the ride was still gratifying until the wind altered direction from the west to the southeast. It was a sign – one that made us fear we might be in for our first storm. We braced ourselves.

The wind velocity increased. It was time to prepare Nausikaa for the worst. We decided to replace the large genoa sail with the storm jib. Then we reefed our main sail. Our course of SW – W was not terrific but the sailing was quite exciting. I felt confident with the current conditions, except I was uncertain and filled with apprehension, not knowing how much pressure Nausikaa's rigging could withstand from the wind.

I think because the storm crept so gradually upon us, we adjusted to it instinctively. But little did I know that we were about to endure the most memorable and uncomfortable storm I was ever to experience in my whole sailing career, including seven hurricanes, some of them devastating. What made this storm so unusually frightening were the gigantic swells, leftovers from a cyclone south of Japan coming out of the WNW, colliding with intense 45 to 55 mile-per-hour gale force winds from the SE, totally the opposite direction.

The two dynamic forces collided with a vengeance. Fierce winds swirled over our heads and confused seas pitched under our keel. I realized early in the storm we were in for a major ride. We were still able to sail but the *seas were building to the point that they now towered much higher than the top of Nausikaa's 58-foot main mast.*

As a result each time we rode deep down into the trough of a swell, the wind was blocked, making the sails flop loose and slap uncontrollably around. The wind that was needed to fill and steady the sails howled many feet above us on the crests of the waves. Then as the next swell charged at us from starboard, Nausikaa would pop up like a cork valiantly riding upward to the wave's crest. Once on top, the full force of the storm attacked us from portside. The wind instantaneously filled our sails with a blast knocking us off the wave's crest and sending us plunging down 65 feet into the next trough.

The ride became so rough that I didn't know which was better, to leave the sails up or bring them down. Having them up scared the daylights out of me when we were exposed to the raw elements on the wave top. On the other hand I felt they were essential to help stabilize Nausikaa while we rode down into the trough of the swell where confused waves would thrash us around like an agitator in a washing machine, before soaring up the next steep swell. It was like a roller coaster ride but this one wasn't much fun and impossible to get off of.

Down below Ann in the main cabin tended to Marci and Cara, while Trevor played quietly in the safety of his bunk in the aft cabin. Shirley was with Trevor but she didn't fare so well in the rough conditions so she did the next best thing. She took a couple seasickness tablets and fell asleep. It was hard to imagine how anyone could fall asleep in those conditions yet she did. It was her only relief.

Jim and I took turns helming the ship, doing our best until the middle of the night when our storm jib tore right down the middle along the seam. I figured the torrential rain must've moistened the seams and weakened the thread. In any case I felt it was a gentle warning from the powers of the universe that it was way too rough for us to be fooling around with so much canvas up. We struggled stumbling around in the darkness to lower and secure all the sails, taking the storm jib right off.

Then we faced another adversity. Nausikaa took on a different rhythm. She bounced, pitched and rolled all at the same time. Every so often, out of the darkness an out-of-sequence wave slammed against us like a huge sledgehammer making a horrible thundering noise, sending a heavy shudder throughout the ship. Each time that happened I clenched my teeth and cringed.

I wondered again just how much impact Nausikaa could handle. *Surely the hull was strong enough but what about the windows?* Even though they were relatively small – 12"x 30" and made out of thick glass I feared how much force they could take. If blown out, we would take on water, perhaps more than the bilge pumps could manage. Then God help us all. I felt so thankful we didn't buy one of those floating condominiums that looked more like an atrium than a ship.

My mind sojourned covering different scenarios. I had to work hard to regain reasonable focus and composure. Otherwise, I feared flipping out – going nuts, since I was physically and mentally exhausted. This wasn't the time to do it.

The entire night I spent outside wedged in a nook between the main cabin and a storage locker, bundled up in a canvas sail cover to protect me from the onslaught of cutting rain. It wasn't as if I could do much but periodically I stood up, peering out into the darkness to watch for the possibility of a freighter or other ships on collision course with us.

What really burned me, was the fact that we were losing ground and helplessly drifting back in a northerly direction. That was a ridiculous concern. After all, in the silence of my mind I doubted if we were going to get out of this storm alive. Tears filled my eyes and pain inflicted my heart. Now all I wished for was to be with Mary and Jakob, my dear parents, secure on their farm where life in the course of the day didn't change much. I visualized my parents playing with their grandson. Then my heart contorted at the thought that they might never ever see us again.

And it was entirely my fault. I felt personally responsible for being in this situation. *How could I get us into this predicament exposing everyone to such danger and adversity?* I wondered. I despised myself for it. My feelings were exactly opposite from some I had a few short days ago when we enjoyed the ecstasy of perfect sailing conditions. Now all I wished was to get everyone off the ship and back to safety.

That night in the cockpit I outwardly conversed with God. *"Please,"* I begged, *"if it's our time to go, please make it quick and painless. But if you just want to make a point, then OK – I get the message. Enough is enough. Just quit with the rough stuff."* I pleaded. I reasoned. I begged.

It didn't make any difference. Periodically water from a breaking wave rushed over the full length of Nausikaa's deck almost washing me away as if it were a response to my pleas. I was drowning, not so much in that water but in my own hopelessness. *"Oh God why me? Why us? What did we do to deserve this kind of punishment?"*

An answer jolted me out of my self-pity, *"You're still alive, aren't you?"*

"Yes I am," I replied, *"but..."*

The conversation continued back and forth throughout the night. In the meantime, there was no sign of a positive outcome as the storm continued to rage. In the midst of this hell on earth I felt my father's presence. I knew that he was with me. I didn't resist the feeling. On the contrary, I welcomed it. Initially I wanted to conceal the truth of the severity of the storm to protect him from worry but then I changed my mind. I needed his guidance. *"What can I do Dad? What would you do?"* I kept asking over and over. *"Please Jakob help me. Please!"*

The next morning Jim spelled me at the helm. Fatigued, I went down into the aft cabin to take a nap. Our cabin looked like a bomb had exploded. Things were scattered everywhere, especially on the floor. Not a single book remained inside the bookshelf. Normally they were so tightly packed on their shelves that it must've taken an incredible force to force them out. Shirley described it later as a scene from the movie, The Exorcist, with books bizarrely shooting off the shelves. Both Shirley and Trevor were sleeping together on our bunk. Drenching wet from the ocean spray and downpour of rain, I collapsed on top of the settee cushions, which had fallen onto the floor. Instantaneously I drifted into a deep sleep.

It was noon when I came around. After I examined our predicament I discovered things hadn't changed too much. The seas were the same size as the day before, and in fact the wind had gained in strength. In order to stabilize Nausikaa and hopefully slow her down, Jim and I decided to rig up warps to drag them off of her stern. Sure enough she became more stable when she was positioned perpendicular to the waves.

However, now with the wind blowing from our stern we had the sensation that Nausikaa was drifting much faster. We would never know for sure if that really was the case. But one thing I knew was we were all still alive and, thank God, not close to land. I actually wondered if it would be possible to get trapped inside the storm and be helplessly dragged along for days, aimlessly drifting without control until we reached a land mass, only to be bashed around in shallow waters by huge waves and pounding surf. Surely Nausikaa would be shredded to bits. I tried not to think about it.

Once Nausikaa was stabilized there wasn't much else we could do – just wait and ride it out. All I remember eating during the storm was Dinty Moore stew. It was much too rough to heat it up on the stove. It took all the effort we could manage to find the stew and a can opener, open it up and eat it right out of the tin. Surprisingly in these conditions, it tasted delicious.

Jim and his family were down below in the main cabin, and Shirley, Trevor and I were in the aft cabin. Both families kept the entry hatches tightly boarded up in case we were rolled or swamped by huge waves.

For two days Shirley stayed below extremely seasick and with the exception of nursing Trevor and changing his diapers when necessary, she kept to her bunk. The discomfort she endured must have been absolutely unbearable. We didn't talk a lot during those moments when we briefly saw each other but I could see she was totally exhausted trying to hang on for her dear life with the ship's motion resembling a wild carnival ride. It was enough for even the bravest to break down, and yet she had to bear the curse of seasickness as well.

I shook my head, amazed that Shirley never complained. She was so courageous. Even though she was as pale as a ghost, I could see in her eyes that she would never consider turning back for a minute. It simply wasn't an option. All curled up in a ball, her tiny 5'4" body looked even smaller. I wondered where all her inner strength and courage came from to endure such hell.

We were married five years and I thought I knew her, but now I realized that I hadn't even scratched the surface yet. I felt so thankful for her courage. I realized that if she were to complain or lose her cool it would be all I needed at this time – the last push to send me over the edge. Instead I found myself drawing confidence from her.

Children must have an inner sense to know when to lay low when danger is lurking and there's no room for fussing. Trevor's bunk was totally netted in. There was no way he could fall out except if he wanted to he could draw the net aside on one corner and crawl onto our bed to join Shirley. He just quietly played in his bunk. I fed him some crackers and juice every so often and then I'd sleep some more on the floor.

Early the third day the wind finally subsided somewhat, as did the swells, but the rain still pounded heavily. With the expectation that the storm was slowly improving we rigged up a spare storm sail and had it ready just in case the weather broke. By evening the wind had subsided a little more, shifting further toward the ENE. We thought if it was possible to pull in the warps and hoist the storm jib and a small staysail we'd be able to slowly cruise in a southwesterly direction, instead of drifting away from Hawaii like we were. However, we were a little too optimistic.

Jim and I worked our selves to the point of exhaustion trying to pull in the warps, only to finally give up because we were still traveling way too fast. It was another 12 hours before the wind subsided enough, shifting to the NE, allowing us to haul in the warps. After much effort we finally raised our sails and were under way.

New energy permeated the air as Nausikaa plowed her way through the massive seas in a fashion comparable to the onset of the storm. But now we were sporting a different attitude. Under the same conditions at the beginning of the storm it scared the living daylights out of us but now we were rejuvenated with new hope. It was all relative. We knew that he worst was over and better things had to be just over the horizon.

Giggles and laughter emerged from the aft cabin. Out of curiosity I looked down into the cabin to see what the commotion was all about. To my amazement I saw Trevor playing *slide* on our bed. Shirley sat on the settee laughing as she watched him have a ball. Our bed cushion had been pushed off on to the floor exposing the smooth wood underneath and Trevor decided to turn it into a slide.

When we were in the trough of a wave, fairly level, he would quickly crawl on all fours to the far end of our bed. As Nausikaa crested a wave the wind would knock her hard to starboard. It created the perfect condition for Trevor to slide the full length of our bed and through an opening in the netting into his bunk, w*eeeing* with delight as he went. He repeated it over and over again, entertaining himself. Our little son had totally adapted to life aboard ship. Shirley looked up and smiled at me, as we shared our joy. It was one of those magic moments when you get that warm tingly feeling. I was happy to see she was feeling better now and was nibbling on soda crackers and drinking seven-up.

Finally there was an imminent sign of change in the weather as the sky cleared completely. At least now we were able to start drying things out. Although the wind calmed down somewhat it was still piping pretty good from the port stern quarter. We briskly clipped along back on course toward Hawaii.

Today was a special occasion. Not only was the end of the storm in sight, but it was Marci's second birthday. One we'd never forget – celebrated at sea at the tail end of our first storm. Happy to be outside, Marci and Cara sat with us in the cockpit bundled up for the cold wind. Shirley pulled out a couple giant lollipops for the girls and the two blue eyed, curly haired blondes giggled as they contently licked away at them.

I was totally delighted that we were all still alive. Things were going to be fine after all. Subconsciously I think we all realized how helpless we were in that storm, being at the mercy of nature, and unable to do anything or contact anyone to advise them of our fate. We could have perished and no one would've known for God knows how long. It was one of those situations that make you realize you don't know how long you've got.

It must have inspired us because we decided to write a note to our parents advising them about our survival and present location. There were also precise instructions how to get in touch with our parents for anyone that might find the note. We placed it an empty wine bottle, corked it, and tossed it overboard in a ritual with great hopes that someone would find it.

In silence we watched, our eyes fixed on the bottle as it bobbed along until it finally disappeared in the post storm spume.

Chapter 17

Trapped in
the Doldrums

"I find the great thing in this world is not so much where you stand, as in what direction you are moving. To reach the port of heaven you must sometimes sail with the wind, and sometimes against it. But you must sail, and not drift, nor lie at anchor."

... Oliver Wendell Holmes

Our jubilant spirits confused me. Everyone automatically fell back into the usual routine just like nothing happened – catching fish, playing, laughing, reading, tending chores, keeping their watches and catching up on lost sleep. No one even talked about the storm in a negative connotation. It was more like, *"Just wait until we tell them back home about the big one. They'll never believe it."*

My thinking as well surprised me. Shortly after the storm I also acted as if nothing had happened. These days my thoughts were more consumed in figuring out how Shirley and I would manage financially in order to continue with our expedition beyond Hawaii, rather than giving up and going home. It was out of the question if I could help it. *So where did that thought go – the one I had in the storm – of giving up? Why could we all forget so easily the horrors of just a few days earlier?* I just couldn't understand it.

On the contrary, my overall memory of the storm exhilarated my spirit as if there was a new kind of energy permeating my soul – a new kind of confidence that accompanied my stride across the decks – a new peace of mind that knew that we could do it! That we could survive even the worst. Now I knew what Charlton Heston felt like as Moses. I felt like a king.

There was only one thing that could humble my confidence. I still doubted myself when it came to knowing exactly where we were. It weighed heavily on my mind. We'd been told the average time for a ship similar to ours to reach Hawaii would be in about 19 days. Since we were at sea for 18 days it meant we should be arriving within a few days. However, my celestial navigation calculations depicted quite a different picture. According to them, we hadn't even gone three-quarters of the way.

When confronted by the others to explain where we exactly were each day, I just wasn't sure. Because of this tensions rose higher with each new day. It was a fact, if I could make a mistake in calculating the distance traveled north to south, I could also make the same mistake east to west. If that were true we could miss Hawaii altogether and have little hope of ever finding the even smaller islands of the South Pacific.

What hurt most wasn't so much the fact that the others didn't believe me, but that I also doubted myself. I tried but just couldn't figure out where I might be wrong in my calculations. So to keep my sanity I was committed to sticking with my positional readings. Our plot line on the chart didn't look promising either. It wasn't straight; actually it zig-zagged and the distances weren't equal. Some days it was twice the distance from the day before. In the area of the storm it didn't even exist only to re-emerge a long way off to the NW and behind longitudinally from my last plot. Based on our strange zig-zag position, each day I had to change our compass heading to compensate for the change in our position.

My days were consumed trying to solve the navigation mystery, only breaking when there was some kind of excitement distracting me. And there sure wasn't a shortage of those times. Now on a regular basis we caught fish – much to Cara's delight. That petite three-year-old could out-eat anyone on board when it came to fish. We also discovered all kinds of flotsam in the water. Old glass fishing balls, used many years ago for fishing net floats, were our favorite discovery. They came in different sizes and colors and when we spotted one we didn't think twice to go off course, retrieve it from the water, and clean off the growth (barnacles and muscles).

We were so immersed in our daily routine that we didn't consciously notice the seas were slowly flattening out and the wind had become so gentle. Regardless of the fact that we flew our largest sails, progress dwindled just about to zero. At first no one complained. After all what was there to complain about? Perfect cloudless hot days, no waves, no rocking, and just a gentle breeze day after day. We were firmly set with the attitude that the engine would not be used under any circumstance, only in the case of an emergency. Our fuel wasn't going to be wasted. Little or no wind was certainly not considered an emergency.

To my skeptical crew I suggested we use our plotted position as our true position and live in harmony until we discovered otherwise. It was a tough sell as the wind had died down completely leaving us motionless in the middle of the Pacific. The calm water reflected an image like the largest mirror we'd ever see in our lives, from one horizon to the next, one continuous glossy surface. It was a stunning sight.

To test our motion I would spit in the water and observe it floating totally stationary along the ship's side until finally dissolving, rather than moving on by. Our sails hung limp, creating an eerie simulation of a deserted ship floundering. It amplified the stillness.

At first nobody really wanted to complain about our condition, perhaps thinking it might jinx us for another storm. However, as the still days added up tempers started to flare. Every little thing was interpreted as an insurmountable problem, sometimes resulting in bitter arguments. I found it ludicrous, as we'd never had those problems previously, even during the storm. So why were we experiencing it now? It didn't make any sense to me.

We tried various activities to break the tedious boredom. Jim and I tinkered with maintenance projects while the Shirley and Ann baked fresh bread and played with the children. Once I came up with the bright idea to swim in the ocean, which was welcomed by all. To ensure the safety of everyone on board we covered all the angles. We had heard stories of whole crews jumping off their becalmed ship to enjoy a swim in the open ocean, only to have a breeze pick up and their ship sail off leaving the stranded swimmers to perish. Shirley volunteered to stay on board with Trevor while the rest of us jumped into the tepid water. Oh how heavenly it felt. At least temporarily it would relieve our irritability and frustration.

For Marci and Cara's safety sake we splashed down our wooden sailing dinghy from the foredeck into the ocean. After flooding it with water, it made a perfect little pool for the girls to play in (wearing their life jackets of course). With fresh memories of the sharks around Sea Mount Cobb, Jim and I took turns snorkeling around Nausikaa to keep a lookout for the predators.

Such a vast array of sea life in waters so deep was amazing. Floating jellyfish encircled us. Enchanting schools of fish, several types and sizes, swam by at different depths. Schools of squid, appearing like aircraft flying in perfect formation, tipped and turned their way through the water dodging the uncoming groups of fish. The quantity of sea life indicated just how plentiful the food was for other marine species. Obviously the food chain was alive and well.

Yes! What a feeling! It was ecstasy! I free dived as deep as I could into the schools of fish, relishing in the joy of being a part of it. It was one of the things I'd always fantasized about – what it would be like to be out in the open ocean amongst the sea life.

From this level the ocean took on a completely different beauty. It was astounding – totally different from being on board. Acting like a prism, the water broke the sun's rays, individually separating them as they beamed down reaching deep into the cobalt blue depths as far as the eye could make out.

It was in that blurry area, off in the far distance, that I made out a large image of a fish. At first it resembled the shape of a large tuna lazily swimming, minding its own business and keeping its distance. Curious, I didn't take my eyes off it. As the image slowly made its way closer towards me it became more visible. Suddenly the image crystallized. The fish darted directly toward us. Panicked, I swallowed a large gulp of salty water, spewed it out and screamed at the top of my lungs, *"Shark! Shark! Everyone out of the water!"*

My heart pounded so hard I thought it was going to beat me back on board. Nobody misinterpreted my warning as a joke. Within seconds the children were whisked back onto Nausikaa. I took another look down in the water. Sure enough the large shark was lurking close by. Obviously it wasn't poised to attack. If it were, there would've been no chance what so ever to escape.

Safely on board we unanimously agreed never to swim again until we got to a proper beach in Hawaii. The girls didn't understand especially Cara who took to water like a little mermaid. She just had to trust us on this one.

We were back to dealing with our becalmed conditions. Finally I also became frustrated with it, to the point that I openly wished for a storm to get any movement, and it didn't matter what direction. *"Let's just get under way,"* I silently screamed to myself.

During the storm I fought the emotion of helplessness and fear. But now I found it was much easier to cope with the trials of the storm than our present state of frustrated tension and stress – due to feelings of complacency brought on by the doldrums. It was the darnest feeling. Even though I was very aware of it, I couldn't fight it off and neither could anyone else.

Many times in my life I would be asked by people the question, *"What were the worst conditions you ever experienced at sea?"* My response would stupefy them when I would answer, *"The doldrums."* They expected it to be some big storm or hurricane.

We would've gone insane had a light breeze not started to blow briefly every sunrise and then again just before the sun set. But in between we just drifted. As the days passed, with each one a little more wind would pick up and last for a little longer than the previous day, then once again die off. Then one day it blew from the east instead of our regular northwesterly direction. Checking our *Sailors Almanac* we discovered we must have been breaking through the other side of the doldrums and close to the easterly trades. Oh the trade winds – the sailor's ultimate delight. The tempered winds that blow steady day and night.

The trades set in and we were back to great sailing conditions. The sky also changed. Puffy white clouds cruised from east to west one after the other, occasionally dumping heavy rain for a few minutes – and then clearing to allow us to bathe in the hot tropical sunshine.

Finally, one day out of the blue, Jim spotted a jet. What a sight for sore eyes. It appeared to slowly descend and its direction was the same as ours. I was thankful for that as it defused one of the worst tensions on board – our whereabouts. We had to be heading towards land. It caused great excitement and sparked speculation of whether the jet was landing and if so, where?

The next morning Jim shouted down from his lookout on the spreaders, *"Land Ho! Land Ho! Off portside!"* It was music to our ears. Puffy clouds shrouded a faint image against the horizon. We speculated it was a mountain on one of the Hawaiian Islands, which one we didn't know. I was tempted to steer directly toward it but decided to stay on course, as maybe, just maybe, my navigation was correct.

Our excitement escalated and blew through the roof; as we moved forward, additional land masses became visible, popping out of the ocean everywhere in front of us. I anxiously took celestial shots hourly and compared and matched them with our charts to the land ahead.

Even though brisk trade winds propelled us at a good clip it seemed to take us absolutely forever to finally get to the islands. By late afternoon it was obvious that my navigation had been correct all along as Nausikaa's bow plowed full speed ahead toward the channel between the islands of Molokai and Oahu. Our hopes to be in a safe harbor before nightfall faded quickly. We could already see lights on shore illuminating the island of Oahu. It was a breathtaking sight.

After all the excitement during the day, and now with darkness falling and the children tucked in bed, we calmed down. A mystical feeling overwhelmed us. Shirley sat next to me at helm, no need to converse, but just to share the magic together. With a fervent sense of pleasure and fascination we gazed at the island of Oahu. Now even more lights were visible. It took on the aura of a sparkling diamond in the darkness of the moonless night.

Now wasn't the time to let our guard down. We were cautious not to get too close to the reefs marked on our charts and decided to take couple sails down to cut back on our speed. As we rounded the south side of Oahu, the impressive sight stunned us – Diamond Head Mountain silhouetted against a backdrop of the bright lights of Waikiki and downtown Honolulu.

It was time to ready our docking lines. *What locker did we stow those fenders and ropes in? Who remembers how to tie the proper knots?* Cracking jokes we wondered if we even remembered how to dock Nausikaa after being at sea so long.

In the midst of our excitement to make landfall, we didn't consider the dangerous move we were undertaking when we decided to try to find our way into the Ala Wai yacht basin in the dark. We weren't aware of the number of boats that ended up on that reef after a long ocean voyage. As newcomers unfamiliar with the waters, we should've waited until morning before proceeding through the narrow channel cut through the shallow reef.

We plainly just couldn't wait. After 28 days at sea, we couldn't wait another four hours for daylight. Strange, but true! The decision was made to push ahead.

It was hard to spot the channel markers and blinking direction lights against the millions of city lights. Shirley manned the helm, and Ann watched for the markers while Jim and I took down the last sail. Then I took the helm and Jim went forward on the bow, peered out into the city's glare and guided me.

We slowly inched our way through the narrow channel. It was unnerving to hear the roar and to see the glowing froth from breaking waves on each side of Nausikaa. Definitely there was no room to change our minds, to turn around and head back. The sensation of each incoming wave lifting us up and then of dropping us down was unsettling. With each drop I anticipated us hitting the bottom. But we did what we were committed to, to keep on moving. Finally we rounded the breakwater and the sea instantly turned into a tame pond.

Nausikaa III, like an inconspicuous ghost, quietly slipped through the jam-packed marina. Finally we spotted a slip. Jim made a valiant leap onto the dock with the bowline. But as he did he made an *ooooooh* sound – his reaction to landing on something solid. Shirley was next with the exact same reaction. We all were to feel it. It had been a while since we stood on a solid surface and it felt totally foreign.

Hugs and kisses of congratulations were in order. A stranger even got out of bed from a nearby boat, coming over to congratulate us. It was 2 a.m. After 28 long days at sea the greenhorns, complete with three little children on board – two in diapers – had successfully sailed to Hawaii.

The next morning a loud banging on Nausikaa's hull awoke me much sooner than I wanted. It was a furious dock master from the Hawaii Yacht Club. Apparently we were tied up to the club's dinghy dock and it wasn't fit for such a large vessel as ours.

"What kind of captain are you? Can't you tell a dinghy dock from a regular dock?" he dramatically delivered his oration. He chewed me out until I felt like the size of a pea. I felt so embarrassed, and truth to be known, I really didn't know the difference. The excitement of arriving in Hawaii diminished quickly as reality of life on land – the tension in the *real world* (as Shirley always refers to it) descended upon me. Finally I got a chance to explain the circumstances of our arrival – of how we came through the channel at 2 a.m.

The dock master started to change his tune. *"You got through the reef for your first time at night?"* Now he was impressed. When I confirmed with a nod that crusty face turned into a smile and he said, *"You're one lucky son of a gun. Cm'on let me get you some real dock space."* What started out as an embarrassing experience turned into the beginning of a great friendship.

By the time Jim and I fully secured Nausikaa III in a slip on the sturdy concrete dock our entire crew complement was on deck. It was a sight to be seen. Three young children hung onto Nausikaa's lifelines. Curiously they peered through the safety net to get a view of the marina surrounding them. Meanwhile their moms were spellbound by the sight of Waikiki beach against the backdrop of modern high-rises and lush mountains.

I picked up Trevor and took him to a grassy area at the end of the dock. I tried to set him down on the ground but his little legs buckled right from underneath him. His bottom lip pouted and then he started to cry hysterically, stretching his arms out for me to pick him up. I couldn't understand what was happening. I thought he would be delighted to be back playing on the grass.

Then I put it all together. The first day we came aboard Nausikaa he cried, petrified to be on the moving deck. He didn't feel comfortable in his new environment, however he eventually adapted to it. It became his norm. And now that he was used to life on board our ship he was petrified by this unfamiliar surface that didn't move. He would have to go through the same cycle again – fearing change and having to adapt to it.

In order to calm him down I put him back on Nausikaa. He plainly wasn't having anything to do with the grass and a surface that didn't move.

After a special breakfast celebrating our Hawaiian arrival we settled down to quiet thoughts and reflections of what had happened in the last 28 days. The bright Hawaiian sun caressed our being and gentle trade winds cooled our bodies. Limber palm trees lining the shore delighted us as their fronds swayed. The brilliant sea, that huge body of water we acquired so much respect and love for, now held a different meaning for us.

I was in heaven. I couldn't believe it, but here I was in Hawaii, with my wife and child safe at my side. What an incredible milestone this was for us in our young lives.

But my quiet reflections were interrupted by a nagging desire to know what the future would now bring? *What was in store for us? How were we going to adapt to our new life in this strange land?*

Chapter 18

Our Ticket
to Freedom

*"One can do without people but
one has need of friends."*

… Chinese Proverb

Arriving in Hawaii was an enormous high for all of us. We were ecstatic – overjoyed after completing our successful 28-day voyage. The fact that we had accomplished such a feat, finding such a little island in the middle of the Pacific, was so gratifying. And I was so personally satisfied, just knowing we were living our dream. It was the ultimate, to test the level of our desire and determination, and it had worked. Now our voyage would continue no matter what obstacles may lie ahead.

I stood on Waikiki beach facing the ocean, looking out in the direction I thought we would sail our next leg. Spontaneously I let out a loud triumphant scream of happiness. It sent shivers through my body. I was on a natural high. For days the feeling of accomplishment, the kind you get when you achieve something you never thought possible, had overcome me. Shaking my head in disbelief I burst out in thunderous laughter wherever I might be. Surely people around must've wondered if I was crazy. But I just couldn't control myself. The feeling was just too overwhelming.

One thing that did bring me back to earth was the cold reality of our finances. After we had provisioned and equipped Nausikaa III for our month long voyage from Vancouver all our money was exhausted. Now here we were, triumphant, in paradise, and with only $25 to our names. For some strange reason the lack of money didn't bother me that much, but it put a damper on our daily grocery budget. Exotic food surrounded us. Don't forget – we'd been at sea for a month without refrigeration, which had restricted our diet. Yummy things like cold ice cream, fresh fruit and surprisingly enough, hot dogs teased our palate. It was the very cuisine we'd dreamed of and craved, but now we couldn't indulge in. How ironic, here we were in paradise, heaven on earth, and totally broke.

I knew before we departed Vancouver that it would be our reality. I knew I would have to find a job along the way to pay for our day to day living in order to continue our expedition. Subsequently, every time we met someone at the yacht harbor, we would inquire if they had work for us. At first things didn't look too promising but we continued to ask. Our determination was driven by sheer need as our $25 reserve dwindled rapidly.

Then one day a small victory. Shirley met a couple named Sue and Frank Turek at the Hawaii Yacht Club. Frank was a local artist who designed *pupule* (Hawaiian for humorous) cards and bumper stickers. He offered to give me a job cleaning and painting the engine room bilge of his 42-foot Grand Banks powerboat. For my effort he would pay me the awesome amount of $7 per hour. I was so excited at the realization that in one eight-hour shift I could more than double the amount of money we'd arrived in Hawaii with.

Of course I eagerly accepted. However, what I didn't realize (but soon caught on) was that cleaning the bilge was the filthiest, most difficult job one could ever get aboard a ship. It was the worst job possible. However I was so ecstatic to find a couple days work that nothing else mattered. Frank gave me his keys to the boat and the paint locker and I never saw him again until the work was complete.

The engine room was so small that it seemed impossible to reach the areas that needed cleaning. To complicate matters I'm not exactly a tiny guy. I had to hang upside down, with my shoulders wedged onto the sides of the bilge. I washed, scraped, sanded and cleaned every nook and cranny of that bilge and underneath the engine. I spared no energy or effort, prepared to earn the money I had the privilege to earn.

Being cramped in the bilge for hours at a time was grueling. I swear the temperature must have been at least 120 degrees. Salty sweat ran down my face into my eyes. It stung so badly but the confined area I had to be in to do the work didn't allow me to reach over and wipe them dry.

Before I was finished my entire body was coated with a black oily sludge and gobs of white paint. I started to regret the day I ever accepted this job. However our need for money was much greater than the pain of it all. *After all, this job will not last forever* I rationalized. Finally I applied a second coat of white paint. When I was finished the bilge and engine was spotless, so pristine, so meticulous I couldn't wait to show it off to Frank.

From that day on, after Frank inspected my work, I would never again worry about being jobless. The news of my workmanship, as told by Frank, swept through the Hawaii Yacht Club and Ala Wai Marina like wildfire. It's funny how life works. All I did was clean and paint the bilge and do a good job. But whatever rumor Frank spread, it instantaneously transformed me into a young ship-maintenance god. I was offered every kind of work imaginable, from overhauling engines, to fixing electronics, to hauling out boats in dry-dock, plus a myriad of maintenance jobs. I didn't know how to do much of it, but I learned as I went along, and what counted was that I was offered more work than I could ever handle.

Now, our expedition was on track. Waiting out the winter, the South Pacific's stormy cyclone season, we had six months to prepare for the next leg of our voyage. While I worked on other people's boats, Shirley kept busy looking after Trevor, who had just turned one, and by keeping our ship ship-shape. Frank's wife, Sue, who had some experience bringing up children aboard boats, shared her knowledge with Shirley and gave her a few tips. One thing was the use of the *cat collar safety formula*. Trevor now sported a cat collar around his ankle, complete with a little bell. That way Shirley could always keep track of him. I was so proud of our little family and our ability to blend into a whole new society and lifestyle.

Like a caring father and husband, at lunch I came home every day. One day we packed up a modest picnic lunch and walked over to the Hilton lagoon on Waikiki beach. Trevor contently played in the ankle deep water, picking up shells and chasing tiny fish while Shirley and I proudly watched the early apprenticeship of a twentieth century Christopher Columbus from the shade of a coconut palm.

Suddenly the tranquility was disturbed by a child's loud shriek. Trevor burst into tears, crying uncontrollably. Wondering what on earth could be wrong, Shirley and I dashed toward him thinking the worst. We had heard stories of the odd small shark or barracuda making its way into the lagoon. I scooped up Trevor and rushed out of the water. Instantly, all the Hawaiian moms at beach with their little ones, gathered to help.

Thank God – there was no sign of blood. But Trevor continued to cry hysterically, kicking and screaming. I checked the bottom of his feet. They were free of any pricks or cuts. Then one of the local women spotted signs of a jellyfish sting between his legs at the dipper line. A jellyfish must've got trapped between his diaper and left leg when he squatted in the water. Immediately we ripped the soaking diaper off, exposing bits of jellyfish tentacles still intact.

Trevor must have been in tremendous pain. The louder he screamed, the more local people came running to help. Unanimously they all agreed, nothing worked better for a jellyfish sting than urine. I was so stupefied by the prescribed remedy that I didn't believe it. *They had to be pulling my leg,* I thought. Making a joke at the *houlee.*

One woman handed me an empty plastic cup and told me to go urinate into it while she and Shirley washed as much of the poison off Trevor's skin as possible. The urine did relieve Trevor's pain somewhat. (Apparently the ammonia neutralizes the poison.) We headed over to Sue and Frank's boat for their help. Sue recommended another Hawaiian remedy – treating it by topically applying fresh aloe vera – the slimy substance inside the cactus plant. Sue had some growing on board, handy for cases like this. We also used fresh papaya.

Trevor calmed down enough for us to take him home and I returned to work. While I rode my bike back to my varnish job I felt deflated. I realized there was yet a thing or two to learn about the sea.

However, things had been coming along just fine with our financial situation improving enough to pay our $287 monthly moorage bill and buy food. And with the help of our outgoing personalities and our friendship with Frank and Sue Turek, there was a constant flow of job opportunities.

More importantly we acquired a wealth of knowledge that would be so crucial in our ability to continue with our expedition.

Chapter 19

Help from
a New Friend

It was a scorching hot day that so far didn't promise relief from midday showers. I really didn't want rain anyway. I was working on the teak deck of my client's powerboat, hoping to sand and varnish the elaborate grid that day without having my work stained by rain.

I was intensely focused on my work when I noticed out of the corner of my eye that I was being observed from the distance by a couple. Normally I would've greeted them, encouraging a conversation, but this time I felt a timeline pressure. I decided not to say anything, pretending that I wasn't aware of them. The couple silently watched my every move and seemingly enjoyed the swiftness of my hands as I worked. It took 20 minutes before my curiosity got the best of me.

Finally I broke down, turned to them and asked, *"Howdy! Where are you folks from?"*

"California," the man answered. *"We have a small powerboat at home to maintain, so we're enjoying watching you work that piece."* He continued, *"Is this your powerboat?"*

"No, I have a 57-foot sailboat down the dock."

I started to share our dream with them. I explained where Shirley and I had traveled from and where we wanted to go. They intently listened with an expression of awe on their faces. Then the man said, *"My name is Henry, and this is my wife Francie. Would you mind showing us your sailboat? We'd love to see it!"*

With enthusiastic curiosity Henry and Francie toured Nausikaa III. It was obvious that they liked what they saw, because what transpired in the next few minutes would change all our lives.

"Would you and Shirley be kind enough to take Francie and myself for a day sail tomorrow? We've always wondered what it would be like to be under sail, rather than under power," Henry inquired.

Immediately I felt awkward – not quite sure how to respond. I had taken friends and relatives sailing before but never had I been asked by complete strangers to take them out. I was caught totally off guard not knowing how to handle this one. These people were sooooo nice! Henry had explained earlier how they had watched me work, wanting to talk with me, but didn't interrupt because they didn't want to disturb me. They were nice people, but even so, how do you give up a day's work and pay to take a couple strangers out for a joy ride?

Something came over me. I couldn't believe my ears when my inner voice spoke out loud, *"Sure. Why not? We can take you sailing tomorrow."*

Then I was really thrown off guard when Henry said, *"How much would you charge us from 8 a.m. until sunset? Naturally we'll bring all the food and refreshments for everyone."*

I wondered how I could charge them. They were so nice. Finally I blurted out, *"You know Henry, I've never done this before. I don't*

133

have a clue what to charge you folks." Then I went numb.

"How about $350 for a whole day-sail?" Henry interjected.

I couldn't believe my ears. Henry was just getting warmed up. *"If you take us out,"* he beamed, *"we'll bring ripe papayas, mangoes, and some passion fruit. Do you like pineapple? Oh yeah, we better not forget some lime to squeeze on that papaya. You know if I can find a nice breadfruit, we'll have it for lunch. We could hollow it out, fill it with honey and bake it in the oven while we sail."*

This guy was speaking my language!

He anxiously waited for my response, *"Would you do that for us? Please?"*

I don't know what stopped me from jumping up and down with joy, grabbing Henry and giving him a enormous bear hug. I was bursting out of my skin with happiness. I tried to answer as composed as possible. Short of stuttering, the best response I could come up with was, *"I guess that would be all right."*

The next day Shirley, little Trevor, Henry, Francie and I set sail at 8 a.m. sharp. Henry arrived with even more provisions than he had enthusiastically promised the day before. All day long while we were sailing Henry was hungry for details relating to our expedition. He was grasping our dream. We seemed to be of the same mind set – having so many dreams in common. And he was as entranced by the history of the early South Sea explorers as I was. It was as though our minds syncro-meshed into one. Little did we know what a big role Henry and Francie were to play in our lives.

Back in port we secured Nausikaa III to the dock. Henry handed over $350 cash. It was the ultimate bonus. Not only did we enjoy their company sailing and playing, we got paid for it. Inside I trembled with happiness although I tried not to let it show, as if it was a normal everyday occurrence.

But truth be known, I had never made so much money in one week, never mind one day. Three hundred and fifty dollars for a day's wages isn't bad today, never mind back in 1979. Perhaps it was at that point in life when I realized how important other people are in making your dreams come true, if only you do your best to make their dreams come true...

Francie and Henry were on the dock preparing to return to their hotel when Henry dropped yet another bombshell. *"Boris,"* he said, *"would you and Shirley consider taking Francie and I and our two boys out sailing for three weeks in January? Just think – we could all retrace Captain Cook's steps throughout the Hawaiian Islands."*

"Sure, why not?" I said not really believing it could ever happened. *C'mon now*, I said to myself, *this is November. Who takes vacations every couple months? I'll believe it when I see it.*

Then Henry added, *"How much would you charge us for 21 days?"* *Here we go again* I thought to myself. *What am I to say to this one?*

"You know Henry, I've never done this before. I don't have a clue," I confided.

He mumbled to himself, *"Well 21 times $350 equals $7,350. How about this?"* he said, his face just gleaming, *"If it's OK with you we'll pay you $5,500 plus we'll buy the provisions, refreshments and fuel for the trip."* Then his excitement escalated, *"And we'll buy scuba-diving tanks and catch our own fish. Hey, we'll get to visit where Captain Cook first landed and where he eventually was killed on the Big Island."*

At this point I confirmed to myself, *I'll believe it when I see it.*

Off Henry and Francie trotted down the dock excited at the prospect of their next vacation.

For us that day was a typical one of sailing in Hawaii, yet it was so special – new friends, new lessons, new hope, and a new revelation. Constantly I put my right hand in my pocket, reaffirming the money we had earned. Every month it was a struggle to save for our expedition by the time we paid our moorage and food costs. However, all things relative, I was happy that we were managing to slowly build up a small savings. This $350 injection would make a huge difference to us.

Shirley and I, not being the type to count our chickens before they are hatched, consciously didn't allow ourselves to believe for a minute that Henry and Francie would return in two months. After all, who had that kind of money to spend on an additional vacation so soon? Yet my subconscious mind desperately craved it. I tried to silence it by reasoning that wishing too hard might jinx it.

One day an announcement came over the loud speaker in the marina. There was a phone call for me. It was Henry jubilantly confirming that they would be coming in January. Even after that conversation I still refused to get my hopes up. But Henry was a man of his word. He delivered everything he promised and more. He and his family came and sailed with us for three glorious weeks exploring the Hawaiian Islands.

Perhaps having heartfelt dreams, hopes and goals and sharing them with others *was* synchronous with the universe. It seemed that the more wishes, desires and goals we had, the more our dreams came true. Our little deed of taking two strangers out sailing and sharing the day with them would come back to reward us time and time again.

Chapter 20

Priming the Prime Minister

"A man can succeed at almost anything for which he has unlimited enthusiasm."

... Charles Schwab

One day, news spread throughout the marina that the Prime Minister of Australia, Malcolm Fraser, was in Hawaii staying at the Ilikai, a hotel adjacent to the marina. Well since we had intentions to visit Australia, I thought it only appropriate to make a few friends there.

Henry and Francie had great day sailing with us so an idea flashed through my mind. I was sure Prime Minister Fraser would enjoy a little sail with us for a few hours as well, especially if we were discreet. Someone in his position would probably appreciate a break from his regular diplomatic routine, to enjoy the freedom of living like a private citizen for an afternoon. Convinced it was a good idea, I decided to attempt to locate him to propose my offer.

The challenge, however, would be to get through to him. That was another story. It was impossible to even come near the floor he was occupying. I tried to talk my way through but his secret service men just weren't going for it since I didn't have an appointment or security pass. I thought it was unfortunate but probably that was the end of it.

Later that evening I shared my idea with a friend, the Hawaii Yacht Club Commodore, Bill Collins, over a drink of scotch. Bill was a retired Colonel of the US Army who had invested in a few apartments at the Ilikai Hotel. At first he chuckled, then agreed it was a good idea but a stupid one. *"You'll never get near him,"* he insisted.

I challenged Bill, *"If I could only get on his floor, I would probably succeed."*

"It would be a nice gesture to take the PM sailing," he said but he also added, *"You're nuts to even attempt to pull it off."* Then he sat quietly, only to break the silence with, *"OK, I can get you in!"* That was all I needed to hear.

Bright and early the next morning I dressed in my usual attire – a faded T-shirt, well-worn sailor's cargo shorts, and a pair of very flat Hawaiian-lava-melted thongs. Bill and I met in the hotel lobby. As a retired Army colonel, his badge and the residential pass got us quickly through the front lines. He whisked me over to the hotel service elevator and using a special key opened the elevator, pushed the penthouse floor button, gave me a good natured salute and wished me good luck.

My heart pounded, as the elevator door opened and I approached two secret servicemen standing guard. They appeared startled by my presence, pale as if they had just seen a ghost. It was obvious my attire was not congruent with the environment.

"How did you get up here?" One of them harshly demanded.

"In that elevator," I replied trying to sound as nonchalant as possible. *"I was sent to speak with Mr. Fraser."* Then I quickly explained my intention. And just in time as the bigger of the two guards held my arm with a determined grip ready to throw me back into the elevator. But the other man was taken by my genuineness

and believed my intentions were sincere. He said, *"Wait here. I'll see if Prime Minister Fraser will see you."* I was in like Flynn ...

They led me into an enormous room and I spotted a distinguished looking gentleman sitting behind a desk shuffling a pile of documents. *"This is the prime minster's personal assistant, Sir John,"* the agent said.

The man rose and smiled, extending his hand to shake mine. Then he started a conversation with me as if we were equals, totally disregarding my apparel, which stuck out like a sore thumb in contrast to his well-tailored suit. *"So I understand you would like to take Prime Mister Fraser sailing."*

I repeated my idea and assured him of my integrity, promising to be discreet. Sir John appeared to be so taken with my offer that I sensed perhaps he himself would've loved it, as he went on for some time talking about the delights of sailing.

He explained Prime Minister Fraser was currently occupied in a high level meeting but would truly appreciate the invitation. However, he then went on to explain that it was the PM's last day in town and he was scheduled for lunch aboard a power-yacht with some dignitaries. But he knew that if it were up to the PM he'd much rather go sailing with me. Sir John confided that if the PM had been able to accept my offer, in the long run I would not be very pleased, because the secret service would basically have to tear my boat apart to ensure his safety.

Feeling so comfortable conversing with Sir John, I took the opportunity to tell him about our expedition plans that included Australia. Judging by the look in his eyes I could tell that he was impressed and a little bewildered. Finally we shook hands and said goodbye.

But that was not the end of the story. It was just the beginning. The prime minister, after being advised word for word of my offer, was so taken with it that he wrote a letter personally inviting us to visit him upon our arrival in Australia. He offered to be our host and to give us a personal tour of his sheep farm.

Once again I felt like life blew me out of the saddle. I was so proud that *l'il ol'me*, an immigrant from Croatia, had the nerve to approach a dignitary such as the PM in the manner I did. I was learning one of life's lessons – it doesn't take an extraordinary person to accomplish extraordinary things. In addition to that, I was happy with now having a good contact in place when we would arrive in Australia.

I felt so uplifted – as if I could fly like a bird. At the ripe age of 25 the experience left me feeling incredibly invincible, as if nothing could ever go wrong, nothing could ever stop us. However, I was to learn life is not like that, nothing is guaranteed. *Nothing is – until it is.* I am not suggesting not to celebrate and savor victories in life, but to be humble in the face of victory and always be prepared for change.

Chapter 21

Hawaiian Adventures with Henry

"What we get from adventure is just sheer joy.
And joy is, after all, the end of life. We do not
live and eat to make money. We eat and make
money to be able to enjoy life. That is what
life means and what life is for."

... George Leigh Mallory

That January Henry and Francie delivered once more everything they promised – and more. We all, including their eight and nine year old sons Aaron and Jason, explored the Hawaiian Island chain. Purposely, we tried to seek out specific areas and anchorages related to Captain Cook's expedition. We blended so well with the local population that they shared with us their perspective of Captain Cook, according to their legends. Later when I would experiment with how to approach natives in the South Pacific, it would confirm my childhood vision. It was a total success. We learned that understanding the culture you are trying to work with can make your experience such a rewarding one – one that all the money in the world can't buy.

The kind of money we were to make by taking Henry's family sailing just boggled our minds. But it was not in the actual money where we received our best value. The true benefit was learning about wealth, being exposed to it and realizing that money is no guarantee of happiness. We discovered that attaining happiness means having to emerge from your comfort zone and doing *that* what makes you happy. We had three weeks to subtly observe and learn.

We were a captive audience. What we realized was that Henry and Francie thought more of us than we did. They had more faith in our ability to run the ship than we had in ourselves. It was a very revealing time for us. It soon became obvious that even though they came across as very humble and down to earth, they possessed a financial independence never before witnessed by either Shirley or me. Any little thing that Henry and his family wanted they simply went out and bought. I am not suggesting that the money was spent foolishly. They were very generous spending it on anything they felt we needed to ensure it was on board for the trip. As far as provisions went, there was nothing we didn't purchase.

When it came to diving gear, Henry wanted to do some scuba diving and spear fishing so we bought two complete sets of dive equipment, one for him and one for myself. Wet suits, lead weights, buoyancy compensators, air tanks, regulators, and spear guns for us and new masks and fins for everyone else. Since Henry was a certified diver and I wasn't, he bought me a complete scuba diving learning system – so I would be ready to write my exam by the end of the three-week charter. Little did I realize those scuba lessons would serve me so well into the future and forever more. It's a sport that not only taught me the art of diving, but also the art of mind and body control.

I was so excited about this charter. I was more eager to get under way than they were. To heck with all this shopping, I thought. But Henry knew exactly what he wanted and would not depart before we had everything we needed on board. When we finally set sail from Honolulu we had to beat against moderate trade winds, making our passage across the Molokai channel a somewhat rough one. But after that ground was covered, it was a relatively smooth trip to Maui.

While the mothers and children visited the island and played on the beach, Henry spent time teaching me dive techniques. I didn't realize I was being groomed for some major diving. I eagerly participated, not believing I could have so much fun and get generously paid at the same time.

Henry must've invested some major time doing his homework before arriving on board because he had a definite idea where we would go and what we would do. Thank God, because I sure didn't!

Our next adventure would take us to the island of Lanai where there was a large Mormon community. Since Henry and his family were Mormons, they were curious to visit it. The warm reception we received by the local Mormons was impressive. Although we had never met them before, it was like a reunion of old friends. Before we knew it they were giving us a jeep tour of the island, including a visit to a local pineapple farm and factory and then they took us for a special lunch. As a bonus we kept the jeep for the duration of our stay on Lanai.

Spear fishing was supposed to be good on the north side of the island. Henry heard that the best spear fishing was at night, and wondered if I was interested in such an adventure. Obviously I was too naïve to know what I was getting myself into, otherwise I would have never been so eager. At this stage of the game it all seemed like a fantastic dream coming true.

Henry suggested we buy a barn-style lantern, one that we could leave on the beach as a reference of where we were while we were diving. It was a good idea. Otherwise the current running along the north shore might carry us away with us not realizing it without a light to guide us back. I certainly wouldn't have thought of it.

As our jeep slowly descended down the steep rugged dirt trail, we bounced around like popcorn in a frying pan. This place we were going certainly was not your average tourist destination. Descending so long to the rocky beach I briefly wondered if we shouldn't forget about it, as the quarter moon had just disappeared beyond the hill behind us, leaving us in total darkness. Not a soul was around. And not an inkling of light, except in the distance across the channel lights twinkled on Maui. Using the jeep headlights, we put on our dive gear and the excitement of our adventure recharged me with positive enthusiasm.

I shivered while Henry set up our lantern on the beach. My chest tightened with anticipation as we walked out into the darkness and finally plunged into the black ocean. All of a sudden, I wasn't so keen to wander far from the beach. The only reason I went was because we were descending deeper and not communicating. Since I couldn't get Henry's attention to express my fear, I just followed him. For a while I was hyperventilating, but then realized if I continued like that, I would run out of oxygen way before Henry. That would not be good.

Calm down. Calm down. I tried to convince myself. Henry turned around and made a *thumbs up* signal, wanting to know if I was all right. I responded with a *thumbs up*. Actually I was regaining control. I relaxed as my mind became focused, not on my fear, but on the cool underwater sea life exposed by the brightness of my underwater flashlight. Henry was immediately into it. He got lucky and speared a grouper and couple of other fish I didn't recognize. Then he zeroed in on a lobster.

I wasn't so capable. In fact it was a sorry sight to see me trying to operate my Hawaiian sling in the darkness of the deep. It took major co-ordination and concentration to point the light at the fish, aim and release the sling, all while fighting the current in an upside down position peering under a coral head. Now I was thankful it was night so Henry couldn't see me miss so badly. I was shocked at how little control I had over my aim – and to see the spear constantly bounce off the coral heads.

Henry performed much better. He gallantly swung by and stuffed a couple of his fish into my empty net hanging from my weigh belt.

Then he pointed up suggesting he wanted to surface. Sure enough, we had quickly drifted westward. Our lantern on shore was barely visible. Wow! It was so dark, without that little twinkle on the beach we wouldn't have had a clue where we were. In fact it was debatable if we could even make out the outline of the island. We decided to dive down again but this time we'd swim against the current along the bottom where it wasn't as strong.

No sooner did we get there than Henry spotted (what I thought was) an enormous shark swimming sluggishly by. (Later Henry would argue that it was only six to eight feet max.) Henry immediately darted behind a large brain coral-head and you can be sure I was right behind him. We turned our dive lights off. All I could hear was the pounding of my heart and the gurgle of air bubbles when I exhaled. I was terribly frightened in that blackness. All I could envision was that shark suddenly taking a chomp out of us and we'd never even see it coming.

Henry turned his light back on momentarily. Relieved, we saw the uninterested shark vanishing into the darkness.

It might have disappeared but in my mind it was right behind me, stalking me, in that dark area where it couldn't be seen. As we swam along the ocean bottom I acted like a suspicious gangster, peering around constantly to check if someone was following. I wished my heart would quit thundering. Surely the noise must be attracting all the predators in the sea. But I was unable to silence it.

Under a large ledge I finally spotted a sizable prize I thought I could spear. In a hole within a coral head I could see its large tail and body, for some strange reason, pointing deep into the cavern. Normally fish keep their tails to the back of the hole with their heads facing the entrance, keeping an eye on potential predators. I counted my good fortune, cocked the sling as tight as I could and came as close to the fish's body as possible to ensure I wouldn't miss. Finally I released the spear. It penetrated my target dead on.

Unexpectedly, a hard tug on the spear pulled me forward making me slam my face against the coral head. My feet floated upward and

I was rendered totally off balance. Before I could react my legs were up high with my head hanging down. Whatever was at the end of my spear was big and determined to pull me into that hole with it. With both hands I hung onto the spear not wanting to let this one get away. Or was it that I was so stunned by the fish's strength that I didn't know what the best thing was to do?

Visibility was a problem. My kicking had stirred the sand up making the water cloudy. On top of that I had lost control of my dive light. It was now dangling by its strap around my wrist, flashing every which way as the fish yanked me about, making it impossible to see a thing. While I was trying to regain my balance and get my feet on the bottom again, my bare legs scratched over fire coral, burning them like hot coals. The only thing making this tolerable was the realization that the big one hadn't gotten away yet.

Obviously annoyed, the fish tugged at my spear, as if it were a big dog trying to yank a stick out of my hand. Now with my fins back on the bottom I was regaining control. My face and knees were still leverage points but at least now I had control with a full grip on the spear. By now I had the flashlight wedged against the coral head using my leg. The light shone to the left. My hands were deep in the hole grasping the spear. But through the cloudy water I could see there was a big commotion to the left of me.

For the longest time I didn't realize what was happening until I made out the gruesome image. Only inches from my left arm, *was a set of giant jaws trying desperately to chomp off my arm*. Suddenly I figured it out. The action of the ominous head on my left corresponded with the tugs of my spear. Those threatening jaws were connected to the tail my spear was imbedded in.

Frozen with fear I realized that I had speared a huge moray eel that had been resting in a two-ended hole. My fear amplified. Just a couple days ago in a tropical fish book Henry had bought for the ship I read all about moray eels – about how they hunt from their holes, attacking their prey, including unsuspecting divers. They lock them in their jaws like pit bulls, until their victims finally drown or bleed to death. Not a nice way to go!

Now I was in the predicament that if I gave an inch, those chomping jaws would be just that much closer to my arm. With all my might I yanked on the spear and gained some ground, enough to be able to look around to see where Henry was.

Consumed with his own pursuit, for a long time, Henry wasn't aware that I had fallen behind. But now I could see him in the distance coming toward me. Now I was reluctant to pull too hard as I envisioned the spear ripping loose and having this large sea creature rush me. By the time he arrived I was exhausted from holding my ground.

Quickly Henry assessed the situation and realized my predicament. He sent a clean shot through the eel's neck. Using his fins he pinned its head against the sand. He quickly pulled out his diving knife strapped to his leg, and punctured the creature's head. Finally I let go of my spear.

Adrenaline rushed through my body as I watched Henry drag the lifeless eel out of the hole, from the other end, with my spear still imbedded in its tail. It looked like a large snake. Henry barely managed to stuff it into his dive bag. He was visibly delighted with our catch. Then I remembered he had mentioned before that he wanted to catch an eel and either smoke or barbecue it. I guess smoked eel was a prized delicacy in his mind and this was one of his dreams coming true.

As for me, all I knew was even though this whole experience was terribly exciting, I wished I had never seen that tail tucked in the coral head. My body trembled and shook uncontrollably from both fear and relief. I was so fortunate the darkness blanketed my fear. I didn't want Henry to see me that way.

Henry pointed toward the beach and like a football coach, indicated a time out. With delight I nodded in agreement. I followed him and could see fish blood streaming out of his dive bag which now made me worry about the shark we saw earlier. Clenching my teeth in anticipation, I followed slightly behind and about ten feet left of Henry. It was that diver's net – full of fish that worried me. Even though I was not an experienced diver I had a notion that it was not the cleverest thing to have, a dive net full of bleeding fish strapped to your waist. Nervously, I kept looking back to see if anything was following the scent of blood. Henry confidently pushed on. It was his confident behavior that slowly revived my shaky nervousness.

A large brain coral formation was ahead of us. Henry, who was now 10 to 15 feet to the right of me and as much ahead, decided to swim around it, whereas I decided to ascend about a dozen feet to go over it. The beauty and the colors of this particular coral head mesmerized me as I glided up its wall. As I crested it the worst of my nightmares came true.

Without warning, out of the darkness a powerful beast charged me from the opposite side of the coral head, knocking me over backwards. In shock, I let out the loudest scream of fear the sea has ever heard. I was in such shock from the shock itself – unable to even feel the pain from a bite or any other injury. I kicked and shoved trying to repel the attacker, but to no avail. It just kept coming at me, forcing me down toward the bottom. I was unable to see the large predator because I had lost control of my flashlight when it was knocked out of my hand. Now it was dangling from the strap around my wrist and shining every which way as I got knocked around.

I tried to inhale a breath of air, only to realize that in my panic-stricken scream, without even realizing it, I blew the regulator right out of my mouth. A rush of water surged into my lungs. I started choking and gagging. In the darkness, with my right hand I frantically tried to find the regulator that was somewhere behind me, while I used my left hand to shove the aggressive attacker away.

It didn't seem to matter how hard I struggled and tried to escape. It was viciously on top of me every step of the way. Blindly I grabbed for the regulator. Oh no. I felt my spear slip off my right arm. I cursed at my carelessness That spear was my only hope for survival against the invader. Suddenly the oxygen tank on my back slammed against the bottom of the ocean. Now I was helpless. The beast had me pinned down.

As I continued to struggle in the black water, the regulator slapped into the palm of my right hand, just as if somebody shoved it there. Quickly I stuck it into my mouth and even though I swallowed and choked on some salt water, I managed to regain some form of breathing. I was puzzled by the fact that I could not feel any pain. I must be bitten somewhere. But then I remembered. I heard surfers say that you don't feel the pain of a shark attack. Your body goes into shock.

Now with both my hands free to fight, I grabbed my assailant and tried to shove it off me. To my surprise whatever I was fighting did not resemble what I thought a shark would feel like. Then I realized that nothing had bit me – yet. With all my might I shoved the creature away but immediately it came charging back to my left side. With my arm now pinned to the ocean floor, the flashlight shone upward. Finally the identity of my attacker was revealed. It was not a shark that I had so vividly visualized in my mind attacking me, *but a giant sea turtle!*

With some relief I frantically tried to wiggle my way out. As I slithered along the bottom creating a huge cloud of soot, I started to realize that the giant turtle was more attracted to where the light was shining than where I was. *Bingo* I thought as I scrambled for control of the flashlight. Immediately I turned it off. That same instant the onslaught ended. For a couple more seconds I lay there motionless and listened to the deafening thumps of my heartbeat. I turned the light back on again and quickly scanned around. Off in the distance I saw the confused turtle hastily disappearing into the deep darkness.

There was no sign of Henry anywhere so I assumed he was waiting for me on the other side of the coral head. Still frightened and confused, I searched for my Hawaiian spear. I wanted to have it in my hand, triggered and ready to go. Once I found it I dashed in the direction of the coral head, this time circling around it. Henry wasn't there. *Where was he?* Hyperventilating, I kicked hard and continued

149

the way I guessed he might've gone. With my eyes bulging from the strain of searching in the dark infinity, it seemed like forever before I finally saw his flashlight shining way ahead of me.

In my eagerness to catch up to Henry, I didn't care how loud my heart was beating, how fast I was breathing, how much air I was using, or how many sharks might be chasing me. I was fixated on the tiny light way off in the distance. Finally I was about forty feet behind him when he stopped, turned around and waited for me to catch up. Of course he could not actually see me. All he could see was my light. He stuck his hand out and made a diver's *Is everything OK?* signal with his fingers. Realizing that he didn't have a clue about what had just transpired over the last few minutes, I shone my light on my fingers and showed the *OK* sign.

My nerves slowly settled down as Henry started to lead the way back toward the beach. I felt so relieved that I actually relieved myself in the water. Henry was still lugging along his *catch bag,* which dragged along the bottom weighing him down.

Thank God, I thought, *he didn't see me panic and fumble in my moments of adversity.* Just as I started to relax, I noticed that I had to inhale harder than usual in order to draw more air out of my regulator. Not realizing what the problem might be, I checked to see if the air hose was kinked. It seemed to be straight so I tried to clear the regulator, reaching over my shoulder to open the valve on the tank some more. But it was already open all the way.

My mind raced. I remembered Henry teaching me to look often at my air pressure gauge to ensure I didn't run out of air. Sure enough I checked it. It wasn't at the empty mark – but below it. My heart jumped, beating wildly. Now aware of my predicament, when I tried to draw a breath of air, my lungs felt like they were going into spasms and I wanted to suck in even more air. The air regulator made a clacking sound each time I tried to take a breath. Finally there was no more air. *What now?* I thought.

Luckily, in my panic, my mind still managed to register on Henry's warning, *"If you run into trouble and you have to get to the surface, never ascend fast or with your lungs full of air. If you hold your breath on your way up, the air in your lungs will expand and your lungs will explode. If you're having any problems, alert your partner."*

Like heck, how am I to do that? I wondered. *He's ahead of me now and I don't have enough air to breathe, never mind catching up to him.*

So I closed my eyes, exhaled the little air I had in my lungs and slowly started to kick with my fins upward. The 50-foot ascent seemed never ending. I didn't know what was going to happen first, if my lungs were going to implode or if I was going to pass out. Finally I broke the surface. Still clenching the air regulator firmly between my teeth, I spit it out, gasped in fresh air and flooded my lungs with fresh oxygen.

To my amazement I could see our lantern on the shore straight ahead of me, barely 250 feet. As soon as my breathing became regular, I made a beeline for shore. I just wanted to get out of this death trap. I kicked my exhausted legs with all my might.

Suddenly Henry surfaced in front of me. We struggled to walk out of the water toward the lantern as if we had been together all along. I'm sure running out of air was a big no-no so I didn't even mention it. Henry was preoccupied anyway, obviously delighted with our catch, as he rattled on about how he couldn't wait to show it to his Mormon friends on the island.

Back on the beach we turned on the jeep's headlights to examine our catch. The eel's colors illuminated in the light. I was shocked how much smaller it looked out of the water, even though it was big enough to drive shivers through my body at the thought that I dared to spear the beast.

In his kind and humble way Henry was so proud of my only catch that he couldn't stop talking about it while we bounced around in the jeep as we climbed up the steep embankment. My mind drifted – recalling the events of the past few hours. Just thinking about it made my body shake and tremble involuntarily. I was thankful that Henry was talking and the jeep was rocking so that he wouldn't notice. Henry continued to plan out loud our future night diving endeavors. What he didn't know was that while he was talking, my mind was all ready orchestrating ways to ensure that we would never go on a night dive again.

The next day, whatever Henry must've said at his church service about our diving efforts impressed a lot of people. In his enthusiasm he invited a few new-found friends over after church for a little afternoon barbecue of fish, lobster and eel. Well it seemed like the whole island showed up. They brought food and drinks of their own but the highlight was definitely our barbecued eel.

Hawaiians love eel. It is their praised delicacy and apparently not many dare to spear it, hence the reason they fussed over me a great deal. My spirits soared to unprecedented heights as they called me Captain Courageous and treated me with a high level of respect. I'd never experienced that kind of treatment before so I felt very uncomfortable. Especially remembering that it was not my courage that helped me catch the eel but my lack of knowledge and inexperience. Little did they know I wouldn't have gone near that eel with a 10-foot pole if I had known what it was. *If they only knew how scared I was,* I thought. But for now, I decided just to take it in and enjoy the party.

The native Hawaiians showed us how to clean the fish and skin the eel. I watched them enjoy every morsel of eel as it came off the barbecue. Being adventurous eaters, both Shirley and I were anxious to try it. It wasn't bad, tasting somewhat like chicken, but our mouths were full of tiny bones. It took forever to pick them out before you could swallow. That task seemed impossible so eventually we spit it all out. Amazingly, we watched the locals smack their lips eating the bones and all.

The party stretched well into the night and the sound of the ukuleles and guitars could be heard echoing through Manelle Bay well after we retired. The next morning it was hard to say goodbye. The locals returned in droves bearing gifts. By the time we sailed out of the harbor, Nausikaa was laden with papaya, breadfruit, macadamia nuts and countless pineapples. We were off to experience our next adventure.

January can be a tough month for sailing in Hawaii. Strong NE trade winds batter the islands for days at a time forcing small boats to be stuck in the marinas. Kona storms, thundering from the south, pound the usually protected lee side of the islands. Our crusty old sailor friend, Dave Silvey warned me before we left the Hawaii Yacht Club to keep a close lookout for those storms, as they were known to instantly appear. We had been lucky. There was nothing to worry about as super gentle trade winds propelled us from anchorage to anchorage and from island to island.

Clear blue skies complemented by the brilliant Hawaiian sunshine welcomed us as we dropped anchor near the Captain Cook monument on the big island of Hawaii. The sea was so calm that it mirrored images of the elegant palm trees scattered along the shoreline.

It was an emotional time for me. I had mixed feelings. I was excited to finally be here and yet I was sad. In my mind, *this was what my dream to go on this expedition was all about.* It was the vision of what happened in this historic place that propelled me to undertake our voyage, exposing us to the unknown. I wanted to be here more so than anywhere else in the world – the place where my hero fought the last battle of his dream. Now a monument that commemorated that occasion was on shore directly on front of us.

I knew that my thoughts were impractical but I could *visualize* the Endeavor anchored right next to me, a dozen sailors rowing a large dory toward shore. Captain Cook stood in the middle with his hands crossed over his chest. I could see the natives on shore waiting anxiously and waving as if trying to welcome the seafarers into their paradise. And finally now I was here – in that paradise. I felt like a sponge absorbing nourishment for my soul.

Over the years, Henry and Francie would return time and time again to join us in our adventures as we sailed the oceans. In the process we learned much about their Mormon faith, their high standards of spiritual and family values, and about life from their perspective. They truly enriched our lives as I'm sure we did theirs.

Meeting Francie and Henry opened doors for us. They would be our passport to continue to live our dream, changing our lives forever.

Chapter 22

Great Expectations

"No pessimist ever discovered the secret of the stars,
or sailed to an uncharted land, or opened a new
doorway for the human spirit."

... Helen Keller

Renewed energy and optimism surrounded our South Pacific expedition plans. When Henry handed us $5,500 in crisp $100 bills after our three week long adventure I finally felt confident that our dream would come through. That money, together with the other I'd earned working on other people's yachts put us into a totally different financial position. It seemed bizarre how not so long ago our situation seemed so hopeless, without much chance. Almost overnight things had changed. Our lack of finances had been a huge obstacle to overcome and most of the time sufficient funds appeared to be impossible to attain. *After Hawaii, 11,000 miles of water would have to pass under Nausikaa's keel before I would have another opportunity to work again.*

Needless to say I was overjoyed with excitement. Our personal self-esteem soared, seeming to attract even more people into our circle of excited well wishers for the success of our expedition.

We had something else to celebrate. Early tests confirmed Shirley was pregnant, and that created much new excitement in our lives. Originally when I proposed this expedition, Shirley had wondered if it would be an act of *juvenile delinquency* on our part. Therefore I had promised that no matter what happened, we wouldn't neglect our family plans. At first I wondered how practical that would be but after seeing how well Trevor adapted to life aboard the ship I didn't worry. On the contrary, once we started to discuss our family expansion plans the whole idea had much greater appeal.

However time was of the essence. We had to carefully plan Shirley's pregnancy with a particular time schedule in mind. Trevor was just over one year old now. We thought if Shirley became pregnant before we left Hawaii, by the time she'd be ready to give birth we would be in the vicinity of New Zealand or Australia where they had excellent medical care in case of delivery complications.

There were a couple minor details to ensure the possibility of this happening. First, whether or not Shirley was able to get pregnant on schedule was to be seen. Second, before we left Canada Shirley had an IUD contraceptive implanted. Not knowing how limited the medical facilities would be along our route, the doctor gave me a quick lesson on how to remove it if we ever wanted to. We decided that six weeks before leaving Hawaii I would remove it, and with a bit of luck, Shirley would be pregnant before our departure.

I'll spare you the details, but other than some deep stomach queasiness on my part, the procedure went just fine. To this day Shirley doesn't like me to discuss this in public. She thinks it's too personal. However, for me it was one of those things I had always wondered about. In case of an emergency would I have what it takes to perform surgery? Not that removing an IUD is anything close to surgery. But I always wondered if I could handle a medical procedure at sea, like administering stitches or setting broken bones, or *(may it never happen)* removing an appendix. In a small way I felt it was a good introduction, to test my nerves for such things. We carried on board reference books and an extensive medical kit complete with scalpels, stitches, bandages, antibiotics and other supplies. We even had a snake bite kit.

The Hawaiian goddess of fertility was on our side. Shirley tested positive after the first go around. We narrowed it down to her ovulating on Valentine's Day. Cupid was working overtime. Our timing couldn't have been better. Delighted, we celebrated at the Waikikian Lanai with a traditional Hawaiian meal, poi and all. Frank Turek, my employment mentor, and his wife Sue were on hand to witness the occasion. I had a personal request in with Shirley for another son so Trevor would have a pal to play with. We couldn't have been happier. Everything was on track.

With our departure planned for the not-too-distant future, it was time to start looking for new crew. Jim and Ann and their little girls had returned to Canada after being in Hawaii about one month. We really realized how much we appreciated and missed them. Now we would be taking a chance with total strangers to help us. We decided to try our luck and posted notices at the local marinas and travel hostels. The response to our efforts was quite promising as some very interesting and capable young men and women came by Nausikaa to apply.

My adrenaline level skyrocketed. I had been worried that nobody would chance going to sea with us since we had such limited experience. Also I wondered if having a baby on board would limit the response. However, my worries were unsubstantiated.

Finally now it looked like all the planning, hard work and promotion of our expedition was going to pay off. I really didn't know how it would all come together, but I knew that there were a heck of a lot of people out there supporting our dream and wanting to take part in it. We made so many great friends in Hawaii and most of them were so enthused about our expedition it almost seemed like they were the ones going on it!

Our departure was scheduled for the later part of March or beginning of April. The only thing holding us back was hurricane season in the South Pacific. We needed to wait for it to end before heading out. That meant we still had lots of time to select our crew and continue building our financial reserves, which we were certain to need with another family member on the way.

Relatively speaking, life was great. Everything was going smoothly, in fact beyond our wildest expectations. On the other hand, on the universe level, it spelled out the calm before the storm. But when things are going so well the last thing you do is spend your time speculating about what might go wrong. Even if I did try to forecast life's next storm, I never would've been able to guess in a million years what it was going to be.

In my state of feeling so accomplished, I had no way of knowing a major change in my life was right around the corner. What was about to happen soon would cause an abrupt stop and cast a dark shadow over the future of our dreams.

Chapter 23

Hit by a
Kidney Stone

*"If you can alter things, alter them. If you
cannot, put up with them."*

… English proverb

I usually enjoyed my bicycle ride routine early in the morning
from Nausikaa through the marina to the boat I was working on that
day. The warmth of the early morning sun blended with the coolness
from the previous night normally made me feel happy, made me feel
vibrant and excited about the day ahead.

I'd swing by the beach to gaze over the horizon just to witness
the birth of each new day on the water. It gave me shivers of happiness
to watch the entire surface of the water reflect hues of red, gold and
blue – the first morning ripples seeming to transform the ocean into
velvet. It was so awesome. Even a Hawaiian tourism magazine
couldn't begin to describe its true beauty. Daily, that was my routine
and my first connection with the sea.

But today was a totally different story. The last thing I wanted to
do was to go down to the sea. This morning I woke up with a sharp

pain in my lower back, just below my rib cage.

Shirley and Trevor were still asleep when I mounted my bike and took off. When I rode through the marina I wasn't very observant. The very things that made me so happy every morning seemed not to even exist now. Being in so much pain, I had tough time to even concentrate on where I was going, never mind to notice anything.

What really concerned me was the fact that the pain kept intensifying. Hunched over, I tried to ride my bike, clutching the handlebar with my left hand while with my right hand, I squeezed my lower right back. I endured the horrendous pain, wishing it would go away – but it didn't.

It became so severe, I found a secluded little patch of grass, fell off my bike and rolled on my back applying pressure to the area of my pain. It seemed to provide some temporary relief but then it intensified. Finally I couldn't stand it any more. I decided it was time to go to Kaiser hospital, a short four blocks away. Riding my bike was impossible. With each step I gasped a deep breath and then let out a long groan, squeezing my eyes shut most of the time, only to take a peek to see where I was going.

For what seemed like eternity I finally made it to the emergency ward. *"Please, oh please give me something for pain,"* I begged the first nurse that came my way. She tended to me immediately sensing that something was awfully wrong. I begged for painkillers but nobody seemed to act fast enough. *"Please I need something for pain!"* I screamed in agony. But the best response I got was a nurse, asking me what I thought were totally unimportant questions. I was in total distress. I needed something now. I realized later that they were following proper procedure to screen street drug users looking for a quick fix.

Once they established the fact that I was not a drug user and legitimately in need, they gave me a shot of morphine. *Aaah...* the pain finally subsided. I lay in the hallway enjoying the relief. After two more shots over a period of some hours I was able to leave for home.

I can't remember what ungodly hour it was when I arrived home. I didn't know what to say but I knew that I really didn't want to tell Shirley anything that could possibly jeopardize our expedition. She always worried about what would happen if someone got sick at sea. At first she wasn't impressed by my late arrival, but then when she discovered the reason why she became alarmed. Apparently I looked pretty ghostly and for some reason my pain was quickly returning. The effect of morphine was subsiding. I could hardly wait for the next morning to return to the hospital for relief. Somehow I endured it.

After a couple days of examinations, x-rays and more morphine it was determined that I was suffering from a kidney stone. It had lodged itself at the opening of the urethra, the tube that connects the kidney and bladder, causing liquid back-pressure in the kidney. The kidney expands bigger and bigger and the pressure builds, causing incredible pain. My doctor thought it was almost a complete blockage. He was very concerned because he felt if the liquid couldn't pass for a prolonged period of time, the kidney would potentially stop working and die off. He suggested surgery to remove the stone.

I was transferred to Queens Hospital, where they had the necessary experts to perform the procedure. They were to enter through my penis into my bladder and up the urethra leading to my kidney to search for and retrieve the stone using a remotely operated basket. With the assistance of x-rays, cameras and ultrasound they would be able to see the stone, grab it with the basket, and drag it out.

There was one snag. I knew the procedure was out of the question. I plainly couldn't afford it. I didn't have any US medical insurance and I knew that my Canadian insurance wasn't good enough.

All of a sudden I could see our dream, our South Pacific expedition, fizzle down the drain. This surgery was going to consume all our funds. Now I had to decide what to do. If I did nothing, I could risk losing a kidney. And if I had another attack at sea I knew I couldn't handle Nausikaa. I'd be totally incapacitated with the overwhelming pain.

The vision of our dream crumbled even more when it was confirmed that our medical insurance would cover only a tiny fraction of the medical cost. The money we'd been saving for our trip would be totally depleted. However with the pain being so severe I didn't have any choice. It was my decision maker. I would go ahead with the procedure.

I was so high on drugs that I can't remember if I went into surgery that day or the next. The last thing I remember seeing was a beautiful smile on the face of a kind anesthesiologist. She held my hand and assured me that I would be just fine. But later, when I awoke, I learned that Mr. Murphy of *Murphy's Law* had paid me a visit.

The following morning my doctor broke the unfortunate news that the procedure had not been successful. The stone was just too big and he couldn't get a good grip on it with the little basket. He was frustrated because he had tried so hard but had to quit because I was coming out of the anesthetic.

That morning my doctor and I really bonded. I told him our whole story – about our dream and about how it was now in jeopardy. He sat at the edge of my bed listening intently as if he did not want me to stop. I pleaded with him to try again. Again, he said the stone was just too big to grab. He suggested another procedure to flush it out. It meant forcing a rubber tube again through my penis to my bladder and up the passage all the way up to my kidney. He hoped it would enlarge the passage tube between my kidney and bladder to allow the stone to pass. That was fine by me except that meant another anesthetic and another procedure, plus an extra three or four days in the hospital. It was an additional expense to be paid with money we didn't have.

Shirley was very concerned about my state of health. She suggested the best solution might be to sell Nausikaa and return to Canada to take care of my medical problem. Now with her expecting a baby it stirred up all kinds of emotions that weren't too conducive to our sailing expedition plans. When I aired my financial concerns to my doctor he said, *"Right now Boris, let's just concentrate on getting that thing out."*

This time when I woke up the pain didn't seem as severe as after the first procedure. However there was a new kind of discomfort that I was experiencing. I couldn't decide if the kidney pain had subsided or this new burning sensation running from my penis inward was overpowering the other pain. On top of that there was a tube still inside my penis, which not only caused me unbearable discomfort but also created the sense of constantly needing to go to the bathroom. The nurse broke the news to me that I had to live with that tube for the next three to four days. At the same time they applied a large flow of IV fluid in an attempt to dislodge the stone and get it moving.

Finally after the four longest days of my life the tube was removed without any anesthetic. What an experience. I had a mixture of conflicting feelings, one of tremendous pain and the other of incredible relief.

But after all that – still no luck. Even with an accelerated intake of IV liquid, that stubborn stone just would not flush out. By now, at least the burning sensation in my penis and inside right passage to my kidney was slowly fading to an ache. My doctor explained that the drainage tube had released pressure in my kidney but the stone still hadn't budged.

Finally the day of my release from the hospital came and I walked the short distance back to Nausikaa III. The bright sun beaming on my face felt wonderful after all those days of lying in the fluorescent-lit hospital room. I was anxious and happy. I was going home to my wife and baby son, and I was feeling better.

Two days later I returned to the hospital for a check-up and to settle the bill. You know I don't even remember that doctor's name now as we write this book, but I am so thankful to him for what he did for us. During my post operation examination the only thing the doc asked me was how I felt. I told him that I had a very faint ache but other than that I was great. Then he changed the topic to sailing and what my future plans were. I explained that we had planned to continue our voyage until my surgery came up. Now since all the money we had earned and saved would be going toward covering my medical costs, we would have to rethink our plans. I also explained that because of Shirley's pregnancy we were on a very rigid time schedule and if our expedition were delayed it would probably mean it wouldn't happen.

At first I didn't think he was listening as his glossy eyes gazed right through me and beyond. Then silently he turned around and for a long while looked out the window. When I finally broke the silence and asked him how much everything would cost, he told me to wait a minute as he disappeared through the doorway. When he returned he said, *"Please fill out these forms. One gives us the right to request payment from your medical insurance. We'll collect as much as they allow for our services. This other document states that you have no further financial obligations to this hospital or to myself."*

I couldn't believe my ears!

"Bon voyage," he said as he shook my hand, holding onto it as if he forgot to let go, his eyes glued to mine. A genuine smile on his face revealed just how clearly he felt about me and the adventure we were about to embark upon.

I didn't understand why he was so impressed. I wondered why someone of his financial status just didn't get a boat of his own and experience the thrill of such a dream himself, instead of admiring someone struggling financially like us. I had always believed that fun and exciting things were reserved exclusively for the privileged and wealthy. In fact I thought we were breaking all the rules. I thought that somehow we managed to pull the wool over the eyes of the supreme powers – and by some chance, possibly a miracle, we had gotten this far without being discovered.

In those days of youthful innocence we didn't understand the basic laws of the mind, like positive thinking, positive action, positive results and such. We just didn't realize. On the other hand we were more accustomed to the opposite of encouragement. Originally, when we revealed our dream we were exposed to discouragement, ridicule and doubt from our friends, acquaintances and even some of our family. It was no wonder we found ourselves dumbfounded now with comments of praise, encouragement, support and empowerment from the wealthy, educated, influential movers and shakers we came in contact with along the way. Why that difference in opinion *now* was still an unanswered question that kept eluding us.

My doctor's action just blew me off my feet. It felt as if our minds connected harmoniously in the spirit of our expedition. With him still holding and shaking my hand I could feel his psychic impulses telling me, *"Go for it kid. That's something I'd love to do but can't. Go ahead and do it for both of us."*

I was beside myself as I rode a bus back to the Ala Wai Marina, so buoyantly happy that I felt like bursting at the seams. For the past few months I'd been riding a huge emotional roller coaster. From the joy of accomplishing our 28 day sail from Vancouver to Hawaii, to anxious feelings over our financial situation when we arrived with only $25 in our pocket, to the exhilaration of earning thousands of dollars on Henry and Francie's charter. Then the excitement of Shirley's pregnancy, and visiting the Australian prime minister's suite at the Ilikai Hotel, to the depths of enormous pain and suffering from my kidney stone. My mind struggled to sort out the magnitude of emotional experiences I'd been through. But right now the level of human kindness my doctor had showed astounded me.

All things considered, now more than ever I realized that we couldn't lose sight of our goal. We had to be strong. We had to be persistent. We had to carry on.

However, truth be known I wasn't free and clear of my problem with that kidney stone. My doc and another doctor friend in the marina, Gene, warned me that this kidney stone would come back to haunt me until I passed it.

Once aboard Nausikaa III I broke the good news about our finances to Shirley. We rejoiced, hugging and jumping for joy. However I downplayed the whole thing about the seriousness of the kidney stone still being in my body, and everything we talked about was in terms of the expedition going ahead as planned.

The next day we announced at the Hawaii Yacht Club that we would depart for Fanning Island and points south. We chose to leave the day after April fool's as sailors are very superstitious. *(We would never leave port on a Friday either.)* It was less than two weeks away.

Our friend in the marina, Dr. Gene, again aired his concern about my kidney stone. He was very critical of my decision to head south. He felt that it was unnecessary to take such a risk. His concern was if I had another severe attack, it could render me totally incapacitated. And in remote areas no doctor would be there to help. It could spell disaster.

Dr. Gene also was concerned about Shirley being pregnant at sea. *"Are you really sure you want this baby?"* he suggested. But Shirley was adamant. After having a healthy pregnancy with Trevor she felt comfortable with the idea. He warned her not to expect much more than a nineteenth century medicine man along our voyage route.

Feeling the intensity of Dr. Gene's concern and listening to all that he had to say, I realized he didn't understand the *depth of our commitment* and how strong our *desire* was to see this expedition succeed.

I am not insinuating that I was not concerned. I was, especially when it came to the subject of the safety of my family and crew. Since I was the only one that could navigate by celestial navigation, I decided to immediately train one of my teammates to assume the duty if I was to fall sick again.

Yes, there was danger related to my health, but I rationalized that the whole expedition was laced with uncertainty, risk, and trial and error. And truth be known, that's really how life is under normal circumstances if we embrace it and live it to its full potential. There are so many variables when one sets out on a voyage through life. If you tried to synchronize everything to ensure no risk, it would probably mean that your expedition would never leave port.

Shirley and I had a serious discussion about the risk-ability factor and agreed that we understood the dangers involved. It wasn't just my kidney stone that was posing a danger, Shirley also had a huge risk to think about – being pregnant on the high seas. None the less we concluded that our expedition must go on.

I was enchanted with Shirley, by her courage, strength and willingness to push forward. Right before my eyes my practical and concerned wife was transforming into a daring adventurer.

In retrospect I don't know if it was our early maturity, or youthful immaturity, that allowed us to sort out the rights from the wrongs to make such a crucial decision. Or was it the passion for our dream and our desire to see it happen that kept us on track?

In the meantime Dr. Gene was able to sleep better at night at the thought of us going to sea after he equipped us with a huge emergency supply of morphine and syringes. Only time would tell if it would be needed.

Chapter 24

The Shark That Never Said Die

*"The only limiting factor to our
achievements is our fear of the
unknown."*

… John Amatt

It was our strong determination to keep our expedition on track that gave us the courage to leave the day we did – even though a small craft warning flag was up, alerting sailors and fisherman to stay in port. The only reason I wanted to head out was I felt it would be harder to deal with the anticipation of departing than to handle stormy weather. In actuality I would learn otherwise.

After experiencing the security of being marina bound for a long period of time, our departure was as difficult as if it were our very first time. Anxiety and fear of the unknown had built up in our minds. But now that we were heading out, even in these heavy weather conditions, it made us think our imaginations might've been overactive.

Even though the winds were reported to be blowing 30 knots, gusting to 40 knots out at sea, it was a gorgeous day on land. Crowds of people gathered to give us a special Hawaiian send off. Even a few friends from Canada and the US mainland were on hand. It was a heartfelt and very emotional farewell. Our local friends tied tea-leaves to Nausikaa's bow, a Hawaiian tradition for good luck. They placed fresh plumeria leis over our heads, layering them one on top of the other until we were adorned in flowers. There were heart-warming good byes with hugs and tears. Then as we sailed out of the harbor we were serenaded by the sounds of ship's bells and fog-horns. A true sailor's send off! It made the hair on our arms stand up. What a contrast it was from our solemn Vancouver departure.

The atmosphere on board Nausikaa was upbeat and positive; however once we were out in the open Pacific we were in for a rough ride. After initially feeling fearful, Shirley and I settled down and became confident. After all we alrcady had our first crossing experience under our belt. Two out of our crew of four, Didier from France, and Deana from California, were experienced sailors. The two green peas, Peter from Moose Jaw, Saskatchewan, and Dan from Denver, Colorado, were university students who showed great promise of becoming first-rate sailors. They were all into it! It was their attitude toward life and their good-natured personalities that made them an asset to our team.

We would realize over the years that building a team for our expedition was a science as well as an art. There is a huge difference between *needing* a ride across the ocean, and *wanting* to, or having a deep desire to, accomplish something great, overcoming the fear barrier, living out a dream, syncro-meshing with nature, and growing from the experience. Beginner's luck was on our side this time because our crew certainly didn't just *need* a ride across the ocean, they were after something much greater. They were on purpose with a deep sense of commitment. They embraced everything with such zeal and enthusiasm that the energy they resonated permeated and enchanted our voyage.

Nausikaa handled the rough seas with relative ease, considering the conditions, as we were running with huge swells that broke just at our heels. Our double reefed main and mizzen sails together with our two storm jibs seemed to give us just enough speed to keep ahead of the rolling mountains that wanted to break over us.

Nausikaa did just fine with one exception. As huge swells picked up her stern, she'd roll on her side, pause, and then drop off the back end of the swell. At that point she had a tendency to turn a bit windward taking the next wave on her beam. Simultaneously, the helmsman had to crank the wheel hard to starboard to keep her bow facing south.

Considering it was our first day out and considering the rough seas, I felt everyone on board was adjusting to the conditions just fine, or as well as could be expected. Peter reported that his forward cabin wooden hutch was leaking excessively making his bunk wet. On closer examination I determined that it was tightly secured, but the wood had dried and shrunk somewhat – a result of being marina bound. Now that huge seas were pounding us, Nausikaa's bow was awash every few seconds and water poured into the forepeak cabin through the dried out cracks.

In the meantime Shirley and Trevor were in the aft cabin. Trevor was just fine, but Shirley was still prone to seasickness. It was a pattern that started to develop. Each time we set to sea after a prolonged stay in port, she would take at least three days to get her sea legs back again. That would become a routine for her. The rest of us didn't feel too great either so when our French crew, Didier, came up from down below offering us dinner we all declined. The thought of food made us even more nauseous.

I can't say that these were the best days of our lives but the experience of being back out at sea was exhilarating. The memory of my kidney stone episode faded. It was the last thing on my mind. We were happy to be continuing our voyage but the discomfort caused by the rough weather was not conducive to any kind of celebration.

I felt we would be ok, but I was concerned about our green crew. Quietly they withdrew as they cautiously observed the mountainous seas. To rebuild their spirits and keep their enthusiasm up I told stories about the early explorers and how they must've felt in adverse weather, not having any charts and with limited provisions on board, and so on. I don't know how effective it was, but it probably kept their minds off throwing up for awhile.

How bad was the weather? How big were the waves? How does a land-lubbing reader get a proper prospective of what rough seas are? And what aren't? One thing was for sure, I wasn't too happy to be in them.

They continued to build. The swells formed higher and higher with big crests on the wave tops as the trade winds continued to blow gale force strength day after day. I began to doubt my decision to leave the safety of Honolulu's calm harbor to endure this discomfort. I wondered if that was such a good call.

Later in our voyage at Christmas Island we met a Dutch couple who were sailing just within a day of us in the same area the entire trip. However they had a much different experience than we had. Two times they pitch polled. (Their 35-foot sloop fell off a wave and into the trough. It knocked them over so badly that the mast was buried into the water, then the hull did a 360 degree roll until the mast re-merged on the other side and the boat up-righted itself.) Apparently the couple were below in the cabin hanging on for their dear lives while their wind-vane automatic steering system did the best it could to keep them on course. They survived but sported gruesome bruises to prove their ordeal. That's how rough the seas were.

Strong 30 to 40 knot winds stayed with us for the next seven days. Nobody felt too great, with the exception of Trevor who seemed happier than a lark. Didier was the only crew that could stay below in the galley, come up with a decent meal and be cheerful about it. Even though we were uncomfortable, most of us managed after a few days to keep our food down. Finally the forward hutch stopped leaking after the wood swelled, a result of water constantly running over it, which made Peter a happy camper.

There was one consolation about the conditions we were

experiencing. We were making great progress! We soared about 140 nautical miles a day, in comparison to the average 100 – 120 nautical miles under normal conditions. With Nausikaa being tossed around it was difficult to achieve accurate celestial navigation readings. I had a tough time hanging on to the ship and holding the sextant still at the same time. But I took three times as many sextant shots as I would've in normal weather. Then I averaged out the results to come up with a decent position reading.

One thing that worried me was the realization that the current heavy seas were pushing us too far to the west. We were headed toward the uninhabited island of Palmyra, which had a bad reputation for its poor anchorage. Very few sailboats stopped there just for that reason.

Finally after seven days my storm worries faded as the strong winds subsided to normal trade wind conditions, about 15 knots from the north-northeast, allowing for a beam reach course towards Fanning Island.

That afternoon, happy to be feeling better and enjoying the fresh air, Shirley volunteered to take the helm. No sooner did she get comfortable than there was a loud bang. The boat shuttered and shook just as if we had run into something big. Shirley let out a loud scream that jarred me out of my nap and simultaneously I felt the strange shutter through the boat. I dashed up on deck only to find Nausikaa III nicely sailing in perfect conditions. Then Shirley yelled out, *"Boris – the fishing line!"*

Sure enough our 200-pound test hand-fishing line was stretched so tight, it was singing like a guitar string. Whatever fish had hit our bait, hit it so hard that it shook the entire boat and rattled the rigging.

When I tried to pull the line in, it wouldn't even budge. Whatever was at the end of it was much bigger than anything we had ever caught before. Peter and Didier were on hand in a flash. The boat's shuttering had alerted both of them. Between the three of us, we were able to slowly inch whatever was at the end of the line closer to us. Much to our amazement we realized we actually had more than we bargained for. We caught sight of a dorsal fin. *It was a large shark!*

Now normally I would've just cut the line and let the shark go but after our not-so-enjoyable week at sea I felt that this experience would inject some new energy and excitement into our daily routine. I picked up the vibes that our new crew wasn't very pleased with our expedition to date because of our very rough start. And after all I really didn't mind having a set of shark's jaws for a souvenir and shark meat for dinner. Frank and Sue had introduced shark to us in Hawaii and we really enjoyed it, so this was the perfect chance to have it fresh. And we could use some excitement.

Sure enough – we got our fill of excitement! Adrenaline rushed through our veins the closer the shark inched toward Nausikaa. Finally it was alongside us. It was a real fighter, which presented the problem of how to bring it on board without anyone being injured.

The problem compounded. Each time we tried to gaff the shark, the gaff hook just bounced off its tough skin. Then as a result it went into a fit of uncontrollable flapping alongside Nausikaa's hull. No fish, large or small, had ever stopped the sharp point of that gaff hook from penetrating its skin before, yet this one did!

Peter yanked on the fishing line while Didier maneuvered the boat hook into the shark's gills. I finally managed to penetrate its skin by the tail. It gave us what we thought was a good hold on the extremely annoyed shark. After a valiant effort we managed to haul it over the lifeline and onto Nausikaa's deck only to be challenged in figuring out what to do with this huge beast thrashing and flopping around uncontrollably.

Nobody dared to even come near the shark's head as the jaws kept snapping and chomping away, its teeth exposed like a growling rottweiler. Whenever I got proper aim I'd hit the shark on top of its head with a heavy wooden fish bat. A big blow that would normally paralyze other fish didn't even slow down this shark one bit. Frustrated, I wished the hell we'd never brought this beast on board in the first place. But now I was unable to figure out a way to get rid of it, so I kept pounding and pounding on its head until it quit flopping. After a couple more pounds for good measure, the shark finally lay motionless on deck allowing everyone on board to inspect it from a closer range.

Little Trevor's eyes were beaming as he said, *"Daddy caught a big shaak, biiiig shaak."* And I felt like a luckiest dad in the world to be so privileged to catch this big shark for his son.

The shark showed no signs of life when we poked at it, so I got my fish-filleting knife out and started to cut the skin around its jaws. Peter held the shark's jaws wide open allowing good access. I was making good progress when out of the blue we all instinctively jumped back as the shark bashed and thrashed once again as if nothing had happened. It was back to the drawing board. Again I continued to pound the shark over its head trying to subdue it. It was a long while before I summed up enough courage to continue to cut its jaws out. Surely there could be no life left in the shark, not after the pounding it received!

I finished carving the outside of the shark's jaws and then I worked on the inside when suddenly *SLAM!* The jaws snapped shut, just barely missing my fingers. The bite was so tight, like a pit bull's, that I couldn't remove the knife still in its mouth. Peter and I were so shattered by the whole experience that I'm sure his heart was pounding as hard and fast as mine. Everyone on board was horrified to witness what had just happened. Shirley even requested that *"we just dispose of the damn thing"*.

An eerie feeling permeated my whole being but now I was determined to finish the job I'd started. To eliminate the possibility of having any fingers or entire hands bitten off, I decided to remove the shark's head from its body. To my amazement, when we finished cutting it off, we discovered that the shark's heart was still wildly beating. I just couldn't believe it. The sight of that beating heart just sent shivers up my spine. It was a grisly thing!

I poked holes in the throbbing heart with my knife. I hoped to stop its heart beat and any agony it might still be going through, but I was unsuccessful. Totally spooked out, I ordered the torso to be thrown overboard. To heck with the shark steaks! The whole experience had shaken us too much. When the shark's body hit the water, to our astonishment *the headless torso wiggled and slowly swam away from the boat!*

In stunned silence and disbelief, we watched as the headless figure disappeared off in the distance. Our mouths dropped open in amazement and I felt more eerie shivers run the full length of my body. When I finished carving the shark's jaws I was amazed to see two additional layers of teeth stored on the inside of the shark's gums. In the event a shark looses a tooth, another pre-grown one automatically pops into its place, just like a knife's switchblade popping out.

After I cleaned and salted the jaws I hung them to dry on the mizzen-sail boom rest, on Nausikaa's stern, thinking that was the end of the shark ordeal. HA!

The experience scarred me. For the next couple nights I had disturbing nightmares of giant sharks' jaws chomping away and headless shark torsos circling around me but my true nightmare didn't come until the third day.

Our wind vane steering mechanism located on Nausikaa's stern was malfunctioning so I went to examine it. When I tried to crawl under the mizzen-sail boom rest, wind blew some of my hair into the teeth of the hanging jaws. My hair became snagged among the teeth. Instinctively I jerked my head backward. As I did, the entire jaws clamped down and closed on my head as if it were trying to bite me. The sharp tips of the shark's teeth imbedded into my scalp. As you can imagine, my wind blown hair looked somewhat like Einstein's, but as cautiously as I tried to untangle it, the more tangled it became.

While I kept trying to untangle myself, I started to get the feeling that this was a bad omen. In my mind I started to believe the shark's evil spirit might be trying to get his revenge for my deeds. It took some heavy-duty reasoning with myself to come up with a sensible answer to my present state. I was in this predicament because every action creates a reaction and it was my hair and carelessness that got me where I was, and not the evil spirits of a shark!

I was so embarrassed by this incident that I never shared the entire story with anyone on board. I didn't want to spook them. But what I did do was wrap up the jaws in a heavy piece of cloth and stow it away for years.

Trevor still has those jaws. Shirley and I gave it to him for a present when he was all grown up and moving into his first apartment. Of course the present was accompanied with the story of how one day, a long, long time ago, *"Daddy caught a big shaaak"*.

Chapter 25

Discovering
the New World

*"The real act of discovery consists not
in finding new lands, but in seeing
with new eyes."*

... Marcel Proust

On the chart Fanning Island resembled a coral atoll, rising merely
a few feet above the sea, but it promised an excellent secure lagoon
for anchoring. I remembered someone telling us in Hawaii that there
was an Australian company operating a coconut plantation on the
island and there was supposed to be a general store. After consulting
with Shirley and the crew I decided to stop at Fanning instead of
going directly to Christmas Island. We were ready for a land break. I
guestimated that in three days we would arrive there.

The next two days were perfect for sailing – absolute heaven on
earth. Gentle trade winds caressed Nausikaa's sun bleached indian-
red sails. Her bow sliced through the sparkling blue Pacific like it
was soft butter. It was hard to believe that this sea was the same one

we'd been struggling with just a couple days before. It was magic. Peaceful tranquility was only broken by the wonderful cries from the helmsman, *"Whales on our port"* or *"Dolphins at our bow"* or *"We have a fish on the line."*

We got so good at fishing it got to the point where we'd fish for a specific fish. As I'd be pulling a fish out of the water I'd yell to Shirley, *"Hey, do you feel like yellow-fin tuna tonight or mahi mahi?"* It just got to be that simple.

Little Trevor adapted just wonderfully to our new adventure. While it had been rough, he was down below with Shirley contently playing with his toys. Now we allowed him to roam on deck because someone was constantly with him. The crew just loved him, always an entertainer – ever the ham. His favorite activities were standing inside a small bucket of water splashing around and observing us catch *"feeeesh"*.

Shirley's original apprehension about whether we should go on this expedition because of Trevor's safety had totally disappeared. I can't tell you how many times she would be holding Trevor in her arms, turn and look at me and say, *"I can't believe you had to talk me into this."*

I was sure I could smell land. Out of nowhere a lonely fly zoomed into the cockpit and took off again. Then Shirley announced on her watch there was a bee on board. Land-based birds flew by. My latest sextant reading put us 37 miles from Fanning Island. We could normally cover 37 miles in six hours. I was disappointed because it was late afternoon and making landfall before dark was out of the question. On top of that the wind died down to a mere breeze. It was impossible to see the island even from our observation point high up the mast on the spreaders.

Night fell and with it heavy humid clouds moved in. Torrential rains started to fall yet there was hardly any wind. Huge tropical raindrops pounded the seas totally flat. It felt strange not to be bothered with huge waves and the ruckus connected with them. We took the opportunity to enjoy a fresh water shower, using the rain water that had run off Nausikaa's almost limp sails. Ever since Hawaii we had been bathing with buckets of salt water scooped from the ocean. Now we had a sweet taste of heaven.

However I had a major concern. We were still travelling three knots in that light wind. I was worried because at that rate we could run into land before the light of dawn. I assigned a person to stand on Nausikaa's bow to watch for breaking seas or any sign of land. The thick clouds made visibility minimal, complicated by the torrential rain that continued to fall.

In an attempt to gain some more headway I decided to take the watch myself on the bow after my 8 -10 p.m. shift at the helm. It didn't take me long to realize that even with a powerful spotlight I was unable to see more than few feet ahead. The harder I tried to stare through the rain, the blurrier my vision became. Large raindrops made a loud slapping noise on the sea, sounding like a thundering waterfall.

A state of panic engulfed me as I thought of an old painting depicting fears of the *Flat Earth Society* – old galleons and square-riggers falling off the side of the earth over a great waterfall. Of course I knew the earth was not flat – that there were no waterfalls cascading off the side of earth. But in my fatigue – caused by straining in the darkness to see more than a few feet ahead, plus the sound of the thundering rain – my imagination got the better of me. Could there be something that remained hidden from man?

It was now after midnight. Realizing that it was pointless, we could not see far enough ahead to prevent Nausikaa from running into an island or a reef, we decided to take our sails down and let Nausikaa drift.

By the next morning things hadn't changed. With the heavy rain and almost no wind it appeared that we had stayed in one spot. The sky remained totally overcast with heavy low clouds, not allowing me to take a sextant reading for the entire day. Therefore we were unable to pinpoint exactly where we were and how far away the island was – or what direction we should head to get there.

On top of that, now the wind totally died and the heavy tropical rain persisted so we just continued to sit stationary. It was very frustrating. We had been at sea 10 days. Land and civilization were right at our fingertips, just over the horizon somewhere. But even during the day visibility was so minimal we feared running aground. Normally water would break over the reefs and expose them, but in flat seas they were impossible to see. We had no choice but to wait.

Another 24 hours passed. Conditions didn't change the next day either so we decided to motor in the daylight in a pattern covering five square miles. That way we'd advance an extra five miles farther south each time we completed the square. Frustration built within us. We were so close and yet so far.

I didn't like the fact that we ran the engine so much. The fuel we had on board was to last us for months. We had rationed ourselves to run the engine only two hours a day to keep the batteries charged – so that we had power for our interior, navigation, and compass lights and such. Running the engine for hours due to frustration and restlessness was not on the agenda. In my mind I justified it, thinking that miraculously we could replenish our fuel supply somewhere before we got to American Samoa, even though we were warned it wasn't possible.

Curious booby birds flew over to check us out, turning their heads to observe us as they passed by. Water, water everywhere and land not in sight. The tallest things on Fanning were palm trees, making the island all the harder to spot.

The danger of being so close to land during the night made our life hell. The wind was ever so light, but the current made us drift posing the threat of running onto a reef. During the day we could at least sail or power a bit and be able to see some distance, but the moonless nights were like being in a dark tunnel. We doubled up on our watches. Our nerves were shot as we strained so hard to see out into the darkness.

On the morning of the fourth day, Denver Dan, who was on the 4 to 6 a.m. watch woke me up. Emphatically excited, he advised me of a small break in the clouds on the eastern horizon. The two of us anxiously awaited the rising sun to make its way to the little clearing in the sky. Finally I took sextant shots of the sun while Dan earnestly tended the timing with a stopwatch. It wasn't a great reading but it provided one line on the chart – our approximate position – which indicated that we were only five to seven miles north of Fanning Island.

YES! Up went full sail complement and within a half-hour, in very light winds, we began to see the faint outline of palm treetops. As we approached the island we spotted outrigger canoes that appeared to be coming toward us. They kept a cautious distance and the dark faces of the natives showed no expression as they escorted us toward the lagoon. My heart soared. *Woooo this is going to be culture shock to the max* I thought.

I immediately told Shirley and Deanna to put on cover-ups over their swimming suits, not aware of what the local customs might be. Meanwhile the men in the canoes only wore small lava-lava wraps made with tropical colored cotton. They were lean and muscular just like the South Seas warriors I'd dreamed and fanaticized about.

We waved to them but received no response. I tried to see inside their canoes to detect if they had any type of weapon but to no avail. The distance they kept from us, their lack of expression and the way they encircled us made me wonder if they might have hostile intentions. I remembered the story of Captain Cook, how the natives first received him and his crew with total dignity only to turn on him afterwards. *God I hope this tribe is friendly.* If they were, they sure weren't showing it.

This was our first landfall, 1,100 nautical miles south of Hawaii and the enormous cultural difference was obvious. *If this is so incredibly different already, what's it going to be like deep in the South Pacific?* I wondered. Later we were to realize Fanning Island is unique because it is so primitive compared to most of the other islands in the South Pacific. It would be a rarity to find natives in such an original state.

Very cautiously we proceeded to follow the natives paddling their outriggers, through the small opening in the *C* shaped coral reef into the lagoon. It was unnerving to see the ocean bottom as we glided through the shallow channel. The water was crystal clear and the bottom seemed much too close to Nausikaa's keel. The thought of running aground gripped my heart. My anxiety was emphasized because now the natives' outriggers were right beside us and I feared running over them.

Their expressionless faces intimidated us even more now that they were so close. I tried to slow down but couldn't. Then I realized the current through the passage was briskly sweeping us in toward the large lagoon. I was relieved to see a good spot to anchor in front of a small village where the current had carved out a deeper channel. Everywhere else it looked only a few feet deep.

Just as we dropped anchor a school of large black stingrays came to check out who had disturbed their turf. Once the anchor was dropped, as silently as the natives arrived, they disappeared. I took that as a good sign, hoping that perhaps they had come to insure our safe passage into the lagoon.

It was here that we discovered something that would serve us well throughout our South Pacific voyage – understanding the tribal society system. After observing the natives that guided us through the lagoon, I realized their society must be similar to the one that Captain Cook probably encountered when he first reached Hawaii. I wanted to do the right thing, to follow proper protocol in their society as guests visiting their island.

I decided we should stay on Nausikaa at anchor and wait until the next morning before going ashore. Captain Cook always waited and observed the island sometimes as long as few weeks before going on land. That gave the natives time to become familiar with them. It was important to me personally as well. Wanting to do things correctly, I decided I would wait until tomorrow to go ashore to pay our respect to the village Chief and ask for his permission to come ashore.

The next morning Peter and Didier lowered our rowing dory into the water and paddled me to shore. Visualizing what Captain Cook would do, I stood in the middle of the dinghy with my arms crossed over my chest. At shore I had the crew stand by the dinghy to await my return.

It felt great to be dressed in a nice clean shirt and shorts. I was on an emotional high, acting out the captain role I had fantasized about for so long. My only fear was that it might not turn out the way I had envisioned it. However this time I wouldn't be disappointed.

When I walked through the village looking for the Chief I was delighted to see traditional native huts made out of straw and coconut leaves. Topless women leisurely sat in the shade. I searched for a less embarrassing place to ask for the Chief's hut. When I did ask, all I received in return was a lot of giggles. It was obvious that the natives didn't understand one word I was saying. I had to stop and think – *this isn't a dream anymore, this is reality!* I felt in total harmony with the way things were unfolding. I was living my dream.

Finally a younger tribe member found someone who spoke a few words of English to help. The young man led me to the village center where more grass huts were set into a semi circle kind of making town square. Some huts even had corrugated tin paneled roofs. The village Chief was well into his sixties if not seventies. He was delighted that I came to ask for his permission to visit his island. Unfortunately, he couldn't speak any English but with the help of Tau, our translator, we communicated. In a very limited conversation we learned from Tau, that the plantation manager and his wife were the only people that spoke English on the island.

Tau spoke very slowly and had a very limited vocabulary. However it was our delight that he could help us, because the plantation manager and his wife turned out to be very unapproachable and unfriendly. It appeared as if our company annoyed them. You'd be pretty unlucky to find such unfriendly people even in New York on a bad weather day. We wondered why. The year before only three sailboats had visited this island. Every six months a supply cargo ship delivered supplies and loaded dried coconuts so it didn't seem as if they were inundated with too much company.

I sensed that having my new translator friend walk along beside me through the village made the natives feel much more comfortable. There was now laughter and lively conversation happening as we passed by.

For the remainder of the day Shirley, Trevor and I, together with the crew treated ourselves by visiting a secluded beach on the lagoon side of the island. Just being on land was such a novelty so we went about playing in the sand and snorkeling. Deana set up her windsurfer and whizzed by us back and forth. Windsurfing was a novelty to all of us and so with fascination we watched her skillfully ride. The locals were impressed too.

The next morning hot rays of sunlight beamed through our porthole and woke us up. Shirley stayed below to nurse Trevor while I routinely climbed up on deck to check Nausikaa's position in relationship to the shoreline, just to see that our anchor hadn't dragged throughout the night. All was well, but I noticed a young native man running off toward the village the minute he spotted me.

A short while later he returned with our translator Tau, the village Chief and a few other villagers. The Chief very formally invited us all to come to a village cultural day to be held the following Sunday, just four days away. I was honored and delighted by the invitation. What we didn't realize at the time was that the whole event was created just for us.

Everyone in the village helped prepare for and then participate in the festivity. The men got up at the crack of dawn to catch reef fish and octopus while the women prepared chicken and pig umu style – covered in banana leaves and slowly cooked in the ground over hot rocks and covered with soil. The celebration was a spectacle never to be forgotten. It was authentic. The island women dressed in traditional grass skirts and young warriors held shark teeth swords, wooden carved clubs and spears, as they sang tribal songs and danced the day away.

The food was spectacular in every aspect – quantity, quality and selection. It was a genuine display of hospitality. Unsuspecting, we truly thought the natives must be celebrating some special annual event and we just happened to be in the right place at right time. We did not realize all the fuss was just for us. What we did notice was the coconut plantation manager and his wife were not present.

Shirley and I gazed at each other in disbelief. Thinking for sure, we must be dreaming. Our crew was also memorized. Expressions of total awe were written all over their faces. We were all bursting with pleasure. Here we were only seven young humble beings, being welcomed and entertained by two to three hundred villagers and their children. It must've been obvious to the natives that we were totally entranced. The more we showed our pleasure, the better they performed.

The party started at 10 a.m. And now it was 6 p.m. and becoming dark. It was time to think about heading back home to Nausikaa to put Trevor to bed. He was getting a little cranky, exhausted from playing with the children all day. Wherever he went there was always a horde of children, of all ages, following close behind him. His unique light blonde hair made him a novelty and the locals couldn't seem to get enough of him.

We thanked the Chief and everyone else and announced that we were leaving. The party suddenly came to an abrupt halt. As we were leaving so did everyone else. It then became clear to us that the celebration had been specifically for us. We were perplexed and couldn't fathom that they had gone to all that trouble just for us. Even though our communication ability wasn't too great we had partied and bonded with our new Fanning Island friends.

Later when we shared our experience with other cruising yachts we realized just how lucky we were as some cruisers never experience anything close to this in their travels. For us it was another lesson in bridging the cultural gap, a lesson in becoming culturally atttuned, a lesson in accepting and respecting others for whom they are.

When we returned to Nausikaa I shook my head in amazement and total disbelief. Whoa, what a treat. Then I got this sensation as if Captain Cook was looking down on us from the heavens, a content look on his face, and nodding his head in agreement as if proud of the way we handled the whole experience.

I looked up into the clear star studded sky. Every square inch of my body tingled and every hair stood on end. I smiled back and said, *"Thanks for the gift Cap!"*

Chapter 26

Lobster Mania

"A little nonsense now and then is
relished by the wisest men."

… Anonymous

Our stay on Fanning Island was a treasureable experience. There wasn't one day that went by without something new and exciting happening. However there was one thing Tau, our island guide, kept evading. He never gave us a clear answer whenever we brought up the question of lobster. When we asked him if there was any in these waters he would simply reply, *"Lots!"*

"But where?"

"Everywhere"

When we asked him to show us where, he'd say, *"The native men like tuna and octopus. No like lobster."*

I think he was sincere about the whole thing. Possibly lobster was unappealing in their culture and he didn't want to insult us. But I couldn't imagine anyone not liking it. Just knowing it was plentiful and in the area made me want some. Even though Dr. Gene had recommended keeping away from rich food because of my kidney stone, my mouth would water instantaneously at the thought of fresh steamed lobster.

I was also obsessed with learning to be a good hunter and gatherer of food, just in case something went amiss down the road causing us to have supply difficulties. I wanted to be aware of how the locals did it so I could too. Finally one day my wishes came true as Tau finally agreed to take us lobstering.

Late one afternoon, using two old decrepit mopeds to transport us to the other side of the island we arrived at a beach where all the action was to take place. The whole thing seemed odd to me. There were the four of us, Tau, his native colleague, with Peter and myself on a deserted beach, dragging our feet by watching the sun set.

"Tau we didn't come here for the sunset. We came to catch lobster," I protested, already knowing that it would be impossible to catch lobster this late in the day, but I played the game.

"Captain today – catch lobster," he reassured me.

I still didn't get it. We had no spears, no nets, and no fishing line. We had absolutely nothing to indicate we'd be catching any lobster and night was falling quickly.

One thing we did have was a brilliant fire-red sunset. I stood with my mouth wide open in awe as we gazed out at the horizon. The colossal red sphere dipped ever so gently into the ocean. Intently we watched it disappear completely. Then for a while we chased each other on the beach, wrestling and throwing each other into the water and plainly acting like kids. We were so carefree, without a worry in the world. The setting, the mood and our state of mind was such that nothing could've topped it.

In those latitudes it didn't take long before it became completely dark. *Now what?* I thought to myself but didn't say a thing. I was curious to see how things would play out. I thought Tau was doomed. He had promised to teach us how to catch lobster and now with no hint of that probability, I'd have ammunition to tease him.

"What are we waiting for?" I tantalized him.

"We wait here more for lobster," he said in his cute way and then in a surprise move he sent me flying into the water. Thinking it was still part of the game, I chased him for a while then suddenly he said,

"Now we catch lobster!" I hadn't noticed before but now I realized the moon was full. Like nature's spotlight it illuminated the night.

Tau walked up to his moped and lit an old barn style lantern. From under the seat he pulled out and put on one glove and then he walked into the knee-deep water. I followed closely behind. Holding a lantern over his head Tao scanned the area ahead. *"Here is one,"* he pointed to a slightly darker area on the grassy ocean bottom. The light was so faint and truthfully speaking, I couldn't really see a thing. Ever so slowly he crept up to a dark spot, with me inches behind peering over his shoulder.

Slam! His hand smashed into the water. Then a loud – *Splat! Splash! Splatter!* Water sprayed all over us as Tau held a humungus lobster up over his head. I couldn't believe my eyes. *"Hold here, take to beach,"* he instructed.

Using my right hand I firmly grabbed the lobster by its back and I felt its sharp spines poke into my skin. The lobster's tail wildly flopped around, pricking me even worse but I just wouldn't let go of our prize until we were safely at the beach. Peter and I cheered and hooted in delight. And before we knew it, Tau called us back to pick up another lobster and then another, and another.

I was in sheer ecstasy. The whole thing, the moon, the lobster, the mystique of the deserted beach, the outline of palms against the moonlit sky, the warmth of the moist tropical air caressing my body – those were only a few ingredients infusing the excitement of the night. It was euphoria – like a non-sexual orgasm.

With lobsters flopping all over the beach Tau decided it was my turn to catch some. With a glove on my right hand and the lantern in my left I spotted one. But I didn't act fast enough or my grip wasn't firm enough. Perhaps I was too hesitant. When I tried to yank the next one out of the water, its powerful snapping tail caused the lobster to jerk loose from my hand. I lost a third one and then a fourth. Tau howled with laughter and yelled smart comments to the others on the beach.

Finally he divulged his secret and told me to yank the lobster out of the water much faster. Sure enough the next one didn't get away.

Once I twigged onto it, I caught all the lobster I wanted. We actually caught so many that we threw the females with eggs and the smaller ones back into the water.

It was time to head home. Peter kept all the lobster herded in one spot on the beach as they were determined to flip back into the water. Oops, guess what? We had absolutely nothing to carry the lobster back to the ship in. Of course, I had my doubts in the probability of catching any so it never occurred to me to bring something, but Tau?

I had to give him credit for creativity as he used palm leaves to make a rope. He tore each palm leaf lengthwise down the middle and then peeled small strands from the core. By weaving together the strands he made a rope which we then used to tie the lobster.

Peter and I, being passengers on the mopeds, slung a couple lobster lines over each of our shoulders and off we went into the darkness of the coconut grove. They hung down our backs to the ground, and as we bounced through the bush I felt some breaking off. The spiny lobsters, still alive, killed us with their prickly spines but neither Peter or I complained. We were on an adventure, a mission. It was like we were engaged in a pain endurance contest.

I couldn't understand how Tao and his friend could see anything in the darkness. The mopeds' headlights didn't work yet they drove like crazy. I feared we'd crash into a tree. We hung on for our lives. They must've known what they were doing because we made it safely back with big smiles on our faces and a dozen lobsters still clinging to our backs.

Our laughter woke everyone when we boarded Nausikaa. They were anxious to hear about our adventure. As we showed off our catch and nursed our wounds we shared our lobster story. Over lots of laughs, we put it all together. Tao had stalled earlier in the month to take us lobster hunting. He wanted to wait for the light of the full moon when the lobsters are easier to catch and also so the coconut groves would be illuminated, in lieu of the mopeds broken headlights.

The mystery was solved. From that day onward we knew where, how and when to fish for lobster.

Chapter 27

Popcorn Madness

*"A ship in port is safe, but that's not what
ships were built for."*

... Rear Admiral Grace M. Hopper

The announcement of our plan to leave Fanning Island was
disappointing news for the islanders, especially Tau. We had
developed such a strong bond with our new friends over a few short
weeks. In that period of time the experiences we shared and cultural
differences we witnessed were profound.

But now the possibility of us departing within three days seemed
hopeless. The village Chief demanded that we stay until after the
weekend so the village could adequately prepare and have a going
away party for us. I had the suspicion it was put off because they
wanted to stall our departure, and we perhaps would re-think it, change
our minds and stay. Even I wondered *why in the world would we
want to leave such a perfect place?* It was ideal, all we ever dreamed
of experiencing in the South Seas. Actually it appeared like a fantasy,
impossible to be happening to us. I constantly had to pinch myself to
see if it wasn't just a pleasant dream.

The islanders adored Trevor. Wherever he went hordes of children
of all ages followed closely behind. Endlessly they gave him gifts of

shells, little homemade trinkets and toys and of course, his favorite – bananas – and other tropical fruit. It aggravated Shirley and myself that there was really not much we could give them in return. We gave plenty of spare clothing, canned spam and corned beef (the islander's favorite treat) and other odds and ends to Tau and a few others, but we really had nothing for the rest of the villagers.

Repeatedly we were asked for liquor but had decided that even though we had plenty stored away, we would not provide it to the locals. We were guests visiting their island and didn't want to interfere with their culture. Most natives weren't familiar with drinking alcohol. Why should we be the ones to introduce them to what could be a possible bad influence?

That remained our policy throughout the South Pacific. Periodically we saw Tau and a couple of his young friends shimmy up their favorite coconut tree and tend to their coconut juice fermenting in half open shells exposed to the heat of the sun. They would sometimes get intoxicated and it was obvious the other locals didn't appreciate it. We weren't going to add to the problem.

I guess I suffered from youthful restlessness or maybe it was that condition seafarers refer to as the *"old sailors rot in port"* virus. I couldn't wait to get under way again. It was agonizing to agree to stay another week but of course once we decided we would stay, how quickly the days flew by! They were filled with interesting activities like exploring the island, fishing for our daily food and watching Deana race the locals with her windsurfer.

It became a popular event, one the islanders loved. Each day another native would challenge her to race against his sailing outrigger. Time and time again she'd win. They were perplexed. How could this contraption, a windsurfer, beat them? They were stumped. And we certainly didn't rub it in. They were proud people. It was evident the native men disliked the fact that a woman could beat them. Women's liberation wasn't big in their culture. Although they never actually confronted us about it, we could feel their disapproval of our women engaged in a seafaring life style.

What really made me content with delaying our departure was the fact that a supply ship was to visit the island. That was exciting news. It was a stroke of luck. A supply ship only visited every six months, and we needed new provisions. All our fresh meat and most of our fresh produce was gone. A few apples, potatoes and onions were still holding out but otherwise we would've had to rely on canned goods if it weren't for the islanders. They constantly provided us with taro root, yams, avocados, breadfruit, giant papaya, bananas, star fruit, passion fruit and other things. So much of it was foreign to us. Unfortunately at that time we weren't aware how to cook half of it and when we tried, the results weren't too appreciated.

I was surprised when the freighter arrived. It was in and out again after only a few short hours. Precious mail, fresh provisions and building materials were unloaded. Then bananas and coconuts, together with the outgoing mail were loaded up, and the freighter darted out of the harbor, quickly disappearing over the horizon.

Our expectation of the ship being a floating Safeway store did not materialize. All we ended up with was couple dozen eggs, a few heads of cabbage and a new bag of rice infested with little bugs. That was it. How disappointing. I had hopes for frozen beef to prepare for the following day's celebration as our contribution to our going away party.

What were we going to prepare now? I wondered. Then Peter came up with a brilliant idea. He suggested we pop a huge plastic garbage-sized bag full of popcorn for the island kids. I wasn't too satisfied with the proposal but after failing to come up with anything better it was exactly what we did. But I just couldn't kick the feeling of being an *el-cheepo*. Fortunately that feeling quickly faded, as the natives were not so concerned with our contribution as with making sure that their show was the best it could possibly be.

The Chief beamed with pride, as young children recited native poetry and sang songs. Not understanding their language, I guessed it was a farewell to mariners. The Chief, Shirley, Trevor and myself were flanked by our crew and sat at one end of the performance area. Opposite us were crowds of natives who formed a semi circle. We all sat on pandanas-leaf mats placed on the ground. I imitated the Chief clapping my hands to the rhythm of the music and periodically yelling along with him, *"Mar-ae! Mar-ae!"* In the middle of the circle little girls danced the hula and young warriors kicked up a cloud of dust as they performed war dances. Laughter and was abundant. Everyone was enjoying it, giggling, laughing, singing, and dancing.

A feeling of ecstasy permeated my entire being. I was only 25 years old and yet felt that life couldn't possibly get any better than this. *How could we have left without this celebration?* I absorbed it all, as the whole event unfolded in front of us, and again, I just couldn't fathom it was all for us. I couldn't shake the feeling that we were not worthy of this kind of honor. It was more like a celebration reserved for royalty visiting their colonies. In my home country of Croatia a festivity like this was reserved for President Marshal Tito, not regular people like us.

Deep down I wondered when we would be exposed. Any minute I expected someone to step into the middle of the circle, point at us and proclaim, *"They are impostors, they are not royalty, they are not celebrities. They aren't even rich."* The accusation would have been right. We were just a bunch of young kids in pursuit of our dream, not worthy of this kind treatment.

The more I shook my head in wonderment the more festive and vibrant the party became. Now old women rose to their feet and did an exotically charged provocative dance, which just caused the onlookers to explode into loud fits of uncontrollable laughter and cheering. It was the first time since our wedding day that my cheeks were sore from so much laughter.

The only thing that interrupted the flow of the performance and settled down the crowd was when the feast was served. Everything was presented on large door size platters, placed on the ground in front of us. The natives rolled out their mats and huddled around their platters. A finger feast was on. We drank fresh juice out of coconut shells broken in half. And ate delicious delicacies, like fish and onions marinated in coconut cream and umu style chicken and pork. Beautiful tropical flowers, hibiscus, orchids and plumeria adorned the food platters.

At dusk torches were lit announcing the arrival of evening. I didn't know where the day had vanished. Tau gathered up the children at my request to receive our treat. I passed out popcorn by individual hand fulls. At first they were apprehensive, not recognizing what it was, but after tasting it they quickly returned for more. Word spread fast and they came in droves. The more popcorn I handed out, the more unruly the children became. Soon the adults wanted to see what they were missing out on. They too tried it and ultimately everyone started to claw at me craving more. I couldn't believe it, but right before my eyes, the curious group turned into a frenzied mob – all after the popcorn.

Things deteriorated so much that the Chief and Tau whisked Peter and myself to their town hall. Peter and I stood inside the building and handed popcorn out a window to everyone lined up outside – little toddlers, young children, teenagers, and adults, young and old. As soon as they got their share of popcorn they'd run back to the end of the line, patiently waiting their turn again. Needless to say the popcorn was a big hit. We couldn't have come up with a better gift. Eventually the popcorn ran out but the celebration didn't.

This party did not end at dusk but continued well into the night. Before it was over Didier, Denver Dan, Peter and Deana did their best to dance the local dances but with marginal success, although it was very entertaining. I hated to be a party pooper, but not wanting to head out to sea in the morning with a party weary crew, I called it a night and we said our final good-byes.

It was like a Jewish farewell. Everyone was saying good bye for the tenth time, but nobody left. Once we did get moving in a concerted direction toward our ship, the villagers followed us. It made my heart wrench. It was if we were saying goodbye to our family, one we'd never see again.

I gazed toward the crowd of people watching us from shore as we rowed our dinghy toward Nausikaa. Tears filled my eyes and I had to swallow hard to suppress a sob. Leaving wasn't going to be easy.

Chapter 28

Hit Below the Belt

*"Never go on trips with anyone
you do not love."*

… Ernest Hemingway

Sailing conditions couldn't have been better. A steady wind blew on our beam at 15 miles-per-hour. Little puffy white clouds graced across the deep blue skies. As Nausikaa gently leaned to starboard Trevor contently played in his bucket of water in the cockpit. Shirley quietly played with him, spending countless hours teaching him to talk. I was so happy she loved this lifestyle as much as I did.

It was a lazy day, the kind that makes your mind tend to drift off. Mine drifted back to the previous day, reliving our going away celebration. I'd never forget Fanning Island and I promised myself one day I would return. Everyone really loved it there except Denver Dan. He was starting to miss the conveniences that civilization offered in North America.

To get my mind focused on things to come, I read some history about the voyages of Captain Cook. Our next destination was Christmas Island, which had been part of the Gilbert Islands, but was now proudly called Kiribati. Captain Cook named Christmas Island because he discovered it on Christmas Day. Interesting enough,

Endeavor was anchored off the island for a week giving them time to study it before they even set foot on shore. I can't imagine the discipline and patience they must've had after spending so long at sea. Captain Cook's hand written log fascinated me; to think I was reading my hero's hand writing while I was re-tracing his footsteps. I was in seventh heaven.

Everyone was as mellow that day as I was, lazing in the shade or catching up on their sleep. Only Didier seemed to have an energetic spark to him. He sang French songs as he puttered in the galley trying to decide on what he'd prepare for supper. Didier loved sailing and being at sea. He was the only one on board that was more content on an ocean voyage than anchored by an island. Don't get me wrong. He loved the islands and the people but his passion was to be out at sea and under sail. Without a doubt, he was the best crew on board, a capable sailor, not at all moody, always ready to help and a darn good cook.

Drowsiness got the better of me so I decided to take a snooze before my evening watch. Since I knew it was one of those great sailing days that I could relax, it didn't take me long to drift into a deep sweet sleep. However it didn't last long. I awoke with a sharp intense pain that ripped through my lower back. Quickly I realized it was the same pain that I suffered in Hawaii. *"Oh no! Please not now. Not again. Not here!"* I pleaded to the higher powers.

The pain wasn't quite as bad as the worst I'd experienced in Hawaii but it was bad enough. It changed my dark tanned face into a pale drawn one. I decided it was pointless to return to Fanning Island, as nobody had medical expertise. Returning to Hawaii was out of the question, as it would have taken too long. *I'd rather live with the pain than risk having to give up on our expedition* I decided. The best thing was to push ahead to Christmas Island, two and a half days away.

I lay in bed and kept a low profile not wanting to alert anyone, hoping the pain would just disappear. I surfaced in the cockpit when it became dark so nobody would notice my discolored face. When Didier served our dinner, the pain was so intense that I felt nauseous.

Instead of eating, I pitched my food overboard when nobody was looking. I barely made it through my watch from 8 until 10, then went straight to bed.

The sharp pain pulsated to a higher degree. It was now so bad I didn't care if anyone knew or not. Shirley definitely became aware that something was awfully wrong the minute I laid next to her. The whole night I couldn't sleep and she didn't either. Agonized, I held my right fist clenched under my kidney and rolled back and forth over it trying to wring the pain out.

Shirley normally did the *sunrise watch* from 6 until 8 a.m. and I then I would start the next watch. For the first time since we left Vancouver I just couldn't honor my watch; the pain was too severe. Since Shirley hadn't slept too much because of the all the commotion I had made she wasn't in the best shape to do another shift but she did anyway.

In the meantime down below I was in total agony and on the verge of passing out. I couldn't wait for Shirley to come down from being at the helm. I was desperate for a shot of morphine and needed her help. I had thought of taking it before but decided to resist as long as I could possibly handle the pain. Now it was definitely more than I could bear. Finally Shirley came down the companion way into our aft cabin.

"Honey please give a shot of morphine," I pleaded.

"What? I can't do that. I'll faint," she immediately responded. Now if you know my wife, you know – yes – she'd faint. She's a brave woman with enough courage to go to sea, but she has one big weakness – needles.

"Sure you can. Remember? Dr. Gene said you can. He showed us how. Come on please honey – I'm hurting real bad."

She went to retrieve the bundle of syringes and a six-ounce bottle of morphine from our medicine kit. Not only were her hands shaking, but also her whole body trembled. I looked at her and through my pain I wondered how was she going to manage it. Neither one of us had experience with giving needles.

The image of Shirley holding a bundle of syringes faded in and out of focus with each pulse of my pain. Through a fog I could see she wasn't accomplishing much so I reached over and pulled out a packaged syringe from the bundle and tore it open. Thank God. Right on the bundle Dr. Gene had written the exact dosage of morphine to be used.

"I can't do this. Let's get someone else to do it," Shirley begged.

"No. I don't want anyone to know how bad I am. Just go ahead and do it." I was getting pretty impatient with her. *"Remember, Dr. Gene said it's not a big deal and not to worry if some air gets injected in the muscle."*

It was a struggle for me to load the syringe because my hands shook so badly. I squeezed the air out of the syringe like they do in the movies and handed it to Shirley.

"What do I do now?" she trembled with nervousness. *"I don't want to hurt you."*

With my right hand I squeezed the back muscle of my upper left arm and I watched the needle approach my arm and then stop. I looked up only to see Shirley's contorted face turn away with her eyes squeezed shut.

It was the most painful laugh I ever had when I saw that sight. Her arms were stretched out in my direction yet she was at least four inches away from my arm. *"Look honey, you are just about there. Come on. Come on. You can do it."* I kept my eye on the syringe as if it was my savior. She must have peeked to see what was happening because the needle came closer to my skin and then barely pricked me, allowing for just the tip to enter my skin. I looked up just to see Shirley's face all distorted and her body stiff. She again turned the other way, except for her arms that reached out to me.

"Come on, you are just about there. Push it in some more."

Nothing happened. I guess she froze with fear, but she held the syringe steady. I shifted my body a bit and leaned on the needle until it was three quarters in. *"OK you are in, squeeze it now."* She squeezed it but the needle came out a bit causing some morphine to ooze out. Again I pushed my body into the needle even more as Shirley continued to squeeze it.

Finally the syringe was empty and I felt waves of relief surge through my body. It was amazing how rapidly it acted. Shirley looked at me with an astonished look on her pale face – as if she couldn't believe she had done it.

"Great. It's all over." I looked at her with a thankful smile of relief and then rolled back and drifted instantly into a deep sleep.

Chapter 29

Christmas Island

"A rough road leads to the stars."

... Anonymous

The minute I woke up I was tempted to call Shirley for another shot of morphine but decided to prolong it as long as possible. The pain wasn't at its peak. Perhaps the morphine was still working. How long I slept, I really didn't know, but would soon learn I was out cold for 24 hours.

I lay in bed expecting the pain to escalate but it didn't. Actually it was more like a stiff ache now. Since I was able to maneuver, I thought I better make an appearance on deck to see how things were going and to try to take some positional sextant shots before my pain increased. Christmas Island in the Kiribati chain couldn't be too far now. I could almost smell it and sure enough the results of my shots showed that by tomorrow morning we'd be there.

As the day wore on the stiff ache in my lower back surprisingly continued to decrease and became so light that I was able to man my 8 to 10 p.m. watch just fine. I was thankful to be relieved of the pain. Now, being so close to land I had to be on the ball to guide us in. Christmas Island apparently had many reefs and rocks to avoid.

The next morning at the crack of dawn Shirley woke me up as Didier spotted land on the horizon. The crew had everything under control with the sails set appropriately for the gentle morning breeze. We glided along smoothly as if sailing through velvet. I thanked the infinite powers above for the wonderful weather we'd been blessed with during my kidney stone attack.

We set Nausikaa's anchor at 10 a.m. outside a picturesque lagoon on the lee side of Christmas Island. According to the information in Captain Cook's log we must've been anchored in the proximate area he originally anchored in on his first visit to the island. That very thought made me quiver with pleasure. For years I had fanaticized and visualized what it would be like and now here I was. Wow! I never expected my feelings to surpass my fantasies but they were.

A beautiful white sand beach ringed the lee side of Christmas Island. Slender palm trees towered into the endless blue sky, the palm fronds gracefully swaying like hula dancers. The sparkling sea gave the illusion that the island was set among a cluster of diamonds. As anxious as we were to go ashore, we waited a couple hours for high tide to try to skim across the sand bar and inside the shelter of the inner lagoon.

From the water the island certainly didn't look like the nuclear bomb ravaged island I expected to see. But on the other hand we hadn't seen any sign of human life so we were eager to explore and find out what the deal was. The chart showed a depth of five feet over the sand bar during high tide. Nausikaa's keel laid five feet under water. This was going to be close. Deana and Peter were on the lookout to detect the deepest route through the sand bar. We traveled half a mile, periodically dragging our keel until we finally came to an abrupt stop, stuck on the bottom.

It didn't matter how persistent we were, backing up or trying another route, we just needed a few more inches. I was becoming alarmed. We were trapped. *Damn,* we had to make it into the lagoon before the tide ran out or be left high and dry. Simultaneously the crew and I agreed to jump in the water to reduce the ship's weight leaving Shirley and Trevor on board to steer.

The inviting water was so pristine and warm. We were all able to stand on the bottom. Deana and Denver Dan were pretty short, but they could bounce off the ocean floor, whereas Peter's head stuck out at least a foot. Shirley managed to inch the ship forward but not quite enough to get us over the sand bar. The drag on the keel was just too great for the engine to push Nausikaa through.

We just had to figure out something. I positioned Deana in shallow water beside us to signal to Shirley. Dan and I took the port side, and Peter and Didier were on the starboard side. We propped our backs under Nausikaa's hull and started to rock and lift her. Bingo! That was enough to shuffle her ahead. For another good half mile we walked across the sand shoal periodically rocking and lifting Nausikaa along until finally she slid into the deep water inside the lagoon. We cheered and hooted over our little triumph. It was amazing that with our combined efforts we could maneuver a 25-ton ship through the water.

The inside lagoon was so deep that we pulled right up and set our anchor on the beach, then hand set another anchor in the deep water off Nausikaa's stern. In the mood for a celebration we dove off the ship into the transparent blue heavenly water. Oh it was ecstasy!

Two other small sailboats in the anchorage sat next to us – an American on his Catalina 26, and a Canadian couple on their 24-foot sailboat who had a little baby on board as well. I guess we felt pretty spoiled on our 57-foot boat and comparatively speaking, with everything put into perspective, we had it very good.

The couple on the Canadian boat was friendly but the other fellow didn't score so high. It wasn't that Captain Ted was so bad, he was just very distressed. In briefly visiting with him we discovered he experienced the same storm as us just south of Hawaii. However, his little boat didn't fare so well. In fact, on a couple occasions it rolled. One of the times he and his cat were washed overboard. He hadn't been able to save his furry sailing companion. But thanks to his harness he managed to pull himself back on board. For the next week Captain Ted had cowered below, locking himself inside and fearing for his survival in the rough weather, unable to go above to take control of his ship. Once the weather improved he found himself close to Christmas Island and sailed in.

Looking at Captain Ted's little Catalina, it appeared to have faired just fine. Inside and out there was no visible damage. After that visit our neighbor withdrew to the point that he appeared *invisible* most of the time. I found that very peculiar. We craved interaction with anyone that could remotely speak English.

When I went to do my *Captain Cook meets the Chief of the village routine* I found that Christmas Island was run much differently from Fanning Island. Even though the villages looked similar it was obvious this was a larger and a more sophisticated society. The island had 2,000 habitants. There was a small town center with a couple stores and a police station. The Police Chief was also the Chief of the village, Fire Chief, Airport Superintendent and Warden for the maximum-security prison for the entire country of Kiribati.

After paying a visit to the Chief, I was delighted to discover he spoke a few words of English and was eager to learn more from us. I invited him and his wife for lunch aboard Nausikaa. But to our surprise he came alone explaining that his wife didn't attend *official functions!* Ooops! Over the *formality* of a simple feast – spaghetti and modest sauce made with tomato paste, onions and corned beef – we realized it was a super treat for him. The Chief was a good looking man, very friendly and let's just say, not the type that would eat and run. He left late in the evening but not before suggesting he had lots of coconut trees and pumpkins he wanted to share with us. We bonded very quickly.

Early the next morning as we awoke, lo and behold there was the Chief and another man already sitting on the beach waiting for us to go with them to retrieve some coconuts and pumpkins. After arriving at his modest house and a quick introduction to his wife, the Chief and I sat against the wall in the shade while his companion whisked up one of the many coconut trees in the yard. *"Which coconuts would you like Captain?"* he asked.

"Which are the good ones?" I inquired.

Pointing high up the tree the Chief gave me a lesson on coconuts. I hadn't thought much before about them. But that morning I learned how to tell them apart. Some were suited for refreshing drinks and some for eating. As I chose some of each, the helper in the tree sent them flying to the ground.

Then the Chief spotted a coconut he felt I should have but it was a couple trees away. To my amazement, instead of coming down his companion in the tree leaped from one tree to the next as if he were part monkey. My heart stopped beating as I watched his acrobatic leaps 70 feet up in the air. In fright I blurted out, *"That's enough. I don't want any more coconuts."*

The helper (whom the Chief had never introduced me to) carried everything while the Chief and I led our way through out the village empty handed. We made plans to go fishing the next morning to another area of the island because I wanted to fillet, salt and dry some fish for our dry goods food reserve.

Early we awoke and started out on our fishing trip. As we motored on the Chief's 50cc moped to the fishing grounds, it became apparent that the island had been used as a major Army base for the British government. I sat behind the Chief and he acted as a tour guide. Pointing toward a perfectly paved road half covered with overgrown weeds he said it was the way to an old nuclear site. He promised to take us there the following week when an airplane would be visiting the island.

Apparently in the early days of nuclear testing the south end of the island had been a surface detonation site for nuclear bombs. The last blast was in 1957. The Army had remained for a few more years and then the island was abandoned all together.

In the area we were passing through now it looked as if the day the order was given to leave the island, everyone drove jeeps, armored personal carriers and a myriad of other equipment into the ditches along the road side, packed up their personal belongings and immediately departed. Some of the barracks were still in tact, and strangely enough, excess personal belongings and suitcases lay scattered about. Shelves of official looking paperwork, faded but still in tact, were strewn within what looked like the command center building. After so many years it was all still here.

An eerie feeling passed through my body making me shiver. Summing up everything I saw, I wondered why the Brits had left so suddenly. And why didn't they take all their equipment with them? If it wasn't practical to haul it back to England why didn't they place it in one of their fenced compounds instead of leaving it like litter? It looked to me that their departure was pretty sudden. I wondered if something went wrong at the testing site, *hmmm...*

Once at the fishing lagoon the Chief surprised me again. While the Chief and I sat in the shade sipping on a coconut, the Chief's companion dragged the fishing net through the bay all on his own. It seemed like a heck of a lot of work for one man but each time I protested and insisted to help, the Chief let me know very decisively that the higher ups weren't to do that kind of work. Not wanting to change the custom of the island, I forced myself to lounge. I would've rather been in the water, but that obviously wasn't how things were done.

It was an interesting relationship between the two men. They seemed to be good friends, yet anything the Chief wanted to have done his companion took care of it, and with efficiency and delight. Efficiency was a rarity in the islands. Everyone seemed so relaxed and laid back. So I thought why try to fix or spoil a good thing. *Go with the flow Boris.*

Back on board Nausikaa III the Chief and I lounged some more under the shade of our tarp while his companion gutted, filleted, salted and hung the fish to dry. From a distance I enjoyed watching him do such an expert job and wanted again to participate, but I didn't want to cross the Chief.

Little Trevor, on the other hand, was in there like a dirty shirt, playing with the dead fish, tossing their guts into the water and coo'ing with delight as he observed the seagulls diving down to retrieve them. I cringed when the Chief's friend, still having a large knife in his hand, picked up Trevor and lifted him overhead. Trevor laughed from the thrill of it. The two were having a ball.

I couldn't resist my curiosity anymore. I felt that by now the Chief and I had developed a solid friendship so I finally asked, *"Who is this man? Why does he do everything for you? Babysitting your kids and doing all kinds of chores for you?"*

"Ooooh," he said, *"he is a prisoner. I take him out of the prison every morning. He does all my chores for me and he gets to be out of jail. It's good for both of us."*

I was surprised. *"What is he in for?"* I was in for a shock.

"Murder."

"Murder?" I gasped.

"Yes, on his island he killed his wife. They sent him here to our jail for his life sentence. We have the only maximum-security jail in the area so they sent him here. And he promised not to escape on me, so I treat him good."

I am sure my face turned beet-red. Desperately I tried to figure out how to get Trevor away from the murderer *(who still was holding a big butcher knife in his hand)* without making it obvious. To get myself out of a speechless state I sputtered, *"How many prisoners do you have?"*

"Just one. He is the only one. Soon we will have to go because I lock him up at sunset."

This was my out. *"You better hurry up Chief. The sun has just gone down,"* I said, totally relieved. I didn't feel comfortable any more. Not with a murderer on my ship around my wife and son. I felt a pang of guilt about my feelings because I had previously befriended him thinking he was truly a great man. It was a peculiar feeling.

That evening in bed proved to be the wrong time to tell Shirley about our prison guest. The poor thing never got any sleep that night.

Chapter 30

Blazing Paddles

"Your own safety is at stake when your neighbor's wall is ablaze."

… Horace

A vigorous elbow jolted my ribs waking me before dawn. *"Fire! Fire! There's a big fire outside!"* Shirley could hardly blurt out the words in her panic.

She had been up nursing Trevor when she noticed it. Brilliant red silhouette forms danced through our aft cabin. A bright glare came from the direction of Nausikaa's bow. All of a sudden my stomach dropped, like I was carrying a lead weight.

Oh God we're on fire! It was a captain's worst nightmare. Naked, I dashed out and stumbled in a stupor around the deck. Suddenly, I realized it wasn't our ship but the Catalina owned by our American neighbor that was on fire.

Dawn was barely breaking so it had to be about 5:30 a.m. The fire's intense heat could be felt from our cockpit. I furiously rang our ship's bell on the main mast. I screamed, *"Fire! Fire! Fire! Off our bow!"* alerting everyone and anyone that could hear.

Immediately the crew emerged with lightening speed. Armed with all four fire extinguishers, I positioned Denver Dan on Nausikaa's bow. Meanwhile Didier, Peter, and I jumped into the dinghy to fight the blaze and to investigate if the sailboat's captain, the sole occupant, was safe.

On the beach we could see Captain Ted sitting on three suitcases staring out at his burning ship in a state of shock. All poised to fight the fire we tried to encourage him to take action as well. *"Forget it. Just let her burn,"* he replied indifferently.

"What happened? How did it start?" I inquired.

"The stove caught on fire when I was trying to make coffee," he replied impassively.

The blaze was so intense I worried Nausikaa would also catch on fire. It could have been catastrophic for us as well. Since the fire had burned both of the Catalina's anchor lines she was loose and aimlessly drifting. Only a light onshore breeze held the blazing boat close to the beach, barely 30 feet away from Nausikaa III. Our bow anchors were set on the beach allowing us to pick them up and drag Nausikaa away a safer distance from the burning ship.

Daylight revealed our 50-year-old neighbor, Captain Ted, was fully dressed in dry, clean, ironed clothes. He was freshly shaven and his luggage was completely packed. An airplane was scheduled to visit the island once a month, now only two days away. Needless to say things appeared a little fishy. Deciding it was a case of arson, the Police Chief charged and imprisoned Captain Ted. A second charge was laid against him for polluting the beach. He was ordered to pay for wreck removal and beach clean-up.

News spreads fast on a tiny island. I decided to visit Captain Ted in jail, taking him some cooked food. After hearing his story it was obvious that he was suffering from depression. He had been sailing single-handed ever since he left the US. It turned out that he was lonely, financially broke and totally distressed over his misfortunes at sea. Clearly, all he wanted to do was go home to his family.

I took great pity on him and tried to convince the Police Chief that there would be no benefit to keep him as a prisoner. The Chief was not so sympathetic. He pointed out the fact that if the guy wanted to go home he should have sold his boat to someone. Or in the worst case scenario, leave it intact so someone there could use it, instead of destroying it and leaving a burnt out mess on the beach.

A couple mornings later, when the plane was scheduled to arrive, I was still unsuccessful in convincing the Police Chief to release the prisoner. Captain Ted cried, threatening to kill himself if he didn't get on that plane. Now I was even feeling desperate since I felt he was very emotionally disturbed and capable of carrying out his threat.

As a last resort I pleaded with the Police Chief, promising that my crew and I would help clean the beach if he would just let his prisoner return home. At the very last minute, after much negotiation and nagging, the Chief gave in.

It was a sight to be seen when the Police/Fire Chief pulled his old 1940 fire engine out of a big barn. Shirley, Trevor and I sat in the front seat and Captain Ted sat in the back. There was no cab to this fire engine, just open-air seats. The red fire engine puttered down the deserted but paved road toward the airport. The only traffic we encountered were hundreds of huge red land crabs crossing the road. They were everywhere. And as we rode along we heard a crunching noise coming from underneath the wheels.

Another surprise was the airport. It consisted of a tiny shack located at one end of a huge runway, the longest in the Western Hemisphere according to the Chief. The Brits had built it during their nuclear testing efforts and now it sat empty like a lonely ghost from the past.

Surprisingly, there were a few other passengers waiting to board the plane as well. Shirley struck up a friendly conversation with an American gentleman who was the supervisor of a satellite tracking station located on the north side of the island. He was thrilled to meet westerners and invited us to come and visit the station and to enjoy few cold beers and dinner. A cold beer hadn't touched my lips for six weeks so the generous offer definitely caught my attention.

Captain Ted thanked us for helping him get released and with his head slumped down he walked off down the runway with a handful of other people to board the plane. We watched the plane until it turned into a tiny dot and finally disappeared in the sky. That was a huge event for us South Sea explorers so we really took it in.

Soon we were back riding the fire engine and on our way to visit the old nuclear blast site. Heading toward the south end of the island the warning signs became more apparent, dramatically alerting us that we were entering a *danger zone*. I was drawn to the bunkers. The closer we got to the blast zone, the thicker the bunker walls were, and the smaller the observation openings were. Walking through the trenches, checking the bunkers and just imagining the nukes blasting off sent shivers through my body. There was really not much else to see, as the landscape was flat and barren.

The Police Chief didn't seem to know anything about levels of radiation. But never mind, the Chief didn't have a clue about radiation – *period*. So I requested that we leave the area. Just imagining what had taken place there gave me eerie goose-bumps. Since we had Trevor with us we definitely didn't want to spend too much time there.

We had been as close as two miles from the blast area and in a way I was disappointed. I expected to see more destruction or something. I guess I really didn't know what to expect except that as a youngster it was something I had been really curious about.

The Police Chief and his red fire engine were a hit. We picked up the rest of our crew and headed for our next exciting adventure – the high tech satellite tracking station. Immediately on our arrival we were impressed with a field of huge white dish antennas facing skyward. All the buildings and equipment trailers were painted bright white. Our host was willing to show us anything we wished to see. Some of the stuff looked so space age, like something out of a James Bond movie. I was amazed that most of it was not restricted or classified information.

Two men sat at control panels littered with blinking buttons and knobs, tracking a satellite on a huge activated screen. They were able to control the spaceships' orbit course and altitude just by clicking on the buttons. We were like a bunch of wide-eyed kids standing there speechlessly impressed. It was a bizarre sight. And an even more bizarre reflection was when I thought about the extreme contrasts on the island. On one side was an original native village. On the other was space age technology and just south of us was an old nuclear testing site. It was all so incredible. It made me wonder why the universe had made this kind of opportunity available to us.

Then it was time to feast. Our host opened up every fridge and freezer in the complex. There was nothing they didn't have. After living on limited provisions on the ship without refrigeration we happily obliged. We ate and drank to our heart's content and played pool in the recreation room. Shirley feasted on ice cream and pickles. Everyone teased her with her choice of food but what they weren't aware of was the heir to our adventurous lifestyle was being nurtured in her tummy.

The scientists took their turns to shoot some pool and eat with us. There were only about a dozen of them in total on the site. And you could tell they were suffering from isolation and loneliness. They enjoyed our company, especially Deana and Shirley. Western women were so rare in this part of the world that the scientists were openly grateful to be in their company.

Being the captain I had an important job to do that day. As often as I could I had to come up with a reason to *toast* to something. Needless to say we made some major beer salutes. That in turn was the cause for many trips to the bathroom. On one occasion I returned from the bathroom absolutely ecstatic. I had a special announcement to make.

"Ladies and gentleman, today I had my baby." I proudly held up a tiny stone in my right hand.

I explained to our hosts the history of my kidney stone attacks including the morphine experience that took place on our voyage to Christmas Island. I guess after Shirley injected me with morphine I relaxed and the stone passed from my kidney to my bladder. Then when I was drinking all that beer, the liquid must've helped to wash the stone completely out. When I urinated I could feel a pain as the stone scraped its way out. But before I could say *ouch* the stone made a *plinking* sound in the urinal. My baby had arrived.

Surprisingly, for all the pain it had caused, the stone was not all that big. It looked like a tiny lava rock, porous with rough edges and the color of a stained tooth.

Now it was truly time to celebrate. With my kidney stone saga behind me we would be able to continue our expedition without fearing another attack.

Before leaving the satellite tracking station, the Police Chief announced that special movie-projection equipment had arrived on that day's flight. Everyone was invited to the village the next night to see the movie *Ben Hur*.

Eagerly, the next night, everyone gathered at the main village hall poised to watch the classic movie. A sea of straw mats covered the town square area. The whole village showed up. But the film was something else. The projector was so old and in such disrepair that it made the images on the screen move in super slow motion. The movie that was supposed to last two and a half hours lasted the whole night. It started about 6:30 p.m. and was still going at midnight when we left. The next day we heard that they showed the movie until dawn and it still hadn't ended.

However, the natives just loved it. The magic of movies captivated them. Slow motion sword fights were so entertaining, the crowds just roared with laughter. Even though the movie was so terrible not many left. It made me realize how very spoiled we are in our own society.

Chapter 31

Crossing
the Equator

"Do not go where the path may lead,
go instead where there is no path and
leave a trail."

... Ralph Waldo Emerson

We left behind an isle of spellbound people on Christmas Island.
The fact was, we were pretty spellbound ourselves. Now as we were
underway and taking in the beauty of our surroundings it was as if
the universe was smiling down on us, proud of its precious jewels, the
islands, safeguarded by nature's biggest moat, the sea. Glancing back
as we sailed toward our next port of call, Christmas Island's mystic
image seemed to be slowly swallowed up by King Neptune.

Shirley and I embraced on Nausikaa's bow. An aura of joy enveloped us as we reminisced. Even though we loved Christmas Island
we were both thrilled to be *on the road again* – so to speak. I don't
know if our delight to be under sail was a matter of youthful restlessness or maybe we really did have gypsy blood in our veins. Or maybe

we were addicted to being able to sail toward the horizon, not knowing what adventures awaited us beyond.

One thing was for sure, we were soul-mates enjoying life together. When we first shared our plans to go off sailing, one of the common responses from friends and acquaintances was, *"My God, how are you going to live together 24 hours a day, nonstop? What a test for your marriage!"* First we were surprised by that comment, but then grew to accept their skepticism and inside we must've started to wonder ourselves. But through thick and thin, the end result was our relationship thrived in each other's continuous company.

We cuddled and pecked little kisses as we compared notes. The only thing that disturbed our mushy moment was Trevor's demands, *"Mo waddie! I want mo waddie!"* Translation for singles – *"I want another bucket of water right now or I will cry for the rest of the day and maybe I'll even fuss the whole night."* With delight I obliged knowing that if I was lucky he would not tip over the bucket for another few minutes.

Then again our faces would break into smiles as Shirley and I went back to recollecting all our experiences since the voyage began. It just made my heart soar. I was so proud of our accomplishments, of how we handled raising our family, and how overall everything seemed to be coming together, even though there had been times when it seemed hopelessly impossible.

Already, our expedition had been much more than we could ever have imagined. Without a doubt, it had been worth every effort, every tear, and every sleepless night to overcome the obstacles to make it happen. If our creator had made it any easier, we wouldn't have felt the strong sense of accomplishment we did. As with any great deed, this one was worth struggling for!

It's the darnest thing how life works. We wondered how anyone couldn't agree that what we were doing was right. How crazy we'd been to give up the security of our jobs and material possessions to embark on this expedition and live out our dream. If that was wrong we didn't want to be right.

I felt a very strong connection with my parents, as I was sure they'd be proud too. I visualized my father nodding his head in agreement, grinning with approval, as if saying, *"You got it right son. That's the way to do it."* I wished he and Mom were with us experiencing this great joy life had to offer – the beauty of the sea, the islands and their people, the gentle trade winds and the freedom of sailing.

It was one of those exceptional sailing days in the tropics. Perhaps King Neptune felt we had paid our price, surviving previous conditions and was going easy on us. Nausikaa swayed in rhythm with the moderate ocean swells gently rocking us like newborns in a cradle. My joy mellowed and I became lethargic from the motion, almost drifting off to sleep.

Twing! The snap of the fishing line startled me. It seemed like ages since we'd caught deep-sea fish. As much as we all enjoyed reef fish like grouper, red snapper, yew, lobster and octopus there was still nothing like a good fresh off-the-fishing-line tuna, mahi mahi or wahoo. It was no surprise that everyone promptly perked to life when Deana enthusiastically hollered from the helm, *"Fish on the line! We've got one!"*

Peter was first to get to the hand line and seemed puzzled by the fact that he couldn't pull it in as usual. Didier and Denver Dan were quickly on the scene to help and with their combined efforts slowly made some progress. The 200-pound test-line was stretched to its limit. What on earth did we catch? Curiosity had the best of us. We had scored large fish before, but this one promised to be a contender in its own class.

Distracted with our dilemma, I totally forgot to take my usual sextant reading at noon. We were anxious to plot our distance from the equator. We wanted to know exactly when to celebrate our crossing. With Christmas Island being only two degrees north of the equator we couldn't be too far from it.

Now exhausted, the fish struggled in the water off Nausikaa's stern where Shirley and Trevor were on the lookout. *"Oh yumm,"* Shirley announced, *"It's a huge yellowfin tuna."*

Huge it was, and we were stumped because we didn't know how on earth we were going to raise the beast on board. Didier was quick to offer a solution suggesting we lower the staysail and use the halyard to hoist the tuna. But Peter and Deana argued that we should cut it loose because it was too big for us to consume it all of it. So why bother killing it? A compromise was struck when we decided to eat some of it fresh, and then preserve the remainder in two different ways, salting and drying it and also by making homemade fish jerky.

The event quickly transformed a peaceful lazy day into a action-packed one. Slipping the halyard around the irate fish's tail proved to be a challenge. We decided to dangle Peter over the side virtually above the fish. We lowered him down using a safety harness, with one end wrapped around a winch. Once Peter lassoed the tuna's tail with the halyard we were home free and Peter was a hero. Triumphantly we hoisted our prize onto the foredeck and scrambled for our cameras.

Our educated guesstimate put the five-foot tuna at around two hundred pounds. Amazing that we could've caught a large beast like that on our itsy-bitsy line. In fact our lure was only a homemade contraption. Since we'd run out of hoochies and other store-bought lures, we used an old tattered Canadian flag, hopeful that the red and white colors might attract something. I had wrapped it around an egg shaped lead weight and then shredded the ends giving it a *squid* look. That old flag turned out to be our most effective lure attracting our biggest catch to date. Sure enough when I sliced open the tuna, inside its stomach were plenty freshly eaten squid.

Being true to our promise to consume the complete fish, for days to come we had our work cut out for us to preserve and eat it. Somehow we managed, I'm sure using the last bits for fish bait. However, with such an abundance of fresh fish available to us, we made a conscious decision never to kill such a big one again.

The gentle equatorial breeze was certainly a pleasant prologue to reaching the South Pacific. Days like this were perfect to relax in the shade, read a book or watch the sea life perform.

Schools of our favorite little acrobats, the dolphins, visited us regularly to delight us. Sea rays, the flying monsters of the ocean, suddenly would soar out of the sea high into the air and then drop lifeless back down, splashing into the water with a big belly flop. It was a strange sight, witnessing their attempt to knock pests off their bodies. As we sailed along, schools of colorful blue and yellow mahi-mahi sometimes swam along side us for hours at a time, like a motorcycle guard racing beside a presidential limousine. Periodically in our travels, we'd even witness sailfish and marlin jump out of the water. When this would happen, a debate always followed as to whether it had been a sailfish or a marlin.

Without a doubt, the whales were our ultimate favorite. It took us awhile to figure them out, but when we did, it became a little game. In the beginning, when we would come upon a pod of whales, in our naïve anxiousness we would immediately change course and try to get as close to them as feasible. We were impressed with their size, both overwhelmed and intimidated at the same time. However, the closer we approached them, the further away they would move, or they would just gracefully dip under the sea and disappear.

Then one day we discovered a sequence of two magic moves. First we made a short attempt to head toward the whales but then we turned away and headed in the opposite direction. What happened next was amazing. At first the whales were alerted when their sonar senses had detected a large object approaching them, causing them to retreat somewhat. But when we appeared to be non-threatening, because we backed off, they in turn followed us. Before we knew it, the pod surfaced all around us, allowing for a close up inspection. Who was inspecting whom, I'm not really sure. There was no question that they were making direct eye contact with us. *It was obvious they were as curious about us as we were about them!*

As much as we adored the whales' company during the day, we respected and even feared them at night. Old salty sailors tell all kinds of stories about whales sinking ships. They have quite a reputation for being temperamental creatures if they are alarmed or threatened. They sleep on the ocean surface and if you should be unlucky enough to run into one or startle one out of its sleep, they have been known to retaliate by ramming the ship over and over until it sinks. Being very protective, they have also sunk boats in the name of defending their young.

Immediately, if we ever realized we were in the same proximity as whales, we'd always turn on our engine in order to alert them of our whereabouts. And especially at night we acutely listened for their spouting. That was our only warning that they were around.

Our late afternoon sextant position shot confirmed that due to light winds we would probably not reach the equator until the next day. After our yellowfin tuna feast that evening everyone lounged lazily on Nausikaa's deck, content with full tummies, staring up at the star studded moonless sky. Didier, riding in the rat catcher net under the bowsprit, was the first one to detect whales spouting in the distance.

Immediately our alarm system for the whales, the engine, was turned on. Everyone stood on the lookout. Spouting whales could be heard all around us. It was obvious we had drifted right into the middle of a huge pod. Terror set in, as we all knew about the whales' reputation and hoped not to run into one. We slowly inched forward. Listening for telltale spouting sounds we tried to navigate Nausikaa around the whales. As there was a large concentration of spouts off our port side we grouped together on that side and peered out into the darkness. Then there was silence.

The tension on board was so thick it could've been cut with a knife. We held our breath and watched intently off our port side.

"Phhhuuuuussshhhhhh!" The thundering sound jolted us. Water spewed everywhere. A huge whale surfaced inches beside us, exploding his fume into our faces. Everyone shrieked with shock. Denver Dan's legs gave up and he started to collapse to the deck. I just managed to catch enough of him to break his fall. We were drenched with smelly salt water. The fishy stench of the whale's breath was overpowering. Our visitor silently sunk back into the ocean. All we could

do was look at each other and laugh.

The next morning I was in for a surprise when I came out for my 8 to 10 a.m. watch. Normally everyone would be catching up on sleep after their night watches, but they were wide awake and buzzing around in some kind of excitement. Today we would be crossing the equator. We were all to experience it for the very first time. While Didier sang French songs in the galley and prepared a special breakfast, Shirley and the crew worked together making a banner. We all teased Dan. He'd never live down his experience the night before, his collapse with fright.

I started to take sextant shots early and continued to take them throughout the morning just to make sure we could pin point exactly the time we'd cross the equator. The day was perfect with a gentle breeze propelling us southward. The deep blue tranquil sea really pronounced the curvature of the earth. For some reason we all gazed toward the horizon as if expecting a magic visible line. Even though there wasn't one, there was an enchanted feeling within us, as everyone cheerfully chatted and waited in anticipation for the big event. We were entering the unknown waters of *down under.*

Finally the *equator* banner went up, pictures were taken and announcements were made. We were entering the South Pacific. To make it official I read a proclamation I discovered in a book on board.

> *"IMPERIVM NEPTUNI REGIS*
>
> *TO ALL sailors and land lubbers wherever you may be: and to all Mermaids, Whales, Sea Serpents, Porpoises, Sharks, Dolphins, Eels, Skates, Suckers, Crabs, Lobsters and all other Living Things of the Sea. Know ye that on this day in the Latitude of 00.00.0 and Longitude 157° 27' there appeared within her Majesties Sailing Ship Nausikaa III bound for the Cook Island of Suwarrow and on to Samoa, Tonga, Fiji, New Caledonia and Australia – BE IT REMEMBERED – That the said vessel, captain, and the crew thereof have*

been inspected and passed on by Ourselves and our Royal Staff.

AND BE IT KNOWN: By all ye Sailors, Mariners, Land Lubbers and others who may be honored by his presence that: Captain Boris and his fine crew Deana, Peter, Didier, and Denver Dan, together with Shirley and Trevor, having been found worthy to be numbered as one of our Trusty Shellbacks, they have been duly initiated into the "Solemn Mysteries of the Ancient Order of the Deep."

BE IT FURTHER UNDERSTOOD: That by the virtue of the power invested in me I hereby command all my subjects to show due honor and respect to them wherever they may be.

DISOBEY this order under the penalty of Our Royal Displeasure.

Signed By: Davey Jones & His Majesty Neptunus Rex"

We cheered, hugged and congratulated ourselves. We were honored and delighted to have crossed the *magic line* and it showed. However, our acceptance into King Neptune's club, didn't guarantee anything ahead of us.

In fact, we were to be plagued with cloudless, windless and therefore, motionless days. For some strange reason we became very restless and edgy under those conditions. They were perfect days to relax in the shade, read a book, or watch the sea life perform.

But instead those circumstances were the perfect ingredients for the hardest condition to tolerate at sea – boredom and complacency. Being at a standstill, or making very little headway was the perfect breeding ground for nit-picking, verbal attacks and even feuds. It was bizarrely ironic because those days should've been our most pleasurable with comfort and safety not being an issue.

Wanting to conserve fuel but feeling tensions rise, I finally chose to relieve our misery and fire up the *iron genny* to propel us to Suwarrow.

221

Chapter 32

Swimming with the Sharks!

"Life is either a daring adventure
– or it is nothing."

...Helen Keller

Arriving at Suwarrow in the Cook Islands was heavenly bliss. It was our first South Pacific landfall, an uninhabited tropical paradise beyond all my expectations. The *Suwarrow* chain consisted of a group of very small low-lying islands covering perhaps an area one mile wide and five miles long. We were able to spot land from about eight miles out.

A huge coral reef stretching about fifteen miles separated the steel blue water of the ocean from the calm turquoise lagoon. The setting was picture perfect with palm trees sprinkled along the white sand shoreline; dense tropical bush covered the interior. Immediately, when we approached the area we spotted literally thousands of frigate birds circling overhead, high above their nesting ground. It was like a clip out of National Geographic. Instinctively they positioned their nests in a very inaccessible area on the ground, protected by a large section of dead coral extending out of the water.

In the lagoon two other yachts sat peacefully at anchor with a distance of about one mile between them. It was obvious they cherished their privacy. Likewise we anchored quite close to shore and at least one mile from the next boat.

As was my regular routine after anchoring Nausikaa III, I jumped over the side to check how well our anchor set. Being so close to shore I didn't want to chance us dragging. If a storm hit unexpectedly and our anchor wasn't set properly it wouldn't take long to be blown ashore.

The results of my inspection confirmed that the anchor had dug deep into the sandy ocean floor so I decided to check the surrounding area, swimming around the ship.

I discovered magic beneath the surface that was breathtaking. Beautiful coral heads, appearing totally untouched, were just 10 to 15 feet underwater. Schools of colorful tropical fish swam among them, some playfully chasing each other, others hiding with a mischievous eye peeking out. It was a fantasy world.

As I continued to explore the area, I came upon an interesting widespread coral formation containing oodles of brain coral. Suddenly, terror jolted me back into reality. Just on the opposite side of a coral head, directly in front of me, was a large shark. Obviously irritated and nervous, it swam in a rapid circular pattern, with its tail jerking erratically. I recognized the pattern. It was my worst nightmare. I was witnessing a shark hunting for its dinner.

My heart skipped a beat as my survival instinct kicked in. Terrified, I swam as fast as physically possible then bolted out of the water and into the security of our dinghy dangling off Nausikaa's stern.

Perched across the dinghy, I got up enough courage to put only my face back in the water. I looked down to see if I had shook off the beast. However the sight I observed was an ominous one. Three more sharks had joined forces with the first shark. They looked hungry, starving in fact. And I wasn't going to volunteer to be their dinner.

Anxious beyond all means, I alerted the crew not to have their sea bath that day. For some reason nobody protested. I guess they weren't too wild about being shark bait.

Later at dusk, Shirley and I decided to go and introduce ourselves to our nearest neighbors anchored at the opposite end of the island. They were a husband and wife team sailing on a beautiful 60-foot boat out of Marina Del Rey, California. After our introduction I excitedly suggested to them that the waters in the atoll were full of sharks.

The captain very nonchalantly replied, *"Oh yea, they're everywhere."*

I felt kind of awkward and thought *OK, if that's the game he wants to play.* I casually said in my coolest voice ever, *"Yea – sure. They are everywhere here – no big deal."*

Nevertheless after a nice visit of comparing notes, the captain and I decided that the next morning we would explore outside the atoll and fish in the deep water. Our food supply by this time was getting pretty low again, especially fresh provisions. With only having an icebox on board, and no place to buy ice, plus the fact that we hadn't provisioned for perhaps two months, fresh food was considered a premium.

The next morning the two of us hopped into our dinghy and motored out a couple miles to the open reef on the outside of the atoll. Both of us were in the water with our snorkel gear at the same time. We took turns fishing and towing the dinghy by the painter line behind us. One person would hold the dinghy line and watch from the water's surface while the other would take a deep breath, dive to the bottom, spot a fish, spear it and return to the surface. Then that person would take his turn to hold the dingy line while the other went down to fish. Everything was going fine until we drifted into deeper water.

The captain's keen eye spotted a large grouper hiding by a massive coral head about 50 to 60 feet deep. Since we were only snorkeling and not diving with tanks this was going to be a big challenge. I held the dinghy as the captain dove deeper and deeper down. Finally he made it to a coral head. *Snap* went his spear gun, obviously spearing a fish. But he dropped his gun, having to surface for a gasp of fresh oxygen.

He waited a few minutes for the fish to die then dove down again to retrieve his spear gun plus the grouper. Down deep he finally wiggled his gun loose from a coral head and then started to slowly swim up toward the surface.

Simultaneously a shark emerged on the other side of the coral head. It was big – five to maybe even seven feet *(and we're not talking fish stories here!)*. Now as the captain was ascending the shark came around the coral head and started toward the bleeding fish at the end of his spear gun. Not knowing if my diving partner had spotted the shark yet, I muffled a scream into my snorkel gear through the water, *"Shark! Look out for the shark!"*

Obviously there was no way the captain could hear me. I felt helpless. My heart started to race because I could see the two of them on a collision course. They were half way up to the surface when the next thing I knew the shark was right on top of the captain. It wanted the fish at the end of his spear. But to my disbelief the captain wouldn't let the shark have it! Instead he raised his feet and started to kick the shark away with his fins.

I was blown away with what I was witnessing. I continued to scream, *"Let go of the spear! Let go of the spear!"* but he wouldn't. He just continued viciously to kick the shark trying to steer it away. I couldn't believe my eyes. I just couldn't believe it. *Was this guy nuts?* The struggle started to slow the captain down. *Why wasn't he coming to the surface?* His lungs must've been bursting, desperate for air, but he wasn't about to part with his spear or the grouper at the end of it.

The indignant shark persisted, rising to the surface and fighting the captain as he went. Finally the captain gave the shark a good boot in its underbelly and it backed off. He then took his spear and swung his prized catch out of the water and into the dinghy. With a burst of adrenaline both of us leaped into the safety of the dinghy. I was frazzled, excited and scared. What a rush! But the captain was unperplexed, very nonchalant, just as if nothing had even happened. I though to myself, *My God, what's the matter with this man?*

Calmly he said, *"Well I guess it wouldn't hurt to motor down the reef a bit to get away from this pest."* Needless to say, I didn't object. That's exactly what we did.

As we continued to fish that morning, I couldn't stop thinking about what had just happened. Here we were virtually thousands of miles from the nearest hospital or from any help what so ever, and the guy was so confident. But I felt the risk he took was totally unnecessary. In my books, it was a perfect example of an individual taking an uncalculated risk.

Even as we fished I couldn't talk the captain out of wearing the little dive bag he had strapped around his waist to carry lobster and small fish in. He didn't want his catch to dry up in the dinghy so instead he carried the half-dead bleeding fish around his waist. I kept thinking to myself – *this guy's got nerves of steel. My God what would happen if that shark followed us? Or what if other sharks are attracted to his fish? He wouldn't have a chance. The shark would go for his fish and at the same time probably take his leg or part of his body with it. How dangerous can it get?* Again the captain sluffed off my concerns and didn't think anything of it.

I never had the opportunity to dive with that captain again because within the next few days he picked up his anchor and set sail toward Western and American Samoa. We never saw him or heard of him again. I wonder if he ever survived the South Pacific. I'd be surprised if he did. However, one thing I learned, was to always treat sharks with respect. And why take uncalculated risks unnecessarily?

We stayed on at Suwarrow for awhile. Although we first thought it was uninhabited, we discovered we weren't alone if you were to count the wild chickens and numerous land crabs. It was obvious that during the war the island had been occupied and then later deserted.

Then one day an American sailed to the island, settled in a small one-room hut, grew a garden, built a swing (which Trevor enjoyed), raised chickens and lived a peaceful life into his old age until he passed away. It was the perfect tropical paradise. Fruit trees were abundant, a few wild chickens ran about, and a supply of fresh rainwater was there for the taking.

Cruisers and explorers who had stopped at this special island continued to maintain the garden and water cistern. A log book explained the history of the island and was used to keep records of who had visited, what improvements were made, and suggestions as to what needed to be done, so the next visitors could continue with the maintenance. It was all done in the spirit of preserving the original home.

With our fresh provisions continuing to deplete, we utilized the island's resources to make our stay more comfortable. A brilliant discovery was coconut pancakes. Since we still had lots of flour we used it to experiment with different ways to prepare coconut – the one thing we always had an abundance of. First we collected old coconuts that had fallen off palm trees and that had already sprouted. After splitting them open, inside where the milk normally was, we discovered a spongy textured mass. We sliced that spongy stuff into cubes and added it to pancake batter. The results were absolutely delicious, tasting a bit like raisins.

Another plentiful resource we discovered was frigate bird eggs. Being without eggs for some time, we really had a craving for them. If the wild chickens laid eggs, we certainly couldn't find them, or maybe the other cruisers beat us to them.

However, there was a large frigate nesting ground located on the reef at one end of the island where the birds continuously laid their eggs. Now frigate birds aren't exactly something you think of and smack your lips with delicious connotations – certainly not like turkey. No, on the contrary, they are relatives of the vulture, being a large black bird with a hooked beak and a very long body with extremely long wings and having a distinct scissor-like tail. As they are predators they commonly rob other birds of their prey. But now the shoe would be on the other foot. We would assume the role of being predators.

Shirley and I took Trevor, who was 16 months old, into the dinghy and motored out to the reef with a 5-gallon bucket filled with water. There we found a multitude of nests with eggs resting in them. As we approached, the frigate birds squawked and made a fuss but then flew off. Very gingerly we took eggs, one by one out of the nests and placed them in our bucket of water. If the egg sunk to the bottom that meant it was good to eat. However, if the egg floated to surface, it was a sign that a hatchling was already growing inside. We put those eggs back into their nests.

As it turned out the eggs were quite flavorful, having a slight fish taste to them, but definitely a delight to eat when you don't have much choice. Physiologically, we had to get over an obstacle, the egg's color. When fried, the egg whites didn't turn white like chicken eggs. Instead they were clear, like plastic. Also the yolk was much bigger than chicken eggs and the color was different. It varied from blood red to bright orange. They looked a little strange but if you closed your eyes, and you were really craving eggs, they tasted just fine. We used them to make our coconut pancakes and were happy that they allowed a variety of food we desired in our diet.

One day I decided it was time to catch more seafood. This time I ventured out alone. It wasn't long before I spotted a good sized, perhaps six or seven pound grouper, perfect for filleting and feeding our entire ship. I decided to pursue it. However each time I came close to the coral head it was hiding in, the grouper would detect me and quickly it would dash to another coral head. The pursuit lasted quite awhile. As determined as the grouper was to shake me off, I was determined to take it home for dinner. It wasn't a quitter and neither was I. We had met our match.

That grouper managed to dodge me until we got in an area of the reef where huge ocean rollers were breaking. Finally when it couldn't find a coral head to hide under, the grouper escaped through a cut in the reef to the calm waters inside. Now it was in a dead end area. The water was very murky, with the waves breaking on both sides of the cut, leaving a residue of foam. Nevertheless I decided to continue pursuing the grouper. As I swam through the narrow cut in the reef, I excepted the grouper to be trapped in the dead end where I would definitely spear it.

Visibility was poor but I continued to progress further into the cut. Suddenly I caught my breath. Right before me, virtually a few feet away, I found myself face to face with a shark lurking in the murky waters. Badly startled, my heart stopped beating. But simultaneously the shark also looked startled. We both stopped, dead in our tracks. Stunned, we stared at each other. The passage was so narrow that all I could do was throw my body to the right and lean against a coral head. The shark took advantage of the space I yielded. It quickly darted by me and escaped into the open ocean.

I don't know who scared whom more. I thought – *Wow, how lucky can you get?* It was the perfect opportunity for a shark to attack if it happened to be in the mood.

Overall, the whole scenario worked out well. Feeling totally humbled, I thanked the greater powers above, leaped into my dinghy and headed back to Nausikaa without the grouper. My face to face shark encounter was definitely one of the most dangerous and certainly the closest encounter I would ever have with any shark.

Sharks were a way of life in the South Pacific, as regular as flies are to honey. The water around Suwarrow was so shallow in places that to get to the beach everyone had to get out of the dinghy and walk a couple hundred feet over the reef, pulling the dinghy behind us. Baby sharks darted from deeper water toward us, their bellies dragging on the reef and their dorsal fins sticking out of the water. We'd all jump back into the dinghy and scare our intruders away by beating our oars on the water.

Respect for sharks was imperative. Thank God it was one of the first things the natives of Fanning Island taught us. The Chief had told us that most shark attacks his people encountered were while they were walking in knee deep water. After all, a small shark's perception of the size of a human leg is non-threatening to them. And chazam, a chunk would be gone. He said the minute you venture in water deep enough, you're to lay down. That way a shark, seeing the size of your whole body, will hopefully be intimidated and swim away.

But with all the sharks charging at us on Suwarrow not one of us dared to lie down. Instead we all jumped into the dinghy and waited until the little brats left.

Chapter 33

Dead in the Water

"Rarely do we achieve complete success in today's world without the help and support of others. The essence of teamwork is to identify and use the strengths of others to offset our own limitations, so that the strength of the team becomes greater than the sum of the individual parts."

... John Amatt

One of the boats we met in Suwarrow was skippered by a good looking American whom Deana took a liking to. He had single-handed his 28-foot boat as far as Suwarrow and was continuing to circumnavigate the world. Even though they were very compatible and mutually cared for each other, the skipper didn't want anyone to sail with him. He was determined to accomplish the feat alone. Heading toward our next port, American Samoa, we decided to make things a little more interesting – to race our heavy cruising ship against his sleek feather-light racing boat.

Our initial departure from Suwarrow was swift and measurable. The two boats closely sailed neck and neck until nightfall. By midnight the wind died to almost nothing and by the next morning we sat dead in the water – absolutely motionless. Our race was obviously over.

With no sight of Deana's boyfriend, we wondered if he scooted ahead of us and was lucky enough to still be sailing with good winds.

King Neptune provided more than perfect conditions, if our mode of transportation would've been a powerboat. Frustrated, we started the engine. Not one of us could bear the thought of being stuck out at sea, two short days away from a western style civilization. Among other things, we were anxious to re-provision. We had plenty nonperishables on board but without refrigeration we craved fresh meat and chicken, vegetables, fruit and our favorite landfall meal, the thing we all craved most – hot dogs and ice-cream.

Our fuel supply was very low but I estimated we would have just enough to get us to Pago Pago, the main port of American Samoa. I was almost right. We spotted the high volcanic peaks of the island after two days of motoring but as luck would have it, Nausikaa's engine sputtered to a complete stop. We sat there motionless for the completion of the day.

That night we saw the lights of Pago Pago but were unable to progress towards them. As much as I tried to restart the engine it was to no avail – there just wasn't any fuel in the tank. The next morning a little breeze inched us slightly closer but another day passed with little improvement. We were immobile and becoming more and more aggravated by the hour. In an attempt to stifle our frustration we decided to busy ourselves by preparing for our landfall. Out came the brushes. We diligently swabbed the decks, tidied below, and took our sea baths.

This was the first time anyone noticed Shirley's tummy was growing. Deana was bucketeering for Shirley's sea bath when she put two and two together. On purpose we hadn't shared our secret with the crew. Shirley didn't want to. She wanted to be just like one of the crew – with no special treatment. The excitement caused by our new revelation helped to make the day more upbeat and pass quicker but we still weren't progressing forward, at least not until that evening.

Finally, ever so lightly a breeze came out of the east just barely enough to cause a ripple in the water. We raised the sails and slowly got under way. As we neared Pago Pago we had a choice to either slip straight through a narrow passage between a little islet and the main island, which was the shorter route, or curve around the outside of the islet, which was a much clearer but longer route. I dithered the whole evening about which route to choose. Finally I made the decision.

Before going to sleep I left orders for the crew on the upcoming watch to take a course that would steer us well around both islands. I surmised if we went between the islands, our wind might be blocked since we'd be on the lee side of the little islet. I didn't want to be in a predicament with no means to maneuver our ship.

When Shirley got up in the darkness for her 6 a.m. watch, she was confused and somewhat alarmed when she went outside. *"What's happened? I thought Boris decided not to go between the islands?"* she questioned Peter.

"No, I don't think so – I was told by the last person on watch to go between the islands." Peter continued on his course, but by now the wind had completely died and Nausikaa drifted dangerously toward the big rollers cascading against the rugged shoreline.

It looked to Shirley that we were exactly in the predicament I had tried to avoid. *"Well I think Boris better check this out – it doesn't look good to me,"* she insisted.

Panicked that we were drifting way too close to the shore of the main island, she rushed down below and shook me awake. At first I thought all the excitement was because we must be close to Pago Pago but when I dashed up on deck I immediately knew that wasn't the case. We had barely inched our way forward during the night. And now, we were on the lea side of the islet, not on the windward side where I had intended to be. A light breeze now came over top of the main island creating a back wind that was slowly sucking us toward the rugged shoreline like a monster about to swallow it's prey.

Cripes! By the time I surveyed our situation and alerted the crew we were just a few boat lengths away from the perilous rocks boiling with the surf's rage. My heart was racing and pounding. I paced back and forth trying to figure out a solution. We were at nature's mercy. *What's a captain to do in a situation like this?* My head was bursting. The thunder of the crashing waves reminded me I didn't have much time.

I raced over to Nausikaa's starboard side and looked down into the water. Dawn was breaking, providing just enough light to see it was too deep to set an anchor. Damn! But that depth was probably our savior. Normally being this close to land we would've been aground for sure.

"The dinghy. Get the dinghy in the water. Quick!" I blurted, hardly able to spit out the words. I hoped that our two horsepower Seagull outboard would have the power to pull Nausikaa. We would have to work fast. But haste makes waste. As we rashly dropped the dinghy into the water from the poop deck one end of it nose-dived, swamping it half-full with water.

Now we were really in trouble! The outboard lay on the dingy floor covered in water. I leaped down into the dinghy and fumbled around in haste, finally managing to mount the motor.

Sailors know all about the legend of the Seagull outboard engine. Its reputation is such that you can submerge it under water, pull it out, crank it up and start it. But not this time. I frantically yanked on the start rope time and time again but it just wouldn't start. The waves roared louder. I agonized as we drifted closer and closer to shore.

I felt so helpless that I almost wanted to give up – to turn things over to the infinite powers to decide our fate. Swear words that had been stored away from my slaughterhouse era fluently and profusely flowed. I continued to pound on the engine but to no avail.

Ahhh...! Then it hit me. If a little two horsepower engine could pull us, why couldn't we? I yelled at Peter, Deana, Dan and Didier to grab their snorkel fins and jump into the water. They scrambled for the gear and were overboard in a flash. Shirley tied a long line to the ship's bow, throwing the other end to the crew. Frantically they swam as hard as possible the opposite way from shore.

It wasn't working. But at least we didn't seem to be getting sucked in like before. Then suddenly it *was* working. It was a sight to be seen. Our beloved Nausikaa was slowly inching away from the rocks.

A new burst of hope revived me and with renewed vigor I continued to yank on the starter rope. Preoccupied with my task at hand, I didn't notice that the dinghy hadn't been tied to the mother ship. But by the time I became aware of my predicament, Nausikaa was a fair ways from me.

The motor still wouldn't start so I started to paddle in an effort to catch up. To complicate matters, the farther away from the islet Nausikaa went, the more breeze filled her sails, and the faster the crew pulled her. Once totally clear of the islet Nausikaa started to sail fast enough on her own and in the right direction that the crew hopped back on board. But what about the captain?

What a sight that was. There was the *big captain*, paddling like heck in his little dinghy, while his ship was sailing away. A humorist couldn't have come up with a better cartoon. However, at the time I felt so stupid and frustrated.

Once a safe distance away from land the crew brought Nausikaa into the wind and waited for me. As I neared her everyone on board laughed their heads off – both with relief and also because of my predicament. *"Here comes our fearless captain,"* they joked. I felt smaller than a pea but happy to be on board and pleased with the outcome of our teamwork.

With a light breeze persisting throughout the day, we managed by late afternoon to reach Pago Pago's harbor entrance. At our request the U.S. Coastguard came and towed us to the fuel dock. It was perhaps one of the happiest arrivals in our sailing history. Having access to some western conveniences and supplies after being without them for such a long time was sheer luxury.

Pago Pago, the capital of American Samoa, is in a setting as tropical and lush as things get. Even when we were sailing beside the island to the harbor entrance we could smell the sweet floral aroma from the humid tropical foliage. Volcanic mountains that rose to sharp peaks surrounded the safe deep-water harbor. It was truly beautiful.

After clearing customs and feasting on ice cream cones, our top priority was for Shirley to visit a doctor just to confirm that her pregnancy was proceeding normally. No appointment was necessary in this part of the world, but we did wait our turn most of the day in a room full of very expectant mothers. Finally the nurse turned her attention to us. *"What's wrong?"* she asked Shirley.

"Nothing, I just came for a regular check up to make sure everything is ok," Shirley explained.

"But what is wrong girl?" the large woman insisted. And sounding a little irritated. *"Are you scared? Are you sick? What's your problem?"*

"No. I just came to get checked out because I haven't seen a doctor since we left Hawaii."

"Honey," she said, *"if you came here for someone to tell you that you're pregnant,"* she stood up, leaned her bulky body over the counter and looked at Shirley's bulging stomach and continued, *"well I can definitely say yes you're pregnant. Now go on home and unless something is wrong don't come back. You'll be just fine."* The nurse ushered us out of the waiting room.

Well so much for that! Our anxiety over not having regular check-ups was obviously for nothing, at least in this part of the world. Anyway Shirley usually felt great except when she faced seasickness from rough weather or when we departed after a prolonged stay in port. It always took her two to three days to get her sea legs back again. But once that was over she felt fine.

The influence of western civilization had its drawbacks. After a few days of being in a town busier than we were accustomed to we all became pretty edgy. We were itching to head out, to get back to face more adventures.

Nausikaa was fully provisioned, complete with ice and fresh meat, which would be a nice alternative to fish. Our dream was that one day we'd have enough money to install a freezer on board but for now that was a big pie in the sky.

After all we were content just to be heading back out to sea, our course set for Western Samoa. YES!

Chapter 34

Conflict with the Natives

"We have met the enemy and it is us."

… Walt Kelly

Life is like that. It seems that once you conquer one obstacle, another pops up and you need to learn how to overcome it quickly or it may give you more grief than you know how to handle.

The bay was perfect – picturesque and at the same time sheltered for safety. Such a calm anchorage as this lagoon, protected from the constant roll of the Pacific swells, was a rarity to find. We were fortunate to be the only vessel anchored in it.

On shore no human life was visible anywhere near the lush waterfront. It looked a little mysterious. If it weren't for the smoke bellowing skyward out of the tropical forest, you'd never guess anybody lived there. Out of caution, we anchored further out than normal.

As usual the crew rowed me in to investigate the whereabouts of the village Chief to request his permission to come ashore. Once permission was granted I sent for Shirley, Trevor and the rest of the crew.

As we all strolled through the village it quickly became evident that the settlement was the most primitive we had visited so far. The huts simply consisted of four stilts complete with woven coconut-palm rooftops. The sides, completely open, allowed us to peer in as we strolled through the jungle. Inside each hut was an open fire pit with a large pot hanging over it.

The men must have been elsewhere – busy fishing, hunting or working the land. Women, children and a few elders were inside their huts. Most women were topless draped only with their *lava-lava* (wrap around skirt). Once they spotted us the younger ones covered up but the older ones never bothered as they went about their daily chores.

There was no big celebration planned in our honor like we had experienced on some other islands, but the people treated us nicely. A few young men spoke some broken English, which was a special treat, enabling us to piece together some information about the Western Samoan culture and its people.

A few young men took us on an adventurous expedition through the topical rain forest into the jungle where we climbed a mountain peak. A special treat was the discovery of a natural water slide tucked away in the heavenly setting. We spent hours cascading down the mountainside into a pristine pool below. Screams and laughter echoed through the rain forest as we flew over the steep cliff, trying not to land a back or belly flop.

Making us look like amateurs, the local boys hung onto vines like Tarzan, swinging off a cliff then plunging down into the water underneath. Finally exhausted, we would regain our energy, wading below through natural water pools with Shirley who had opted not to play to protect her unborn child. For what seemed like an eternity we frolicked like young children in the coolness of the deep tropical rain forest. Without our local guides we could never have found such a treasure.

The older folks treated us with a similar generosity. They shared their fruit and vegetables, which was of huge importance to us. Finding fresh produce on a regular basis was very infrequent with most of the islands not having a commercial way to distribute it. Also many of the islands we chose to visit were uninhabited. This was a great but rare re-provisioning opportunity.

The next day, Sunday, we decided to invite all the local villagers to come and visit us aboard Nausikaa. It was going to be a new experience for us but we all agreed it would be a great gesture to show our gratitude and appreciation as we constantly struggled to think of methods to reimburse the local populace for their genuine kindness and hospitality.

Our guided tour was to take place in the afternoon following the local religious ceremony. It was our intention to run our dinghy back and forth to the beach, pick up a group of four to six people, give them a tour of Nausikaa, and then return them to the beach to pick up the next group.

News of our invitation spread like wildfire throughout the village and by noon the beach buzzed with people. Obviously it was going to be an active day. But to our surprise, we made only one pick up. By the time we returned to Nausikaa with our first group, the remaining village people were afloat, heading toward us. Hundreds of them of all ages swam, floated, or were being towed toward us. I am sure every peace of flotsam in the village was being utilized – outriggers, logs, inner tubes, even bits of styrofoam. Anything that could float was being used as a vehicle to carry people in our direction.

I feared some would drown. It was obvious that many couldn't swim. And once they arrived I had more worries. Crowd control was virtually impossible, with nobody understanding us. Over the sides they climbed, all around us like pirates. I couldn't believe the ages of some that tried to climb up our rope ladder. It was overwhelming. As hard as we tried we couldn't stop the blitz.

At first we managed to form a flowing line that led people through Nausikaa from the aft cabin into the main and forward cabins, and then outside. The crew spread themselves through the ship guiding our visitors through, while I tried to fend off others climbing on board. It was an impossible task, as no one cared to understand a word I was saying. I tried being loud and gruff but got no results. And once people were on board there was no way to get them off.

Nobody budged. At times Nausikaa III was listing so much I feared she might capsize. I wasn't comfortable with the situation but could do very little to change it unless I started to throw people off the ship and that was easier said than done. Young well-built Samoan warriors, totally tattooed from just above their knees up to their necks, were huge. I was intimidated just looking at them, never mind confronting them.

In amazement, we watched the child-like people admire the things we considered our meager possessions. A favorite of the ladies was Nausikaa's high-gloss varnished wood. They stroked it as if it were precious, their eyes glazed over expressing awe and disbelief. Something as simple as a dozen mismatched coffee mugs hanging from ceiling hooks in the galley blew them away. I couldn't fathom the mystery or attraction but it was obvious they were fascinated with them. I don't know if the fascination was because the cups hung off hooks suspended high up or if they found the cups beautiful in comparison to their home made coconut-shell ones.

The men, on the other hand, were more intrigued with such things as Peter's backpack, the toilet, spearfishing spears, and the ship's sails and rigging.

Commotion, chatter and laughter were in abundance. In fact it would have even been enjoyable had we been able to control the number of people on board. Instead every inch of the ship, from the bow to the stern, was filled, and more people continued piling on board over the sides and shinnying up the rigging.

As I watched them pile on, the more panic-stricken I felt. We were totally besieged with no practical way of dealing with the situation. Again I shook my head in disbelief at the age of some of the people that made it all the way out to the ship. Old toothless ladies grinned at me with at hint of shyness but proud to be on board. They were so adorable but all I wished myself was for everyone to get the heck off my ship. Thankfully, even though so many people were on board, the ship was laden but balanced.

Needless to say the afternoon dragged on until finally the sun dropped behind a mountaintop which motivated people to leave.

We finally had Nausikaa back to ourselves. Frazzled but relieved, we all convened in the cockpit, looking at each other and shaking our heads in disbelief. We began to swap stories, mulling over all the events of the day, when Denver Dan happened to notice his expensive hiking shoes were missing from the cockpit. Then it was a chain-like reaction. Didier noticed his thongs were gone. And then Peter, Deana, Shirley and I noticed some of their possessions missing as well.

Once we finished taking inventory it was obvious that anything that had not been tucked away in drawers or tied down was gone. All our footwear that had been lying about, t-shirts, some cutlery and even fishing gear. But what infuriated me the most was that our dinghy paddles were missing. Incredulously, we had been robbed in broad daylight right before our eyes.

My mind raged knowing that we could not go to sea without dinghy paddles. Having no inflatable life raft on board, we depended on our hard catamaran dinghy and little sailing dingy not only for transportation but also as a lifesaving device. Going back to sea without paddles was not negotiable. Furious over the whole incident, I went to sleep that night only to dream of boarding pirates with knives between their teeth.

The next morning I was determined to retrieve our stuff. When I rounded up the men I knew spoke a little English they denied that anything could've been stolen. Looking puzzled they had no solution to offer but vigorously and at great length chattered in their native tongue. I was exasperated – determined to retrieve our belongings and bring the thieves to justice.

Finally I chose to go directly to the Chief to request his personal intervention. Using our local translators I investigated for hours trying to uncover the mystery of our missing stuff. We seemed to be getting nowhere, but on the other hand I was starting to get a picture of what had actually happened. Difficulty in understanding each other was evident since the Chief couldn't comprehend such terms as *stealing, theft* or *banditos*. Clearly we were deadlocked in a cultural misunderstanding.

From the beginning I approached the issue from the viewpoint that the culprits must be found, our stuff retrieved, and the thieves punished. The Chief and I didn't seem to be communicating on the same parallel but by reviewing the situation, I started to realize there was no such concept as stealing in their culture.

They believed – what is mine is yours and what is yours is mine. If you need something of mine, just help yourself. If I need something of yours, I'll help myself to it. To accuse or punish someone just for taking something would be totally against their belief. In the name of community sharing, everyone on the island unselfishly helped each other.

Once I started to grasp the concept of their system I started to re-configure my tactic for my request with the Chief. Still the remaining challenge was to retrieve our stuff. Who was in possession of it? Instead of feeling and acting like a victim, I started to change my focus on the circumstances. My new approach to the Chief went something like this.

"Chief, tomorrow my ship go bye-bye, to a far-far away island. We need paddles for our boat because the big sea is dangerous. We can't leave without paddles. When we get to a far-far away island we need our shoes and clothes because over there we are going to meet another great Chief, like you. To survive we need to catch fish so we need our fishing gear. You are a great Chief. You call your people and ask them who has those things? Ask them to share it with us so that we can leave." What can I say? It was worth a try!

After spending most of the day conversing, I felt our cultural gap had closed and I had a better understanding of why the incident happened. The Chief did a great job saving his community's face considering the limited translation available to us. The natural evolution of our cross-cultural seminar opened my mind and the lessons I learned will continue to serve me for the rest of my life.

By the time I bade the Chief goodbye I felt somewhat like a jerk for barging into his community – accusing, threatening, demanding and insisting on imposing the laws of my society on his. I will always wonder if it was an accident that we stumbled on a solution to our problem or if it was the Chief's philosophical ability and intuitiveness that took me, spun me around, and made me understand his culture, which ultimately changed my opinion of his people. In any case I was satisfied with his suggestion that he would see what they had to *share* with us.

The first thing the next morning I woke up, walked out on the aft deck and looked off our stern. To my delight just about everything missing was in the dinghy, complete with the paddles. Denver Dan's hiking boots, a pair of thongs and a couple other small articles weren't returned but overall we were ecstatic with our newfound situation. Not a sound had been heard during the night, but obviously the natives came, deposited the stuff into our dinghy and quietly left. I asked the crew if they wanted to stay to ask for the remaining missing items, but Dan and Peter jokingly agreed to *share* their shoes with the islanders.

We all learned a lesson, an invaluable one of tolerance toward others. It was a paradox. Things hadn't been the way they looked. On this special island we discovered not only beauty in the surroundings, but beauty in the people – a special human quality the locals possessed, when in fact we thought it had been the reverse.

With the oars back in our possession and with a lesson well learned, we set sail toward our next unforeseen adventure, in search of Tonga!

Chapter 35

Onions Did It!

"Every gift, though it may be small, is in
reality great if given with affection."

… Pindar

I never understood why the local South Pacific populace rose so early, but I was especially reminded of it one morning as a jolting rap on Nausikaa's hull jarred us all out of our sleep. Usually an abrupt early awakening meant our anchor had dragged overnight and a concerned neighbor was warning us, or we had anchored in a prohibited area, but this time it wasn't the case.

Just the evening before we had chosen this peaceful looking cove to anchor in but now I wondered what the rude arousing was all about. Shirley's automatic reflex, her elbow jabbing my ribs, signaled that she wasn't the one going up on deck.

Coming outside I couldn't help but notice a spray of pink in the eastern horizon announcing a fresh day about to begin. Not pleased to be up so early, I was prepared to growl at the responsible culprits, but for some reason didn't. I discovered two men standing in their hand chiseled outrigger canoe. They looked as if they'd barely woken up themselves and had come straight out to see us. One man spoke a teeny bit of English and after a long bout of hand motions and facial expressions I began to get the drift for the reason of their visit. The King of Tonga's birthday was coming up and the men wanted us to contribute some food for the celebration. *"This occasion – special. Big holiday in Tonga. Need food – make party good,"* one man explained.

I shook my head bewildered at their request. I wondered how sincere they were. On one hand I was still a little annoyed and feeling defensive because I wondered if I had a couple early morning scammers on my hands, but on the other hand I was sorry that we didn't have much to offer. We had a limited amount food for ourselves with provision opportunities being few and far between. Our canned food supply was plentiful but we were very low on fresh produce, which spoiled quickly in the tropical heat.

I chuckled to myself at their ingenuity to scam food from us but I just couldn't bring myself to say no. After all, through our travels it was the native people that shared their locally grown food with us. Things like yam, papaya, taro root, pumpkin, banana, passion fruit, breadfruit, mango, oranges and other stuff we didn't even recognize. *Perhaps this was our opportunity to give back,* I thought to myself, or maybe I just wanted to get rid of them so I could go back to bed.

I returned with a couple cans of corned beef but the men just frankly stood there waiting without saying a word. I got the message. Back I went for a few boxes of spaghetti, but apparently that wasn't enough either. The older of the two men explained there would be many people at the celebration, giving me a clear indication to cough up more stuff. I was becoming more annoyed by the minute, astonished at their boldness and ungratefulness. In my opinion they had scored big already and here they were demanding even more.

I tried to think what might satisfy them. Then I remembered we had tons of onions, the better part of a 50-pound sack, since out of all the fresh fruit and vegetables the onions had lasted the longest. I decided to share half of them with the men. As I handed the onions down into the outrigger, they beamed with delight. *Bingo!* They thanked me profusely and, ecstatic with their results, rowed back to the village.

Since we were up anyway, we decided to go ashore to explore the village. Tonga was known for its quaint islands and villages. We had briefly stopped to clear customs at the capital of the Vavau Group, but found that the town was much too busy for us. This outer island was more our pace where the donkeys ruled the roads.

Before long we bumped into one of the rude men responsible for waking us up that morning. Eagerly he shook our hands, and beamed with pride as he offered to take us to meet the village Chief. We were to learn that he was not only the Chief's brother but also a cousin to the King of Tonga. Wow, had I ever figured him wrong.

We were introduced to the Chief as *the people who had contributed the onions.* Cringe! At first I wanted to crawl under a rock and hide, embarrassed for contributing so poorly. But then I realized something major must've happened when the Chief eagerly welcomed me, shaking my hand and embracing me. Never did any Chief do that on our first meeting!

That event was the catalyst for the quickest bonding experience ever with the natives. From that moment on we had an open invitation to eat and play with the Chief and villagers. Wherever we went on the island, we were introduced as *the people who had contributed the onions.* It caused the natives to gleam with delight and there was nothing they wouldn't do for us. To this day I could never figure out exactly why.

The young native men introduced us to a new way to hunt lobster. Contrary to the Gilbertese people further north, the Tongans loved lobster. But the trick was to find their holes, usually in 20 to 60 feet of water, where they gathered in large numbers. Normally the holes were protected by small openings and were camouflaged, but what usually gave them away was a pair of telltale tentacles poking out. Once a hole was discovered a great catch was assured. Diving down to it, the natives used a slingshot to fling a narrow two-foot steel rod with such precision that it would zap right through the lobster.

The Tongans also introduced us to kava. It was a drink made from pulverized root mixed with water. It was in essence a tranquilizer.

It didn't look very appealing, as the brownish-gray substance resembled muddy slough water. It makes me gag just to be reminded of it, but it could've been worse. Apparently in days gone by, instead of mixing the dry kava with water they used to chew it, get their saliva juices flowing, and spit the whole lot back into a halved coconut shell, just to pass it to the next person.

In an effort to relax through the mid day heat or after dinner in the evening, the natives would consume a few swigs of the muddy concoction, become tranquilized, settle in a comfortable position and *veg*. I felt kava fell into the drug category so I encouraged the crew not to use it.

Throughout the South Pacific, the Chiefs looked at my status of a sea captain to being equal with them, and therefore the Tongan Chief felt insulted when I wasn't too enthusiastic to share some kava with him. (A similar parallel would be, refusing to smoke a peace pipe with a North American Native Indian Chief while visiting their tribe.) Realizing the importance of the ritual, I sat next to the Chief and pretended to slug back the odd tasting liquid. Instantaneously I felt my lips and tongue turn numb just from touching the liquid so I could only imagine the numb state my hosts were in for after an hour or two's indulgence.

English was a rarity with the out-island natives so it was a delight to meet Johnny, the Chief's cousin, who spoke a few words of English. Johnny's wife, Mary, really took to Trevor, constantly playing with him, feeding and looking after him. Never hard to locate, Trevor had (as usual) an entourage of children and adults alike keeping an eye on him. It was then when Johnny invited us to come and visit his home at the far end of the island, just a few miles away from the village. We promised to stop for a couple days on our route out of Tonga toward Fiji as it was along our route.

Finally, it was the day of the king's birthday celebration. I didn't realize that little island would transform into a major cultural extravaganza, as it was the epicenter for Tonga's northern Vavau group of islands. Chiefs and elders from other islands and villages came to celebrate. Boats, dangerously overloaded with people, came from every direction. Foreign dignitaries and business people, likewise the media – radio and television crews from New Zealand and Australia miraculously ascended.

The natives dressed in their traditional clothing, and visitors dressed in light suits and other fine tropical outfits. Even the local island priest dressed in a black suit complete with white collar and offered blessings for our mid-day feast. Since Nausikaa's complete crew was officially invited to attend the celebrations, we too dressed in our best shorts, t-shirts and whatever footwear we could scrounge together, after our *sharing* experience a few islands before. Needless to say I felt uncomfortable amongst the well-dressed and influential foreigners who attended. In comparison, we probably looked like a band of rag tag hillbillies.

The morning was filled with traditional events. Young warriors, their bodies painted and tattooed, performed loud energetic war dances, while young women with enchanting and gracious body movements, danced and sang songs about life in the islands by the seaside. A good natured tug-of-war between the rival island tribes was a hoot to watch as the losers wound up in a hole filled with thick mud. The crowd cheered as they watched the enormous men, their bodies covered in muck, trying to crawl out of the pit. It was no wonder so many had come from far and wide to witness this spectacle.

Then it was time to feed the crowds. Seated at the head table, under a straw covered roof propped up by stilts, were the village Chief and his entourage. On each end, two long rows extended outward with straw mats placed on the ground for people to sit on. Between the two rows was another row of mats, heaped with food. The head table was actually raised off the ground, coffee-table height. On top of it, specially prepared dishes were displayed – roast pig, chicken, lamb, fish, octopus, lobster and you name it. I also noticed that there were a few things not offered to the others – watermelon, floral arrangements, and the ultimate feature, cigarette bouquets.

It was an example of the local people's creative ingenuity. The *bouquets* consisted of long skinny straws extending from simple wood vases. At the end of each straw a filtered cigarette was attached. It looked pretty decadent for these latitudes, a definite sign of prosperity and obviously the ultimate treat for smokers. Normally they cut their tobacco leaves with a sharp knife or machete and hand rolled each cigarette. Very few people could afford, or even have the opportunity to buy, filtered cigarettes.

I looked for signs of our contribution, but so far there was no evidence of it amongst the mountains of food. Then the shock of our lives came. The Chief's brother who had awakened us so early came to fetch us and lead us to the head table. Apparently the Chief and village elders requested that we be seated with them.

We were bewildered as to why! *How come we deserved such special treatment?* I wondered. Thrilled but at the same time feeling unworthy. *Can't these people see we're just nobodies, a bunch of idealistic kids in search of a silly dream? Can't they see that we're not influential or wealthy and that by all the laws of universe,* as I understood it, *weren't even supposed to be here. Whoever's doing this please stop it. It's not funny any more.*

It was a constant struggle in my mind, making me feel uncomfortable and self-conscious. *How could we be worthy of all this?* I wondered.

The Chief distracted me. *"Mar-ae! Mar-ea!"* he hollered out, motioning me to do the same. We clapped our hands and cheered. A member of the New Zealand news team stopped by and whispered in my ear as I munched on the goodies at our table, *"How come you and your crew get to sit at the head table?"*

"I guess we just got lucky," I replied. What he didn't know was the onions must've done it!

Chapter 36

Johnny and Mary's Paradise

"I have no special gift, I am only passionately curious."

… Albert Einstein

If there is such a thing as an ideal place on this planet, I think we found it!

A lonely hut, simply composed of palm leaves and straw, sat tucked beside a coconut grove. Directly across from it was a beautiful expanse of white sand, the beach stretching far out to a point. Serene turquoise-blue water encircled the numerous islands that sheltered the bay. Nausikaa III peacefully rested at anchor parallel to the grass hut to complete the enchanted setting. It was a scene I had yearned to be in years before we ever set out on our voyage of discovery. And now we were.

Shirley and I couldn't help but fall deeper in love as we walked hand in hand along the beach watching Trevor contently play in the sand on the shallow water's edge. As Shirley became tired we lay in the shade under a coconut tree, both touching her stomach to feel our baby flutter in her tummy, pondering over his or her name. Without a doubt these days were times of excellence – the best in our lives.

Close by was an older local couple, Mary and Johnny, who watched Trevor intently. They were absolutely entranced by him. That was actually the reason why we had come to spend time with them. In the South Pacific the whole society revolves around children, with them being the most significant parts of their lives. Mary and Johnny's desire to have children was obvious but unfortunately they had been unable to, and now they were too old. Since they loved being around Trevor, they were delighted that we anchored in front of their property.

Originally we thought we'd stay only a couple of days just to recuperate from the king's birthday celebration, but Mary and John were so sweet, asking us to stay forever. It was a tempting thought. So it wasn't surprising that we were well into our second week before we decided it was time to leave.

Even though Johnny and Mary lived so close to the water they didn't know how to swim – which wasn't an unusual thing for the locals. Through a comical dance of sign language and a few understandable words of English, we got the message across that they were invited onboard Nausikaa for lunch, but only Johnny agreed to come. We assumed Mary wouldn't risk the dinghy ride out to the ship.

Once on board it was obvious that it was Johnny's first experience aboard a sailing yacht. Nausikaa was a simple ship but to Johnny she must've been a palace. He walked around in a daze examining everything with incredulous awe.

Incredibly, he had a hard time figuring out how to slide onto the bench seat under our dining table. Even though I demonstrated how to do it, Johnny bent over and with a puzzled look on his face could not for the life of him figure out how to sit down and slide in. When I continued to demonstrate he looked under the table and broke into laughter when he discovered where my legs had disappeared.

Once we managed to sit him down we all feasted on canned corn beef and sauerkraut, which he devoured with great pleasure. He followed our example of eating, using plates and forks versus coconut shells and fingers.

Finally we broke the news that we were planning to depart the next day. Johnny lowered his head, stared down at his feet and became very quiet. It was going to be a difficult departure but I knew we had to keep up the pace for two reasons. In Fiji we planned to hook up with Henry, Francie and their two sons for another two-week charter. Being low on funds, we desperately needed that charter to ensure the necessary finances to continue on. Secondly, we needed to be in closer proximity to New Zealand or Australia, in time for our new baby's arrival.

We dropped Johnny off on shore but within minutes he caught our attention, hailing us back to the beach. He cheerfully announced that he and Mary wanted to prepare a big farewell lunch for all of us before we left the next day. Even though we had planned our departure for first thing in the morning we agreed to delay it until after lunch.

The next morning about nine o'clock Johnny hailed us to the beach once again. Wildly upset, he was trying to express that something was wrong. I tried to figure out what! He was so disturbed, that I realized leaving today was out of the question. Then he proceeded to describe something about a pig that got away. For the life of me and for the longest time I couldn't understand what a run-away pig had to do with our departure but each time I motioned with my hands for Johnny to explain again, the more upset he became.

Finally I got it! For our going away lunch Johnny and Mary had planned a big feast consisting of seafood and the local specialty, umu roasted pig. It was one of our favorites. The locals would dig a deep hole in the ground and partially fill it in with fist-sized rocks. Then they built a hot fire over the rocks. Next they would clean and season the pig and dress it in herbs and then generously wrap it with banana leaves. After removing the hot coals from the fire, the wrapped pig would be placed on top of the hot rocks and then liberally buried with dirt. And presto, after six hours of slow cooking the succulent pork was ready to eat.

The thing that infuriated Johnny was his wife not being able to catch a pig that morning. Being semi-wild, the pigs roamed in the coconut grove during the day. However, at daybreak Mary would feed them husked and dried coconut meat (like the grated coconut used for baking, but it was in chunks). For special occasions, when they wanted to eat pork, it was Mary's job to catch a pig. To succeed she would get a rock, fling it at the pig, hit it on the head and knock it out, butcher it, spice it, wrap it in herbs and banana leaves and put it on the hot rocks that Johnny had prepared. Bingo, a feast would be on the way.

The reason Johnny was upset this morning was because Mary's aim was off. Her rock didn't hit her target. Instead the scared pigs scattered into the grove. Regardless of how hard they tried to lure the pigs back, they were unsuccessful. Sometimes life is not easy. And I guess living in the tropics has its own trials as well. Rats! That meant we would have to delay our departure so Mary could have another try. Not wanting to offend Johnny or Mary, I agreed to wait for the feast that was now rescheduled for the next day.

In the meantime, there was something else in the area I had heard about which intrigued me and now I was motivated to check it out. One of the natives in a nearby village had told us about an uninhabited island just a few miles from Johnny and Mary's. *"There you can take your dinghy and paddle your way through an incredible maze of caves,"* he had said.

But what really interested me was his account of a special hidden cavern. Describing the cavern's precise location, he explained that it was possible to free-dive deep down along a rocky bluff and swim underneath it, to surface inside in a beautiful large cave. He recommended that the best time to attempt it was in the afternoon because the sunlight would reflect through the water, illuminating the underwater cavern.

Our afternoon excursion proved to be even more beautiful than we imagined. The conditions were mild, cloudless and wind free. Sparkling like a diamond, the turquoise blue ocean seemed to blend into the infinite sky. The sun's rays were bright and warm, yet gentle. Motoring over to our destination, we positioned Nausikaa adjacent to the caves.

Playing like children, the crew dove off her bow into the tepid 80-degree bath-like water, performing somersaults and cannon balls and swimming into the caves. I rowed Trevor and Shirley into a large cave in our dinghy and as we glanced back we saw a perfect picture – a silhouette of Nausikaa framed by the cave walls *(see the back book cover)*. We were captivated. The day, the whole experience, was definitely one of those special *magic moments in life* one never forgets.

Later I snorkeled the area, exploring for an entrance to the underwater cavern. But regardless of how hard I hunted, I couldn't seem to detect any signs that revealed it. As far as my eyes could see the side of the cliff went straight down deep into the water. After discovering the above-water markings, which indicated the entrance area, the only option was to free dive to see if what the native said was actually true. Sensing this might be a dangerous maneuver; I left detailed instructions with Shirley and our crew about what to do if I ran into difficulty.

One thing I prided myself for was my ability to deep dive free style, without the use of an oxygen tank. So with youthful determination I resolved if the natives could do it, why couldn't I? This proved to be foolish thinking on my part but for sure it was a big lesson.

After several relaxed deep breaths, I inhaled a big gulp of air and submerged, head first kicking my fins to propel me directly down the bluff into the dark deep water. After quite awhile the bluff started to curve under. I thought – *Yes! Soon I'll start my ascent and be inside the cavern.*

But the farther I followed the curvature of the bluff, the further it stretched under the island. The deep water was cold and it was hard to see in the darkness. I was starting to run out of air but was sure that any time now I would be able to surface inside the cavern. No such luck!

Time for Plan B. *I'm out of here* I thought. Then on second thought I realized I was too far-gone to turn back. If I tried, I'd surely be in trouble. My lungs were bursting as it was. I had no choice. My only option was to keep going forward and to hope to God that the native's instructions were accurate. And hopefully I was in the right location!

One thing I did know for sure, *I was trapped and if I didn't find the cavern soon, I would pass out and this was going to be my graveyard*. I wasn't ready to die at such a young age. My mind raced to find an answer for my predicament. By now my lungs burned and the bursting pressure behind my eyes was beyond human tolerance but somehow I continued to press forward feeling my way as I went. I tried to control the overwhelming panic that wanted to take my body prisoner. *Where was the end of this thing? Was there an end?*

Then finally the curvature abruptly ended allowing me to ascend. At first I was relieved but there was still a long distance to cover before reaching the surface inside the cavern, assuming there was one. I prayed, desperately hoping for a pocket of air somewhere. Strangely, the higher up I went, the darker it became. Overcome with dizziness and in a mental haze, I wondered if I was passing out or if the light just couldn't reach this far.

In my panic I thought how stupid this was and how my mom and dad's prophesy was coming true. No wonder Dad was so concerned. He must have intuitively known that he would lose his only son. *The news of my death and not being able to say a final goodbye would break his heart* I thought. The words *I am so sorry Dad* loudly echoed through my mind. I wasn't fearful any more. I was too busy apologizing to my loved ones. I was giving up and didn't really care.

Then suddenly my hands broke through the water's surface and for a brief second I could see a dark outline of a cavern. I gasped uncontrollably for air but then instantly everything turned white as if I had been submerged in milk. The first thing that crossed my mind was the absolute whiteness must be the bright light en route to the hereafter. I felt light-headed and weak and could hear myself gasping for air but all I could see was total whiteness. *So this is what it's like to die* I thought.

Then as quickly as the whiteness appeared it disappeared. Now, with a clear vision I could make out stunning images inside the cavern. They were accentuated by reflections of light that danced off the cavern walls and ceiling and penetrated into the water. Then once again, I quickly drifted back into total whiteness.

I was confused. Was I dying or coming back to life? The longer I was able to breathe, the more revived I felt, so I rubbed my eyes and massaged my upper body in an effort to revitalize myself. Sure enough the whiteness disappeared and it was clear again. *Perhaps I was drifting between life and death* I thought.

After a couple more episodes of whiteouts and clearings, I realized that the whiteness had nothing to do with me dying but with the water surge. Even though there had been no wind and the sea was totally flat, the deep ocean swell still surged in. With each swell, the water level in the cavern raised, compressing the trapped air. For whatever reason, within a few seconds the air went from being clear to totally milky, like a thick San Franciscan fog. Then as the swell receded, the air cleared up again. It was such an interesting phenomenon that once I realized I was safe I actually enjoyed studying it.

The secret cavern would have made a perfect hideout for a pirate's treasure. Under different circumstances it would've been a great place to explore. But now I had to focus on the challenge of overcoming my fear of how I was ever going to make it back out of this hole. For a long time I meditated and rehearsed over in my mind the swim back to the ship. Even though I was not cold I had difficulty controlling my trembling body.

Resting on a rock, I shook my head, disbelieving my stupidity. How could I have allowed myself to get into this predicament? It was my second closest encounter with death, the first one when I was electrocuted on the roof of my home in Croatia at the age of 14.

Frozen with fear but knowing there was only one way out, I

mustered up my nerve to finally do it. I gave up on my first try when I was barely under water and became panic stricken. After a second and third very good try, I had to return again. I started to fear that I'd be stuck in the cavern until a rescue party retrieved me.

On my fourth try I didn't have high expectations of success, but then, like magic, I got the courage to continue and swam like crazy until I saw the brightness in the water from the sun on the other side of the bluff. This time the pain in my lungs was just as excruciating, but I knew I wasn't going to die.

When I made it back on board Nausikaa, I didn't intend to tell the mother of my *heir to be* what happened because there was no need to frighten her. I am sure she wondered what went on because I kept chuckling to myself the rest of that day recounting what happened in that cavern. What she didn't know was the sheer fact that I was just happy to be alive.

I was surely content to be once again anchored in front off Johnny and Mary's point that evening. With a totally different zest for life I relished the sight of the red-tinted sky as the sun dipped beyond the horizon. I hugged Shirley with my right arm, feeling some of the first movements of our tiny baby in her tummy with my left. Every couple minutes I found a reason to peck a little kiss somewhere on her body. I was very thankful to be still alive, spending another day with my sweetheart and son.

Early the next morning Johnny was again sitting on his beach patiently waiting for us to wake up. That was his signal for us to go see him. As I rowed the dinghy toward the shore it was evident he was a happy man. *"Mary's aim – perfect today,"* he told me. *"Feast soon."*

And we were delighted to do so.

Chapter 37

The Cannibal
Encounter

"There are places to go beyond belief."

... Neil Armstrong

Suva, the capital of Fiji had perhaps the best health care out of all in the South Pacific islands we had visited so far and we took advantage of it. Finally Shirley had her first real pregnancy examination and we were delighted to hear that our new addition to the crew would be joining us in less than six weeks. By now she was quite big and was feeling the humidity and extreme heat of Suva but generally she enjoyed good health.

We reveled in the modern world conveniences Suva had to offer. It was by far the most advanced of the islands we visited. Trevor, not seeing cars for so long, would point at the passing traffic and say *"boats"*. Obviously we had to update his vocabulary now that we were back in civilization.

We shopped and re-provisioned Nausikaa for what I predicted would be a fast voyage to New Caledonia. There was no time to waste. Shirley looked as if she were going to have the baby any minute. Her stomach stuck out a mile in front of her. For some reason I felt she had never been so big with Trevor but she insisted that I just didn't remember. Perhaps this time I cared for her well being in a different way, feeling that it would be my responsibility if something went amiss.

Fiji was a wonderful place and had so much to offer with hundreds of islands to explore. We wanted to do it all but were plainly running out of time. For two weeks our crew enjoyed land-lubbing and taking in the city nightlife. Meanwhile Shirley, Trevor and I took our American repeat charter guests, Henry and Francie, for a two-week cruise through some of the Fijian islands. The charter couldn't have come at a more perfect time as our money supply was quickly depleting. Just when I had started to wonder where the necessary money was going to come from to continue our voyage, we'd received a letter announcing their wish to join us. Yes!

Fiji wasn't a place to get easy work like Hawaii was. I felt that if we could only make it to New Zealand or Australia, it would be easier to replenish our meager finances. We had been so blessed to meet Henry and Francie in Hawaii. Again they were our saviors, providing the financial fuel necessary to continue our voyage.

While we were in Fiji it was wonderful to receive mail from our family and friends as well. Needless to say we felt a lot of anxiety in our parent's letters, with phrases like *"We hope you get to read this letter. We worry about you."*

They were also ecstatic to receive our correspondence we had sent along the way, confirming we were still alive. But in their letters it wasn't hard to read between the lines – they couldn't wait for the whole episode to come to an end. My father was so concerned for the safety and health of our unborn child that he kept begging me to send Shirley and Trevor to their home. They would've been delighted to have them until I was finished with the expedition. It was obvious how much pain, heartache and sleepless nights it was causing them.

I thought that my mother was exaggerating when she wrote that Dad was quite sick and not taking to our adventure too well. Her first letter that mentioned the problem come to us in Hawaii but then, like now, I just interpreted it as a plot to make us stop sailing. After all, any memory related to my dad's health was – other than the odd cold – he never went to see a doctor.

Our goal continued to be our focus and with replenished finances we were more determined than ever to continue as planned. Our course would allow us a few more stops in the Fijian Island chain before spring-boarding off to New Caledonia. From New Caledonia it would be a maximum two-week hop, skip and a jump to reach either Auckland or Sydney where our Kiwi or Aussie would be born.

Once again Shirley didn't take too well to our first day at sea. Her proneness to seasickness was hard to watch, especially when she was going through her throwing up attacks. She heaved so hard and long that I feared it would bring about premature labor. I was amazed she was so sick this time. The sea wasn't all that rough. In fact it would be considered a great sailing day under normal circumstances but I guess her pregnancy just made it tough on her. Unable to watch her suffer any more, I decided to pull into the closest island we'd been tacking alongside.

As we pulled into the lagoon, I noticed the lush tropical jungle setting. At first glance it looked as if there were no settlements near shore, which we assumed meant nobody to visit. Also there was no beach. The crew craved going to the beach after being stuck in town for two and a half weeks. My choice of anchorage, not a popular one, caused a great deal of tension. However, Shirley instantly recovered when we anchored in the calm lagoon.

Being too late in the day to explore the island, we stayed on board and bickered among ourselves over the poor choice of our stop. Immediately I realized that the continuity of our team had been broken because the crew had left the ship and spent so much time on land. Now it seemed like it was just *old hat* to be out here sailing again.

The crew's focus had changed. Deana missed the friend she had first met at Suwarrow and then left behind in Suva, Figi. Didier now considered going to Tahiti rather than continuing to Australia. Denver Dan wanted to meet up with friends he met in Suva who had flown on to Raratonga in the Cook Islands. Peter was the only one that was still into sailing but his time was limited and he would soon have to go back to university. Before he did so he wanted to squeeze in a quick visit to Australia.

Restless tension raged the whole evening and left us all feeling somewhat bitter. The next morning Shirley and I woke up early, wanting to take Trevor for a walk before anyone else got up. Quietly we paddled our dinghy to shore. Discovering a small dirt trail, we followed it up a hill. Since it didn't appear to be well traveled, we didn't expect to see much, especially not many people. From our vantage point on the hill top, we saw streams of smoke trailing skyward from the forest in a valley. Curious as ever, we decided to explore further.

Ooops – I thought as we entered the village. Not only was it unexpectedly large, but what was so striking were the people. Large men, dressed in traditional grass skirts, threateningly held wooden war clubs and spears studded with shark teeth. Their faces were painted with war-like expressions making them look even fiercer. When they spotted us, they appeared puzzled and surprised as if we had just landed there from the moon. Likewise we felt as if *Scotty* had just beamed us down onto a strange planet among ferocious-looking people.

I cringed. Shirley gripped my hand firmly. Somehow I felt we were too deep into this and an attempt to retreat perhaps would be interpreted as weakness by the armed onlookers. I decided to do the next best thing and walked through the village looking for the Chief's hut. He didn't look any tamer or less surprised to see us than the others. It was clear we had a problem. We couldn't communicate in English but the message was definite – he was not thrilled to see us.

It seemed we were in big trouble. I couldn't shake off the feeling that we were interrupting something big.

An elder who had come to visit the Chief spoke only a few words of English, but in our situation, I felt he spoke fluently. Fumbling for words and excuses for being there, I explained we were off a ship anchored on the other side of the hill and had come to ask the kind Chief for permission to visit his island. The elder translated my request and in a long narration the Chief expressed his displeasure for us interrupting their sacred celebration. The elder translated overtime, trying to convince the Chief to change his mind. As an end result Shirley, Trevor and I were invited to stay and watch the celebration.

I don't think they understood that there were other people on board the boat over the hill anxiously awaiting for us to return. I tried to explain it was unnecessary for us to stay. In fact, I tried to tactfully suggest we would be more than happy to leave their village and the island but to no avail. *"That is out of the question."* Now the Chief was getting angry.

"If you decline his offer to stay," the elder explained, *"he will be insulted."*

We were trapped, unable to leave. Our little early walk was promising to turn into a whole day event. Something was different about these people. The expressions they painted on their faces, the ritualistic movement of their bodies and the wild look in their eyes told me that this was not just an amusing event.

Finally the elder started to shed some light on what was happening. He explained we were witnessing a cleansing ceremony. Originally their tribe had been cannibals. The ritual they were now performing was to scare away evil spirits that tempted their cannibalistic urges. Bigger-than-life sized rosewood carvings, like totem poles, encircled the ceremony depicting elongated faces with exaggerated tongues hanging out. The dangling oversized tongue symbolized that human flesh was distasteful.

To demonstrate their fervent courage for the evil spirits, the men bravely walked on red-hot coals and over broken glass. Other men set the mood by creating an ominous rhythm, beating sticks over logs, and chanting and yelping war-like cries. It was enough to drive shivers up my spine and make the hair on my arms stand at attention.

All kinds of strange thoughts crossed my mind as I watched the warriors glare at us with their piercing eyes. I wondered if we looked like Big Macs to them, making their salivary juices flow. *Were they tempted, or was this ceremony really curing them? Or was it just a traditional ritual?*

The elder still sat next to us and I wondered if it was for protective reasons – perhaps to stop us from making an innocent mistake like interrupting the ceremony, or perhaps he just wanted to practice his English. Whatever the reason, I was utterly grateful to have him beside us.

It was surprising how he wasn't shy about revealing their cannibalistic ways. He confessed they had practiced cannibalism as late as 1943. Then Christian missionaries came and converted them, and hence the woodcarvings.

Overall the missionaries were successful but in the early days some weren't so lucky. The elder continued in a light hearted manner to tell us a story about a very ambitious missionary who had lived with their tribe for two years teaching them Christianity and steering them away from cannibalism. He was well liked by the tribes' people, but one day during a village ceremony the missionary made a fundamental mistake. In the process of blessing the Chief, the missionary rested his hand on the Chief's head. In cannibalistic terms that was a signal to eat the person.

Of course the village Chief was the *almighty one* to the tribe's people, therefore no one dared to put their hand on his head. In retaliation, the infuriated Chief put his hand on the missionary's head, giving the signal to the others to eat him. The crowd was so worked up that by the time the ritual was over they had eaten the missionary completely – leather boots and all.

By now all I could think of was how to get the heck out of there. I thought that if I were Shirley, I'd be ready to have the baby now. Was I imagining it? Or were the warriors licking their lips as they gazed at our tender young, white-like-goat-cheese son? On one hand I was scared out of my wits but on the other I felt appreciative and privileged to have stumbled upon this experience. *As long as we make it out of here alive!* I thought.

I remembered my childhood fantasies of wanting to meet cannibals face to face one day. And now I wondered if the infinite powers of the universe had answered my call. As I think back, I don't think our lives were ever in danger, but the heavy dark jungle setting with the overcast clouds hanging just above the treetops created an eerie atmosphere. And the natives looked so sinister in their costumes that it set the stage for our terror.

We stretched our ears trying to absorb every word of the elder's stories. Before we were to leave I had one question for the elder. *"What does human flesh taste like?"* I asked. He looked at me. A peculiar smile covered his face. He was prepared for that question. I sensed he had been waiting for me to ask him for long time and now I finally did.

"Human meat tastes just like chicken!" he snickered. Nervously we all burst into uncomfortable laughter. Shirley gave me that *let's get out of here* look.

Finally by mid afternoon, feeling we had pleased the Chief with our presence, we thanked him for his hospitality and our translator for his help and prepared to leave. Now I could sense the Chief was satisfied. He was proud that the ceremony had been performed with more dynamics and vigor because the warriors had us as guests to present to. For him it was a well-done routine ritual, whereas for us it was a stimulating but startling experience.

As we walked through the village I looked around wide-eyed in an effort to decipher if we were dreaming or was it the real thing. Once out of the village our pace hastened out of fear that we still might be ambushed in the thick deep forest. At the same time, overwhelmed with excitement, I felt so fortunate the way life had blessed us with such a unique and unforgettable experience.

I couldn't believe what had just happened. Deep inside I struggled with my feelings. *Why was life bestowing such fortune and riches on us?* In my lack of *understanding the law of compensation* I didn't feel we had paid an adequate price to be enjoying such ultimate rewards. There was a deep conflict within me between what I wanted out of life and the results I felt we were worthy of.

I just couldn't shake off my inferior feelings that we were only impostors that had just connived and faked our way. That we were thieves that had taken something that belonged to and was reserved for the rich, famous and privileged.

Chapter 38

A Run for the Finish Line!

"Only those who dare to fail greatly
can ever achieve greatly."

... Robert F. Kennedy

After Shirley and I discussed it, we decided the best option was to return to Suva in Figi and she and Trevor would fly either to Australia or New Zealand. She was just too pregnant and I didn't want to take any more risks that might jeopardize her and our unborn child. It really killed her not to continue on Nausikaa as she wanted to complete the trip sailing, but we both knew it was not the right choice to make.

Unfortunately the decision deteriorated our relationship with our crew even further. They decided if we returned to Suva, each one would go their separate ways. It killed me to think of them leaving after all the months we'd spent together and after all the experiences we had shared. But perhaps it was time to part as friends rather than to force the issue, becoming adversaries. That would truly make the rest of our voyage miserable.

By this stage of the game I had developed much more self-confidence in running the ship, but still, I wondered, how was I ever going to pull this one off? My heart wrenched with the pain of uncertainty and rejection, as we became crewless. Seeing them leave was a heartbreaking experience. But it compared nothing to how I felt when Shirley and Trevor boarded the bus in Suva to head to the airport in Nandi. It was as if part of my being left as well. Swallowing hard, I controlled my tears, not wanting to expose any signs of weakness or insecurity. After all I was *"The Captain"* and captains don't cry – right?

Shirley and Trevor were flying to Sydney. It had been tough to decide which country they would fly to because we wanted to visit both Australia and New Zealand. But at this crossroad in our life, the question was – do we want a little Kiwi or a little Aussie? Australia won. Deep inside I reasoned if we made it there, our expedition and dream would be fulfilled, without losing face. After all, we had told everyone Australia was our goal, our ultimate destination, before we even set out from Canada.

Since our early days of falling in love and being inseparable, Shirley and I had constantly connived to elope to Australia to get married. When her parents got wind of it, they talked us out of it, and really pushed for a traditional family wedding. To this day I'm glad they did, as it turned out to be the nicest day of our lives. It had been the proudest day of my mom and dad's life as well. We flew them over from Croatia to celebrate with us and it was as if a heavy weight had been lifted from their hearts to know that their beloved son would finally settle down to have his own family.

Well it didn't immediately go like that. Three years after our wedding, Shirley and I made a second attempt to go to Australia. After working three jobs each and saving our hard-earned money, we took a year off to travel around the world. Heading south from Canada, the first leg took us along the west coast down to the United States to Long Beach, California, on our way to Central America and Panama.

While we were in Long Beach we visited the historic ship, The Queen Mary. Afterwards we sneaked into the commercial cargo ship docking area, seeking a ride south to Central America aboard a freighter.

We had no luck finding a ship heading south. However, the captain of the cargo ship, Lloyd Brazilero, had his wife and two daughters traveling with him on board. He offered us passage to Australia in exchange for teaching them English. Difficult to resist such an offer we were tempted to go, but declined because we would've arrived in their winter. We still planned to get there in the sequence of our year of travel around the world. But the year went by and we never made it to Australia.

Now once again, for a third try, we were on our last leg to Australia. But the simple 2,000-mile voyage, with a quick re-provision stop in New Caledonia, was now jeopardized by the crew's departure. *When do problems ever end? Never!* I thought. With everyone leaving I had secret doubts if I would ever make it to Australia. However, I was determined to complete the voyage and promised myself to do it single-handed if I didn't receive any response from the crew notices that I posted throughout Suva.

With Shirley and Trevor gone I felt so alone. Days felt like years and I started to panic that I wouldn't make it in time to be with Shirley for the birth of our child. I worried about how she was going to manage in Australia on her own. There was only one person she knew in Sydney, her childhood girlfriend Nancy, who happened to be visiting a boyfriend. *At least she knew someone,* I thought. Sometimes I felt like just abandoning Nausikaa to join them but I just couldn't bring myself to actually do it.

One day, just as I was losing hope, I hit the jackpot. Four young British women in their early twenties, travelling in the area, were looking for a ride to Australia. Then the same day a strong young Belgian man signed on. The ship was completely provisioned with the exception of fresh produce, meat and ice. While the new crew topped off the tanks with fuel and water, I finished provisioning and cleared customs. Now it was like a race and before the day was over we headed out of Suva harbor and started our passage to Noumea, the capital of New Caledonia.

I was impressed with the diligence of the women as they executed their responsibilities at the helm. It was kind of amusing to watch them become upset if for some reason the ship went off course a solitary degree. They acted as if something disastrous would happen. Sure, there were reefs to dodge. They were our greatest challenge throughout the South Pacific. But a little variation to the left or right of our assigned course was nothing to worry about.

During my watch I couldn't control my right knee. It just rocked away, wanting the ship to go much faster. By regularly plotting our progress on the chart, I realized I had nothing to complain about as we were cruising well-above average speed directly toward Noumea. The winds were perfect and the largest sails were raised to take advantage of every breath. Nausikaa, just like a racehorse sensing it had to give its best, plowed through the South Pacific waters. The faster she went, the faster my knee rocked.

We literally came to a screeching halt in Noumea, New Caledonia, 10 days later. Being a French colony, the Noumeans spoke absolutely no English, which added a unique flavor to our stop, but wasn't very helpful when I wanted to quickly find the necessary supplies to continue our voyage. It was an extremely progressive city so I was amazed with my difficulty in finding anyone to give us directions in English. I became frustrated with the people's attitude, as it seemed as if they were either really stuck in their French bubble or were just playing head games with me, wanting me to address them in French. I wasn't in the frame of mind to play games. I just wanted to provision the ship and leave. In one day flat our *rest and relaxation* was over and again we headed full speed toward Sydney.

However conditions deteriorated as we entered the strait between New Zealand and Australia into the Tasman Sea. The wind died down and changed direction, coming from the south, right on our nose. I decided it wasn't a timely situation to let my *sailing purity syndrome* stop me from running the engine full speed. It allowed us to sail under complete sail, cutting closer to the wind without compromising our speed, which was of utmost importance to me.

I worried Shirley might go into labor without me being there with her. She was due any time now, any minute. I remembered her going through three long days of labor with Trevor, with her back killing her and needing someone to walk her around to help relieve the pain. We still managed to motor-sail along just fine but were forced to head too far west.

Finally one of the women eagerly announced she could see land. I dashed to Nausikaa's bow to witness my first glimpse of the Australian coastline.

What a rush! After everything that had happened to get here – all the challenges, obstacles, adversities, and all the pain, uncertainty, discouragement, and ridicule – after all that, and now my eyes were feasting on Australia. Wow!

Oh how I wished that my sweetheart were here with me. To be hugging her tight right now was all I wished for. To kiss her lips and whisper in her ear how much I loved her. And to share with her the excitement of the moment we had dreamed of for so long. I felt proud, in less than one month we would be celebrating my birthday – in Australia, at the ripe age of 27.

In the distance we could make out cliffs close to Sugarloaf Point, just north of Newcastle. My sextant position shot pinpointed that we were 100 miles away from the entrance to Sydney harbor. I couldn't believe how all of a sudden it was so close. For so long it had felt impossible and untouchable but now I was almost upon it.

My body was tense, as if tied in a colossal knot, trying to hold my insides from jumping ship. I warned myself not to let my guard down. After all we actually hadn't arrived safe and sound yet. My mind raced through space and time to visualize Captain Cook and his crew shipwrecked on the shores of Australia. He thought he had made it but then a storm blew his ship ashore, stranding him and his crew.

"Captain what went wrong? What should I look out for?" in my mind I asked for his direction.

I didn't feel we were in the clear. *We can't just arrive without something going wrong,* I thought. *But what would stop us? What could go wrong? It just can't happen like this* I kept telling myself. At this stage, it appeared too good, too easy. Something had to go wrong. I wanted it too badly. I begged my dad for his assistance. He had always offered me good advice and now I needed some more. *Where was he when I needed him?* Then I spoke to God asking for guidance.

I could feel their presence – both of them looking at me, smiling, without saying a word. In the midst of my mental confusion, self doubt mixed with the ecstasy of our achievement, I felt grateful to our creator for allowing me to get this far. I thanked Him and declared, if for some reason the ship now floundered and sunk under our feet, I was content just to be here – this close to shore to swim to safety if need be. But nothing happened. Just smooth seas and gentle winds.

Even though the winds were pretty much straight on our bow, they were so gentle that Nausikaa's engine and sails continued to propel us forward at a steady speed. I was so excited that I wondered how I would be able to sleep my last night at sea. Finally I reasoned if I slept, time would go much faster.

At daybreak one of the crew come down to my cabin, shook me out of my slumber and announced that a high circular tower and some other high rises were now clearly visible. In the magic of the early morning Nausikaa slowly approached the striking harbor of Sydney. Rising behind us the sun cast a red blanket over the eastern sky creating a mystical feeling.

Within, peaceful bliss overwhelmed me, as I became conscious of a great revelation. I realized it had been worth every effort to keep a firm grip on our goal. There were so many times Shirley and I just about lost our dream, had we not hung onto it with both our hearts and soul. Perhaps it had been just a foolish one, but now I affirmed to myself it was a dream worth striving for.

"Yes!" I screamed with all my might. My enthusiasm must have rubbed off on the others on board as we all jumped up and down cheering and laughing. Good thing Sydney harbor was so huge, giving us enough space to air out our excitement.

Now with our sails down and protected from the ocean swell, Nausikaa III gently glided toward Rushcutter's Bay. The water, flat and glossy, beautifully reflected the outstanding splendor of the city. In the distance we could see the famous Opera House and the historic Sydney Bridge.

As I stood, perched on Nausikaa's bowsprit observing the view, I yelled at the top of my lungs, *"Can you see this Dad? It's beautiful."* I felt as if I couldn't have done it, if it weren't for him. The success of our expedition was proof he had done well raising me. All the tough jobs he and Mom had me do and insisted I finish had tempered me to endure and overcome even the toughest challenges to succeed. What they had taught me was paying off.

Mom had also guided me, through her example of hard work, as she struggled in the fields working side by side with all her children. As a child I had wondered why we worked every day so long and hard, that at the end of the day there was no time left to play. It sure didn't look to me like my friends had that problem. When I would challenge Mom she would say, *"Son, don't look at what other people are not doing, just do whatever it takes to survive and reach your goal."*

As I reminisced about my parents, I promised myself that somehow I would figure out a way to bring them over to Australia so they could share with us the fruits of our achievement. That was, I felt, something I had to afford them regardless how much and how hard I had to work to make it happen.

Now at the closing minutes of this monumental event in our lives and on the threshold of our goal, I so wished that Shirley and Trevor could be at my side to share it with me. But soon, I reasoned, we would be together.

Nausikaa III gently slid up to the dock at Sydney Yacht Club in Rushcutter's Bay. The minute all the lines were secured to the dock, I congratulated my crew on a job well done and once again we jumped, hugged and made a fuss. Our new neighbors, on their 80-foot powerboat docked next to us, must've thought a bunch of young kids were just carrying on. We didn't bother to explain. There was no way they could ever relate to the depth of, or reason for our joy.

I walked to the end of the dock, dropped down to my knees and kissed the ground. Finally, we were in Australia!

Chapter 39

Changing
of the Guards

*"To live in hearts we leave behind is
not to die."*

... Thomas Campbell

With a quick phone call to Nancy I learned the whereabouts of
Shirley and Trevor and was relieved to hear she hadn't delivered the
baby yet. Immediately I rushed to the youth hostel to see them, but
when I got to King's Cross, I realized it was a pretty seedy part of
town. I spotted a couple eager hookers hanging out on the street trying to snag their after-lunch customers and the odd bottle-hugger
leaned up against a building. Groups of young punk rockers strolled
down the streets, their spiked blue-dyed hair making them look like
something from outer space. I felt like I had landed on Mars.

I was amazed that Shirley would stay in a neighborhood like this
on her own, pregnant and with a small child. *Where did she find the
courage?* I wondered. The fact that we had been unexposed to this
side of life for so long I'm sure compounded my shock. Just the busy
traffic and other loud city noises were traumatic, never mind the

characters that were hanging about.

The youth hostel was locked, obviously for security reasons. A big woman, looking like she ran the show, answered the bell and sized me up for a few seconds. Before I had a chance to say a word she said, *"You must be Boris looking for Shirley, right?"* It was obvious that everyone knew why Shirley was staying there.

I realized later, deep inside Shirley thought I would not arrive in Australia so fast, on time for the birth of our child. She had limited funds and thought best to stretch them as far as she could, in case she had to provide for herself even after getting out of the hospital. Right there I knew that I was married to a special woman with a lot of courage and common sense. The hostel, full of young travelers from all over the world, was surprisingly clean and friendly, but just one step outside on the street it was a different story.

Shirley and Trevor were not to be found. I was totally disappointed – crushed! I was bursting at the seams, not able to wait another minute to see them, and now they weren't here. Chills rushed down my spine with the thought that Shirley might be giving birth, in the hospital right that moment. After all, she was already overdue.

The hotel manager explained Shirley had lost her wallet, complete with passports and money, while shopping downtown. She had been distracted by a temper tantrum Trevor had when he couldn't understand why he couldn't take home an expensive toy. Fortunately some honest soul had found the wallet and turned it in to the consulate. Shirley and Trevor were now picking it up.

Deflated, I returned to the marina. The next couple hours dragged on, seeming to take forever, while I wondered how Shirley was making out. Again I feared she could go into labor any time, anywhere and unbeknownst to her, I was here to help. Every so often I strained my eyes intensely scanning the dock, but there was no sign of my precious family. Searching for a pregnant lady with a kid at her side,

I didn't notice a little blond boy walk up to the ship alone.

"Hi Daddy!" he squealed in his child voice. Kind of shyly he stood on the dock with his fingers in his mouth looking as if didn't really recognize me. From my point of view *he* looked so big and so grown up that I had to do a double-take before I leaped onto the dock. I hugged him, kissed him and spun him around. I just couldn't get enough of him. It seemed unbelievable that we were together again.

Then I saw Shirley waddling down the dock. She was bigger than big. From a distance her appearance also looked different. Wearing a nice dress, with a new hair do, she looked like a regular landlubber, only pregnant. Waving at me, she picked up her pace. It was obvious she was as anxious as I was for our long awaited reunion. I had to do another double take just to make sure it was she. I was surprised how, in such a short time, they both looked so different.

Hugging and kissing, laughing and crying, I couldn't believe she was in my arms again. It was a challenge to get in a good hug with a third party wrapped around our legs. *"Daddy's here,"* Trevor squeaked.

I was so overwhelmed – words just couldn't come. I wanted to tell her so much and yet all I could do was shake my head in disbelief and gaze at her. I was thrilled to be there in time for our baby's birth. But concerned with her being overdue, I couldn't help but wonder if the child inside her was still alive. Resting my hand on Shirley's tummy, I realized I had nothing to worry about. The little being inside kicked and squirmed as usual. One thing was for sure. This one was going to be active.

Trevor looked a bit confused, as he became re-acquainted with the ship once again. But it didn't take long before he found security back in his netted bunk and especially when I brought out his toy box. He was back home.

We all celebrated our successful arrival in Australia late into the night sharing details of the voyage with Shirley. It was obvious she really wished she could've also sailed the last little stretch with us. But on the other hand, I was delighted the whole plan worked out and everyone was safe. The next day the English women left to continue their world travels.

With Jacques, our only remaining crew, I took Shirley and Trevor on a cruise back out to the harbor entrance and re-enacted our arrival, then we continued to tour the harbor, viewing the famous sites of Sydney. Every so often, like when we sailed beside the Opera House and under the Sydney Bridge, Shirley eyes locked with mine and we burst into laughter, in our disbelief of finally being here. It was so moving.

Finally we opened the mail Shirley had collected from the consulate. Amongst all the letters of well wishes was one from my mom and dad. My father sounded more upbeat and congratulatory, wishing us a happy arrival in Australia. I could sense his pride in his writing. But Mom was a bit more revealing. She thanked us for writing so consistently but expressed her concern about Dad's health, suggesting I phone him as soon as possible, to help calm him in his concern for our safety.

Immediately I wrote a long letter back to them, proudly confirming our arrival in Australia and describing some of our most recent adventures and experiences at length. I was very confident and upbeat, promising to send them an airline ticket to come visit us and to meet their new grandchild. When Trevor was born we had brought them over to Canada, likewise I felt I could earn enough money in Sydney to afford a special treat for them.

I decided to hold off phoning them until we had news of our new arrival. After all, that was bound to happen any day. However, that proved to be only wishful thinking. Days passed without any change, no new bundle of joy. Each day we walked from Rushcutter's Bay up a steep hill to the Paddington Hospital for Women, hoping the effort would bring on Shirley's labor. But all that seemed to do was make her even more fit. According to the doctor her progress was great and he didn't feel there was any reason for intervention.

Time dragged and Shirley was now two weeks overdue. I would have paid anything just to get the labor under way, but the doctor insisted the baby was better off maturing in the womb rather than rushing. He suggested we continue to walk in an effort to induce labor, but all we got was more exercise.

However, our walking routine turned into an excellent opportunity to window-shop. We dreamed of being rich, of buying lots of wonderful things and taking them to share with our friends in the islands. The reality was that our budget could only afford the necessities in life, like food.

A heavy weight hung over my head. How much would the doctor charge for Shirley's visits and how long would she be able to stay in the hospital? We were down to our last bit of money with no immediate prospects of employment. However, nobody at the hospital seemed to be concerned about the charges. I thought if they weren't concerned, why should I worry? So I tried not to.

The day after we arrived in Sydney I had contacted Prime Minister Fraser's office to announce our arrival. Sir John, the PM's assistant, sounded genuinely happy to hear from us and extended an invitation to visit the prime minister's sheep farm for a few days. I promised we would after things settled down with our baby's birth. I had great hopes that our visit with the PM would yield a good job prospect.

When on earth is this baby going to arrive? I wondered. I was becoming very anxious, the days feeling like the longest ones of my life. Besides worrying about everything else that you do back in civilization, what concerned me the most was the safety of our child. As much as I tried not to, I became possessed with the feeling that something was wrong and I just couldn't shake it. Trevor had been two weeks early and I just had a hard time buying the doctor's claim that such a late birth was a normal occurrence.

Then one day my heart skipped a beat when Shirley calmly announced she was experiencing mild labor pains. Insisting on walking to the hospital, she labored up the steep hill, her pains intensifying to the point that she had to periodically stop and do some deep breathing. Just as I would be ready to flag a cab, the pain would ease and we would continue on. She was adamant about walking, as she wanted to ensure the labor was well on its way.

Finally at the hospital she settled into a room but again nobody inquired as to our finances or our medical coverage. I found that strange, but frankly that was the last thing on my mind. I was boiling over with excitement as the big day was finally here.

With a tight grip on Shirley's hand in the delivery room, I hit the top of the world when the doctor held up a little blood-smeared body high into the air and announced, *"It's a boy!"* I wiped the sweat off my wife's forehead, kissed her and repeated, *"Did you hear that honey? It's a boy."*

Not to sound chauvinistic, but if you were ever a part of the older European upbringing you would understand the pinnacles of excitement that shot through my body. I had goose bumps that had goose bumps. Not only did we have a son, a new heir to our family, but someone to look after us in our old age. That is the old European belief, the one I was raised with. This was Jakob's grandson we were looking at here. I could just envision the happiness and relief on my dad's face when he would hear the great news.

Emphatically, I counted all the fingers and toes that belonged to our little boy, while the nurse wiped his tiny body. A little tap on his bum revealed that the baby was very much alive and with a voice that would knock your socks off. One thing was for sure, his lungs were working! I couldn't believe such a little creature could belt out such a sound with so much volume, but it was music to my ears. I smiled from ear to ear for so long and hard that my cheeks started to hurt.

It's fascinating how life works. It's like a roller coaster ride. After the high we experienced on our arrival to Australia, we plunged into such a low – two weeks of anxiety and anticipation, both over our finances and our son's health. Now we were at the peak, after our son's birth. Ask any parent – it is the utmost natural high one can experience. As a bonus, we were told the hospital care was gratis, and Shirley could stay as long as she wanted. WOW what a relief that was. Where else in the world could that have happened?

With excitement I kept pacing the room and every so often I would drive my right fist into my left palm, out of sheer disbelief. All our plans – our expectations of the expedition, our encounters with the local population, and our efforts in raising a family – they all happened as we had visualized them.

There seemed to be some kind of paradox happening in our lives. In fact, the more we defied fear, the greater was the reward. The greater the adversity, even greater was the victory. The more we defied conformity, more spectacular was the discovery. Right now I just didn't dig it, to really understand how life works, but I felt we both were enjoying it and getting hooked on the adventure.

Trevor was entranced with his new little brother, not quite understanding how he, all of a sudden, appeared on the scene. Our new son wasn't the shy type; if there wasn't a breast close by when he was ready to dine the whole hospital knew about it. At first we wondered what to name him and finally decided on Ryan. Picking his middle name was a natural. We had named Trevor John, after Shirley's father and now Ryan's middle name would be Jakob after mine. I visualized how happy my dad would be over this great news.

Now that we had Ryan's name chosen, it was time to phone home with the happy news. I smiled to myself as I envisioned the joy our good news would bring our parents. The relief my father would feel knowing we were all fine, that we survived the crossing of the mighty

Pacific Ocean. And especially to hear of yet another grandson, this one bearing his name.

Feeling light-hearted, I skipped from foot to foot and clicked my heels in search of a public telephone booth in Rushcutter's Park. I passed a large tree with hundreds of huge fruit bats hanging upside down from the branches. In my carefree state of excitement I blurted out, *"You know guys, even I didn't believe we would make it as far as we did, but we did. We just kept dreaming and moving forward, and now we're here! And now I have another son! Yeee Haa."* Then I whispered, *"And you know, I don't think we've been found out yet. Sushhhh! Don't tell anyone."* I put my finger across my lips.

Then sheepishly I looked around but there was nobody close enough to hear my conversation with the fruit bats so I added, *"You know, dreams can come true for anyone."* Then I skipped off toward the phone booth.

By nature I'm a very positive person (in case you haven't noticed) so to be a bearer of great news delighted me to no end. It was already too late in the evening to phone Europe but I could still schedule a phone call with the telephone office in Croatia. They in turn would send word to my parents to come to the telephone office at a specific time the next day to receive my call. It was a bit of an ordeal to phone, but I missed them a lot.

Leaving home at such a young age I didn't really have time to grow out of my childhood, and still felt the need for their affirmation, recognition and approval of my actions and accomplishments. I just couldn't wait to hear their voices again and to share all the exciting news. At the cost of $4 per minute it was a stretch for our budget but it was going to be worth every penny.

The timing was perfect to phone Shirley's parents in Edmonton. My heart beat loudly, as I anxiously waited for only three rings. But it seemed like an eternity before Shirley's dad answered.

In my excitement I blurted out, *"Hello Grandpa! Grandpa guess what? You're a grandfather again to a little sailor boy we've named Ryan Jakob. He was born yesterday at one o'clock and he's 21 inches long and seven and a half pounds. And I swear, today he's even bigger. Soon he'll be our new crew. He's pretty content, as long as he isn't hungry, and he sleeps whenever he feels like it. Grandpa he's just beautiful. And Shirley's doing great too."* I chattered on but at the same time, I wondered why Shirley's dad wasn't responding. Nothing – no *that's great, how wonderful, super* – nothing!

Then he broke the silence. He cleared his throat a couple times and then started talking, *"Congratulations to both of you, Boris, but I have some bad news. Yesterday, I guess around the time Ryan was born, Shirley's grandfather suddenly passed away from a heart attack."*

My mouth just dropped open and my excitement instantly dissipated. *Oh no! Why now?* I thought, concerned for Shirley.

This was supposed to be a time for celebration, not mourning. I really liked her Grandpa Matt and Shirley thought the world of him. He was a stern, tough guy, a strong leader, who was loved and respected by everyone in the family. He had also been one of the very few genuine supporters of our expedition. He had respected the fact I had the chutzpa to take my family on such a daring adventure because I believed in it.

Before we departed he had taken me aside and said, *"You know Boris, my family came from Idaho to the prairies in Alberta in the early 1900's. In Idaho we had a great life, lots of land, a grand house of such prestige that it is still a great feature of the town. My father sold that large house, packed up his children into a horse drawn wagon and traveled hundreds of miles to homestead land in Alberta. Everyone thought he was crazy, but he wanted to clear land, build a log house and grow grain. He believed his children would have a better life there. He followed his dream."*

He continued, *"Now I don't know anything about the open sea, but I do know when I go sailing with my son, Orville, on his 16-foot boat in the bay it makes me very happy. If you think you can do it and if you want to do it bad enough, Boris, go live your dream. Just remember, take good care of your family and things will be fine."*

His words echoed in my head. Why now? Why did he have to die now? Why couldn't he wait to hear the good news, that we lived out our dream and survived just fine, and that he was once again a Great Grandfather.

In the background Shirley's dad was talking, but I couldn't really hear what he was saying. I was there but I wasn't. Everything seemed to be in slow motion. I could decipher the odd word about a funeral and the family going to it, but my eyes were full of tears and my soul filled with sorrow and sympathy. My mind raced, how was I going to break the news to Shirley?

She told me of stories of when she was young, Grandpa Matt would come over and play the violin and all the relatives would sit around the piano for a big sing-along. He was the catalyst that held his big family close together.

"Can you hear me? CAN YOU HEAR ME?" John startled me out of my thoughts.

"Yes Grandpa, I can hear you, tell Grandma I'm so sorry about her father. He was a great man."

John seemed concerned, *"Did you understand that Boris?"*

"Yes. Yes I understood that. Shirley's grandfather died yesterday," I answered.

"No, No, I mean yes Grandpa died," John struggled, *"but didn't you hear the part about YOUR dad?"*

"No. What about my dad?" I asked for clarification.

John cleared his throat again, *"Yesterday your father passed away as well."*

Something must've been wrong with the phone. I couldn't be

hearing right. *"You mean Grandpa Matt is dead. But tell me about my father. How is he?"* I asked again.

"I am sorry Boris, Jakob is dead. He died yesterday as well, I'm so sorry I have to be the one to tell you." John's voice broke.

My hand holding the telephone dropped down like a lead weight and my back slammed up against the glass in the phone booth. Tears poured down my face like rivers. My heart wrenched. I felt sick to my stomach.

"It can't be possible. Dad can't be dead. He is only 54 years old, he's too young to die. Nooooo," I wailed, *"Not Dad!"* Defeated in grief, I stooped over in the phone booth and cried. I don't remember hanging up the phone.

My mind raced over many thousands of miles to my home, needing to confirm the fate of my father. In seconds my whole life replayed itself in front of my eyes, but regardless of how hard I tried I could not realize his death. All I could visualize were happy moments from my childhood. I could see Dad holding me up by my waist, helping me master the dog paddle, in the little creek that flowed beside our house. He took me on my first tractor ride, on a tractor so old it had steel wheels.

And he taught me the art of riding an adult-sized bike, clinging on the cross bar and pedaling with all my might. When I fell down and hurt myself, I wasn't interested in riding any more. Now, as a parent, I know he would have gladly taken that fall for me to take away my pain. But he encouraged me to try again saying, *"Son, try it just once more. I know it is hard but once you learn how to ride a bike you will be able to go much farther from home, see many new things, explore like you can't on foot. You can do it son! Just try it one more time."*

I just could not realize my father's death. I remember the day I raced against him and won. It was a moment I had waited to cherish for the longest time. Even though I gloated in my victory, deep down I knew he let me win, and he never tried to regain his crown, making a clear indication to me that I was maturing to be a leader.

My father wasn't the type to lecture. He taught me through example. When he was the Director of a building material company I had the opportunity to observe his character. Since there was so much construction going on, it created a shortage of cement, so my father kept a list of people waiting their turn for the precious commodity. One day a local businessman come to our house and asked my father if they could speak in private. *"You can talk in front of my son. Everything I know, he knows and he is very trustworthy,"* my father assured him. I was 15 at the time and felt so proud and mature.

Boldly the man proceeded to offer a bribe worth a huge amount of money, staring into both my father's and my eyes as if we were partners; he requested his name be moved to the top of the cement list. I couldn't believe his offer. In my youthful innocence I felt we needed that money badly and nobody would ever find out how we got it. Expecting to hear my father accept the offer, I was dumbfounded when he thanked the man but refused. Later when I asked him why he said, *"It's unethical to accept a bribe. I didn't earn that money and I like to sleep at night."* At the time I didn't understand but those words forever echoed in my mind and to this day I am so proud of him for being the honest man he was.

I searched my mind and found only fond memories, yet sorrow still engulfed me. Dreams of any future sailing expeditions just crumbled in my mind like a falling house of cards. My enthusiasm for our present accomplishments meant nothing any more. Life no longer had the same meaning. I realized that as much as I wanted to live a dynamic successful life for my family and myself, I was doing it for my parents as well. They had such hard lives and I knew they would have preferred to live rich, satisfying lives full of dreams and goals just as Shirley and I were doing.

Now our expedition didn't make sense any more. Our dream to continue sailing around the world came to an abrupt stop. All I could think of was returning to Canada.

My heart really contorted when I had to break the news to Shirley about her grandpa and my dad. We hugged and cried. Gently holding Ryan in our arms, we looked at him as a gift from God and a welcome relief at our time of pain and sorrow.

Returning to the ship from the hospital that evening, I walked again through Rushcutter's Park. The fruit bats still hung upside down from the branches.

Tears ran down my face as I confided to them, *"I guess the cat's out of the bag. We've been discovered!"*

> *"Do not stand by my grave and weep,*
> *I am not there. I do not sleep —*
> *I am a thousand winds that blow,*
> *I am the diamond glints on snow,*
> *I am the sunlight on ripened grain,*
> *I am the gentle autumn rain.*
> *Do not stand by my grave and cry.*
> *I am not there. I did not die..."*
>
> .... Author Unknown
> (In memory of Dad)

The Beginning!

The Unsinkable Spirit
Episode II

Episode I came to an abrupt halt as did the King's expedition and their life. Regardless of their fears, hardships, knockdowns, trials and errors, their voyage had been a total success with their dream being realized far beyond their expectations. One could never put a monetary value on what they had experienced.

One thing was clearly evident – good things don't come easily. Boris and Shirley knew that was a major factor in why so few experience the kind of triumph they were able to so far in life. You might wonder why would they subject themselves to the kind of adversity they faced during those stormy days and nights. But when the *unsinkable spirit* moves you, you're compelled to go for your dream regardless how tough the road might be. And they did just that.

However, what they didn't understand was why the infinite powers were being so cruel to them now. This was supposed to be the time to celebrate their accomplishment, the victory over their fears and the un-known, and to celebrate a new life within their growing family. It was supposed to be the time to reap their rewards, to explore Australia, the place they had longed for and dreamed of so much. The time to visit the outback, the prime minister's sheep farm and Ayers rock; to ride camels through the arid desert, to explore the wild jungles of Queensland and to dive the world famous Great Barrier Reef. But now that all meant nothing. Now they were devastated by the cruel blow life had dealt them.

They felt their whole expedition had been too good to be true anyway as they felt unworthy to be *getting away* with experiencing life in full color. How could it continue? They sensed something had to go wrong. Surely they'd be caught. But they didn't expect this – not this kind of an end to their expedition.

Jakob was too young to die and Boris was too young to be fatherless. Even though Boris had left Croatia at such a young age and thousands of miles had separated him from his father, he now realized how much he relied on his dad's guidance and craved his approval. The pain in his soul was just too much to bear. He was deeply wounded by the loss of his father but could never imagine the depth of pain that ravaged deep within his mother's heart. And Shirley mourned her beloved grandfather. Their only relief was their newborn son, Ryan.

But they felt such a void in their lives. Boris and Shirley felt deserted, isolated from their home by thousands of miles of water. With their thoughts so focused on the loss of their loved ones, they lost the desire to extend their expedition to circumnavigate the world. On the contrary, they felt trapped. All they could focus on was how to get out of their predicament without losing their shirts.

The world recession of the 1980's firmly gripped Australia's economy. Money was tight. It was impossible to find a buyer that would consider offering the Kings much money for their ship, never mind enough to cover their outstanding debt to Shirley's brother and sister-in-law. They were stuck.

The only option was to sail Nausikaa III back to Canada from Australia. It would prove to be one of the greatest challenges in their lives. They were warned it would be a battle, like climbing Mount Everest. It was a known fact that it was much easier to sail *around* the world, *with* the trade winds, versus *against* the fierce winds and currents, and against the gods.

And the gods would test them to the utmost, putting the Kings through the ringer before they were deemed worthy of personal sovereignty. Their lives would be threatened as never before; their ship battered every inch of the way with the crew barely hanging together, bonded only by a strong will to survive. Before they would finish, the Kings would curse the day they ever dreamed of their sailing expedition.

However, never in their wildest dreams could they have imagined that the lessons they were to learn were merely stepping stones to prepare them for their future. They would discover:

- Their struggles and adversities would be the actual seeds of future opportunities.
- Sailing would become their ticket to personal independence and business success.
- They would become one set of the very few parents on planet earth to have the opportunity to grow up with their sons.
- They would actually develop a love for the sea as potent as their love for each other.
- The sea would provide them with an overwhelming abundance of food, fun, funds and never-ending experiences. Experiences so enriching that no dollar value could be placed on them, so unbelievable you wonder – *could that really happen?*

The King family would live a dynamic lifestyle with no time for boredom or complacency, always keeping a sharp eye on the horizon for their next great adventure.

**Look for Episode II sailing into
your harbor soon!**

Share a Gift

Enrich the lives of those around you with this entertaining and inspirational book. Share the adventure with your friends, family or employees.

Five easy ways to order The Unsinkable Spirit, *Episode I,*
*In Search of Love, Adventure & Riches***:**

1. Fax this page to 1-604-618-5270
2. Mail this page to: 111 East 1st Street, #20,
   North Vancouver, BC, Canada, V7L 1B2
3. Call toll free 1-888-414-5464
4. E-mail: borisking@attglobal.net

	Description	Price	Quantity	Total
Code 1231	Trade Paperback	US $19.95 x		= $ ____
Code 1232	Trade Paperback	CDN $24.95 x		= $ ____
Sub Total				= $ ____
Plus Shipping and Handling ($5 per book)				= $ ____
TOTAL				= $ ____

Your Name _____

Address _____

City _____ State/Province _____

Zip/Postal Code _____

Country _____

Home Ph: (   ) _____ Work Ph: (   ) _____

Fax: (   ) _____

Your Profession _____

Payment Method   ☐ Mastercard   ☐ Visa   ☐ Amex

Credit Card # _____ Exp. Date _____

Cardholder's Name (as it appears on card) _____

Signature _____

Coming soon!

The Unsinkable Spirit, *Episode II*

Four easy ways to pre-order:
1. Fax this page to 1-604-618-5270
2. Mail this page to: 111 East 1st Street, #20,
   North Vancouver, BC, Canada, V7L 1B2
3. Call toll free 1-888-414-5464
4. E-mail: borisking@attglobal.net

	Description	Price	Quantity	Total
Code 2231	Trade Paperback	US $19.95 x		= $ ____
Code 2232	Trade Paperback	CDN $24.95 x		= $ ____
Sub Total				= $ ____
Plus Shipping and Handling ($5 per book)				= $ ____
TOTAL				= $ ____

Your Name _____

Address _____

City _____ State/Province _____

Zip/Postal Code _____

Country _____

Home Ph: (   ) _____ Work Ph: (   ) _____

Fax: (   ) _____

Your Profession _____

Payment Method   ☐ Mastercard   ☐ Visa   ☐ Amex

Credit Card # _____ Exp. Date _____

Cardholder's Name (as it appears on card) _____

Signature _____

Speaking Services

Boris King is a sought after professional motivational and inspirational speaker presenting to corporations and associations throughout the world. He motivates his audiences with empowerment strategies, thought-provoking content, laughter and lasting inspiration! He teaches:

- Foolproof techniques to achieve the power to earn top money and enjoy peace of mind!
- How to make change work for you!
- How to turn every challenge into a new success!
- How to make your dreams and goals come true!
- How to discover your own unique potential to reach new heights never thought possible!
- How to get rid of fear, build self-confidence and personal drive!
- How to develop healthy self-esteem!
- It doesn't take an extra-ordinary person to achieve extra-ordinary goals and live an extra-ordinary life.

Described as one of the last great adventurers, Captain Boris King tells remarkable stories of his sailing expeditions at sea, including fighting killer hurricanes aboard his ship. He uses those experiences as powerful metaphors for:

Change	Teamwork
Adversity	Risk-taking
Sales & Marketing	360 Degree Success

Book Captain Boris King to present...

- Your Unsinkable Spirit Takes You to the Top
- Risk-Take or Stagnate
- Embrace Change & Enjoy the Voyage
- Overcome Adversity - Be A Survivor!
- Riding the Wave to Success
- The Secret to Living Your Life in Full Color

Contact *your favorite speaking bureau,* or
Email: borisking@attglobal.net
Web: www.borisking.com
Phone: (604) 983-4338

Boris and Shirley King have shared their lives and adventures for twenty-seven years as soul mates and business partners. Trading their professional careers to become adventurers, they spent many years cruising the world, raising and educating their young family along the way. Eventually they turned their lifestyle into their livelihood and settled in the Caribbean. There they restored two wooden ships and ran a charter yacht business aboard their two traditional 100' sailing vessels, Latina and Maverick.

Today Boris is a professional motivational keynote speaker presenting to corporations and associations throughout the world. With Shirley's keen organizational skills, detail-oriented nature and her love for antiques, she was inspired to start one of the largest antique import and retail businesses in western Canada. After spending years on the high seas they now reside in beautiful Vancouver, BC. Inspired to share their formula for living life in full color, Boris and Shirley King wrote *The Unsinkable Spirit*.